THE MOSES
OF ROVNO

THE MOSES
OF ROVNO

The Stirring Story of Fritz Graebe,
a German Christian Who Risked His Life
to Lead Hundreds of Jews to Safety
During the Holocaust

Douglas K. Huneke

PRESIDIO
PRESS

BALLANTINE BOOKS • NEW YORK

A Presidio Press Book
Published by The Random House Ballantine Publishing Group

Presidio Press is a trademark of Random House, Inc.

www.ballantinebooks.com

Designed by Erich Hobbing

Library of Congress Cataloging-in-Publication Data

Huneke, Douglas K.
  The Moses of Rovno.

1. Jews—Ukraine—Persecutions. 2. Holocaust,
Jewish (1930–1945)—Ukraine. 3. World War, 1939–1945—
Jews—Rescue—Ukraine—Rovno (Rovenskaía oblast´)
4. Graebe, Fritz. 5. World War, 1939–1945—Germany
—Biography. 6. Rovno (Rovenskaía oblast´, Ukraine)—
Ethnic relations. I. Title.
DS135.R93U354 1985   940.53'15'0392404771   85-7077
ISBN 978-0-891-41457-5

Printed in the United States of America

144915995

I dedicate this book
to my Family,
Jane, Karen, and Jason

No act of kindness,
No matter how small,
Is ever wasted.
—AESOP

Es geht alles vorüber   ("*This too shall pass*
Es geht alles vorbei   *This too shall be over*
Nach jedem Dezember   *After each December*
Folgt wieder ein Mai.   *A May will follow again.*")

—CHORUS FROM A SONG POPULAR
WITH GERMANS DURING THE WAR

Contents

Foreword

Rabbi Harold M. Schulweis

Founder, Center for the Study of Righteous Acts,
Judah L. Magnes Memorial Museum, Berkeley, California
Rabbi, Congregation Valley Beth Shalom, Encino, California

It is told of Rabbi Nachman of Bratzlav (1772–1810) that he knew of the persecutions and pogroms against the Jews in the Ukraine and yet said nothing. The master listened to the tales of horror and shook his head: "I know what you want me to do—you want me to shout with pain, to howl with despair, but I will not." After a long silence, he began shouting louder and louder, "Jews, for God's sake do not despair." Generations after Rabbi Nachman, the Jews of the Ukraine again faced despair and death, but this time there was one who would protect them— a German who neither thought nor acted like the majority of his people.

How, in our days, can we heed the counsel of Rabbi Nachman and that of the sages and not despair? How can we be faithful to the victims of the Holocaust, retell their unspeakable fate, without succumbing to melancholy? How do we transmit trust and faith to our children and to our children's children when the Holocaust, which looms so large in our lives, offers evidence of massive betrayal and cruelty? Can hope rise out of the crematoria?

When it comes to telling the story of the years of atrocities (and tell it we must) to our children, we are torn by ambivalence. We feel compelled to tell the truth that we lived in an era that was a nightmare of uncivilized criminality. But we grow steadily uncertain whether it is sufficient to relate the disaster and end it there.

As parents who must tell our children why and what and how this unspeakable outrage was visited upon the Jewish people, we are left wondering, what are we doing to their morale, to their will to live as Jews in this world, to their trust and belief in God and humanity, to their moral strength? After the lesson is over, and the nightmare reviewed each year with greater detail and more evidence, we remain perplexed. Do we lay a terror upon their hearts, a stone of fear?

It is not easy these days to speak for humanity. It is easier to believe in God than to believe that we are in God's image. Our contemporary problem is not with the justification of God's ways but with the justification of our own ways. It is important but not enough to quote biblical, rabbinic, or Chassidic texts to sustain our faith in humanity. Morality cries out for evidence, hard data, facts in our time and in our place to nourish our faith in humanity's capacity for decency. Villainy broadcasts ample evidence on its side. Is there another side to the evil dimension? Was there no spark of human decency, of human concern in the Holocaust? Was there no one who cared enough to move, to act, to speak, to help?

A body of literature that is far too small reports significant accounts of incredible heroism during the Holocaust years. I have myself read documents and heard from Jews who were rescued by non-Jews; who were protected, fed, clothed, hidden in bunkers, attics, cellars, ovens, couches, stables, cowsheds, pigsties, cemetery graves, and open fields. These rescuers were raised in hostile anti-Semitic environments; they lived in fear of their informing neighbors and the merciless Nazi killers.

Fritz Graebe was a civilian German contractor who followed the German forces into the Ukraine, building railroads, roundhouses, and other structures. He learned of a massive pogrom in Rovno where thousands of people were rounded up and murdered. Once, following the war, he told me of his concern for what his son might someday ask him: "What did you do in that time when people were in danger?" He knew what he had to do, then and there, to be able to answer his son tomorrow. His acts of righteousness were not impulsive, solitary gestures, but involved sustained commitment over a long period of time and entailed incredible risks.

The acts of the "righteous non-Jews" lend a needed dimension to the revelations of atrocities. The purpose of the telling is to strengthen the young with a mature understanding of human beings, both of their limitations and of their potentials. The tale of barbarism cannot end with twisted wire and torn bodies. We all must come to see and appreciate what these gallant non-Jews did.

We must, for the sake of our sanity, make use of history to restore a sense of balance, to provide some moral symmetry to humanity. For non-Jews particularly, knowledge of the conduct and behavior of their contemporaries who rescued is no less essential. Let no one turn a deaf ear to the sound of accusation, to the noise of villainy, or to the voices of heroism. Instead, let us be justifiably proud of such nobility of character.

The world is hungry for moral heroes like Fritz Graebe. Because of him, they who knew the sadness of the disillusioned heart know also that there is an alternative to complicity with the enemies of humanity. They know that there is meaning to our belief that humanity was created in "the image of God."

It is my privilege to know well this extraordinary man, Fritz Graebe, and his wife, Elisabeth. The Reverend Douglas Huneke has written an ecumenical book in the profoundest sense of the word, for he has drawn upon Mr. Graebe's "humanly holy" (from Martin Buber's distinction between a life of holiness in the present world and an angelic or otherworldly holiness) responses to totalitarian intimidation and to acts that transcend race, religion, creed, and class. Reverend Huneke's remarkable text is for every man, woman, and child. Its truth derives from no theoretical construct or superhuman being but from the celebration of the human spirit that resides in each of us.

Preface

I had to know. After nearly ten years of research, study, tormented reflection, and teaching, I had to know if the final word belonged to the Nazi murderers. I had to know if the roles of the Holocaust were to be reduced to just three: murderer, victim, bystander. The murderers, with their uncomplicated one-dimensional mission, were not of interest to me. Their aggression and unthinking obedience to authority belonged to another domain, the purview of some other science of human behavior. The victims were of profound importance, but I knew that I could only listen, absorb, and be changed by their testimony and their lives.

The third group concerned me the most—the masses who remained silent, unmoving, indifferent. Had they acted, they most certainly would have lowered the human toll exacted by the death camps. I had to know why they remained inert, their eyes averted from the arrests, tortures, and humiliations. Why were their hearts closed, their bodies frozen? The bystanders lived lives as simple and one-dimensional as those of the murderers. The killers killed and the bystanders pretended not to see, know, or understand.

In 1976, while on a spiritual and academic pilgrimage to the former extermination camps in Poland and the German Democratic Republic, and to the Israeli Holocaust archives at Yad Vashem in Jerusalem, I became aware of a fourth role played during the horrors. I had not begun the odyssey with the intention of searching for other roles, but rather for the purpose of preparing a personal, Christian response to the Holocaust for its victims.

The fourth role was formally introduced to me by the taxi driver who transported me from the city of Krakow to the former death camp Auschwitz. During the ride he inquired about the purpose of my visit and, in a very caring gesture, elected to be my companion as I entered this most vile of the extermination camps. He said, "No one should enter this place alone." Together we viewed a sequence of films from the Soviet and Allied liberations of the camp and from captured Nazi footage of the camp in operation. After viewing the film, the driver was terribly upset and left me for the remainder of the day. When we met, hours later, he apologized and explained his emotional outburst. As it happened, his sister, a devout Roman Catholic, had served during the war as a nurse in the Polish equivalent of the Red Cross. She had regularly made rounds in the Jewish ghetto in Krakow. She had precious few medical supplies and almost no medication.

The plight of the children moved her to create a means of removing them from the ghetto and placing them in the homes of friends on the outskirts of Krakow. Her rescues followed a strict pattern. She would walk with a child hidden between her legs under the large hoops of her dress. Once this walk was mastered, she could take the child through the ghetto, past the militia-staffed guard post, and on to safety with an adoptive family. She had done this six or seven times, when she tried to evacuate a child with tuberculosis. The child let out a muffled cough at precisely the wrong moment. A militiaman heard the noise and grabbed the woman. He knocked her to the ground, and before her very eyes, he and the other guards who had rushed from the shadows yanked the child into the air and shot him. They next turned their weapons and summarily executed the nurse.

Even though I remained faithful to the primary purpose of my pilgrimage, this deeply moving story became a haunting counterpoint to the inhumanity of the Holocaust and was the genesis of my interest in those who courageously performed the fourth role, the rescuers. For several years I had read various incomplete accounts of the rescuers, but it was not enough for me only to know the stories. I was compelled to know what led the rescuers to take such risks on behalf of total strangers. In 1979 and 1981 I received grants from the Oregon Committee for the Humanities and from the Memorial Foundation for Jewish Culture that enabled me to begin a systematic study of the moral and spiritual development of the rescuers. I went to Jerusalem and with the support and cooperation of the Department of the Righteous at Yad Vashem, I was able to review case studies and to interview some of the rescuers, who were in Jerusalem at that time to be honored, as well as many of those whom they had rescued. Returning to the United States, I continued gathering the stories and interviewing the men and women who had lived out these dramas of human compassion. As I left Yad Vashem, the parting admonition by the director of the department was, "Be certain that you meet Herman Graebe in San Francisco."

While conducting my research in the archives, I found frequent references to this compassionate, tenacious German Christian who had taken remarkable risks as he developed and maintained a rescue network that saved the lives of hundreds of Jews and peasants. In accomplishing this feat, he had been required to virtually abandon his family in order to protect them, and he had depleted his personal resources and suffered serious health consequences as a result of his work. Then, as if what he had already done were insufficient, he sought justice for those thousands whom he was unable to save. Fritz (as he preferred to be called) Graebe's depositions were read to the International War Crimes Tribunal at Nuremberg, and the attendant publicity caused Graebe and his family to be ostracized in Germany. Subsequently, the depositions have been quoted in more than one hundred texts and translated into nearly a dozen languages.

From our first meeting in his San Francisco office, it was clear that Fritz Graebe embodied a Christian faith grounded in Biblical teachings to "love your neighbor" and "care for the sojourner in your midst." Here was a man who had resisted the combined forces of culture, nationalism, and state authority solely for the purpose of saving the lives of desperately endangered strangers. Fritz Graebe used his position as a civilian employee of the Reich, an engineer, to conduct his humanitarian efforts.

In spite of these monumental considerations, Fritz Graebe, like most of the other rescuers, disdains the label of hero. He refers to his acts as simple, often inadequate, gestures of human decency. He tells visitors that, in these worst of circumstances, he had simply done what he could to help; "I did what anyone could have done, should have done."

The impact of his deeds and, by implication, the acts of other rescuers are best stated in a simple and profound tribute to him by Tadeuz Glass, the leader of a group of thirty Jews who were rescued by Graebe. The tribute, engraved on a gold case presented to the rescuer, reads: "To Mr. Engineer Herman Fritz Graebe whose actions in the cruelest of historical eras gave back to me to a belief in humanity. Wiesbaden, 1 February 1947." The rescuers gave the victims back their human dignity and a sense of hope in a hopeless time. Today Herman Graebe also keeps a photograph, perhaps as a reminder, in the case that holds the tribute. The blurred image on the bent paper is of a Jew hanging from a makeshift gallows. That lone, murdered Jew is a symbol of all that Graebe resisted.

What motivated Fritz Graebe to resist and disobey the directives of the Third Reich? How was he able, in the face of rampant, murderous racism, to engage in activities that opposed the forces of anti-Semitism and that made him the quarry of informers, malcontents, and the dreaded Gestapo? Why, in one deeply Christian culture after another, were there not more people with the vision and resolve and commitment of Fritz Graebe? Why, with the essential work of rescue completed and the war at an end, did he jeopardize his place in German society by seeking to bring to justice those fellow citizens who had masterminded and perpetrated the evil acts that he had witnessed?

Though his efforts were audacious and gallant, risky and expensive, it would be a mistake to seek some complex psychosocial explanation for his compassion. It would be a great disservice to treat him as a deviant simply because his was a minority action. Fritz Graebe had learned the skills he needed and the moral values of compassion. His motives in the Nazi era can be traced back to the instruction of his mother, Louise Graebe. She taught him to be an independent thinker and to care for the less fortunate and for those who were the victims of society. She showed him how to be hospitable and instilled in him a profound sense of justice that enabled him to resist ill-willed, inhumane authorities.

He had life experiences that crossed over political, religious, and social boundaries. He maintained an egalitarian outlook toward people of different creeds and races. His spiritual life was informed by the Christian tradition of the Golden Rule and the Christian parable of the Good Samaritan.

Furthermore, his activities in the Nazi era would not have been possible without the selfless, unquestioning support of his wife, Elisabeth Graebe. She knew only a little of what was happening to the Jews and almost nothing of her husband's mission, but when she learned that many lives depended on his honoring his promise, she stepped aside and urged him to fulfill his vow. She did this after an absence of several years and while she and their ten-year-old son were visiting the Ukraine, hundreds of miles from the safety of their home in Germany.

I present this account of his life partly in his own words, in the words of many whom he rescued, and from the archival records of his deeds. The purpose of this book is to provide a public record of his valorous behavior; to offer the horrified, post-Holocaust generations an account of one who resisted evil, who took the side of the oppressed, and who lived out the admonition of St. Paul to "be not conformed to this world" (Romans 12:2); and to tell the story of one who bears the honored title "Righteous Among the Nations." On August 20, 1965, Herman Friedrich Graebe received the highest honors bestowed by the government of Israel through the Holocaust Memorial Center, Yad Vashem. The honored title came to him as he planted a carob tree in the Garden of the Righteous, on the Avenue of the Just. Today, in front of the tree is a modest black plaque bearing a simple inscription in Hebrew and German, *Hermann F. Graebe, Germany*. Before Fritz Graebe received these honors the Yad Vashem Commission for the Designation of the Righteous carefully considered the accounts of Jews whom he rescued, pored over his testimony before the International Military Tribunal, and his sworn testimony prepared for their commission. In addition to the tree, he was presented with a certificate that testifies to his honor, and finally, he was given the highest distinction, the specially cast medal from Yad Vashem and the people of Israel. It bears a saying from the *Mishnah*: "He who saves one life, it is as if he saves the whole world."

I hope that the readers of this testimony will identify with Fritz Graebe's values and commitment to life. I hope too that his actions will be an example for those who wonder how they would act in similar circumstances. Now they have a model of one who is not far removed from them, not a superhuman being, but rather one in whom we can see ourselves.

To Fritz Graebe, human suffering was inappropriate and unnecessary, and through most of his life he has resisted the forces that cause suffering. There is a consistent perspective that has informed his behavior over the years, a perspective that was best described by the late Dr. Martin Luther King, Jr., in his last public address:

> The first question that the Levite asked was, "If I stop to help this man, what will happen to me?" But then the good Samaritan came by. And he reversed the question: "If I do not stop to help this man, what will happen to him?" That is the question before you. . . .[1]

It was precisely "that question" that was before Fritz Graebe when, with great care and planning, he placed the rescue of Jews, Polish peasants, and other refugees before his own personal security. This book is the testament of one person's struggle to be moral and caring in the cruelest of eras and a denial of the final word to the murderers and indifferent bystanders.

DOUGLAS K. HUNEKE

Acknowledgments

The initial study that led to a meeting between the author and Herman (Fritz) Graebe was made possible by a Faculty Summer Research Grant from the Oregon Committee for the Humanities. A portion of the initial research was also funded by a grant from the Memorial Foundation for Jewish Culture. I am profoundly grateful for these two grants, which came at a period when virtually no scholars were considering the acts and the motivations of rescuers in the Nazi era.

THE MOSES
OF ROVNO

1. Actions Taken Against the Jews

In the spring of 1941, the Reich Security Service established four battalion-size mobile killing units called *Einsatzgruppen* (Special Action Groups). These forces, of nearly three thousand men each, moved rapidly into Poland, the Ukraine, and parts of the Soviet Union. Their assignment was to summarily execute all Jews, Communists, dissidents, and the infirm. The autonomous *Einsatzgruppen* were relatively free of normal military constraints and protocol and pursued their task virtually without consideration for any routine wartime military objectives. They regularly followed the German army into an occupied area and killed Jews or hunted down "undesirables" who had eluded the army. In some circumstances the *Einsatzgruppen* were even permitted to precede the army with a lightning raid that surprised the population, allowing the units to kill the Jews before they could either flee or hide.

Einsatzgruppe C, the smallest of the four units, positioned itself near the Ukrainian city of Sdolbonov late in the first week of August 1941. The unsuspecting population was not prepared for an Action; only an unbelieving few had even heard of such a thing happening. The Jews believed that they would be relocated or, at worst, roughed up by the German soliders. At dawn on August 7, 1941, the unit invaded the city. As was their custom, they rounded up only the Jewish men. The Action took the entire day to be completed, but it was thorough and successful. As the Jews were found, they were beaten and then forced to sit in a squatting position in the heat of the late summer sun with their hands clasped behind their bowed heads.

Between four and five o'clock in the afternoon, two hundred fifty Jewish men were taken to a mass grave behind the cement factory and shot to death. *Einsatzgruppe* C left Sdolbonov the next morning to continue its assignment of exterminating the entire Jewish population in that region. In an Operational Report to Reich Security Service Headquarters dated December 12, 1941, the *Einsatzgruppen* claimed to have eliminated 55,000 Jews. Actions conducted by other mobile killing units accounted for an additional 245,000 Jewish victims in that period.[2]

Also in August 1941, while the *Einsatzgruppen* were doing their work, engineer Fritz Graebe was completing an assignment on the West Wall fortifications in Kronenburg near the Franco-German border. Between 1938 and 1941, the West Wall had been constructed and strengthened by the Germans in order to repel any military action initiated by either the French or the British. This range of fortifications had radically altered the strategic maps of Europe and was to play a critical role in the defense of the western flanks of the Reich when its armies later invaded Poland. The West Wall was also a source of great dissension. Adolf Hitler saw it as an impenetrable defensive line as well as the launching point for a future western offensive. Others in the Reich military command knew that the line could not hold for more than a few weeks even under optimum conditions. The five army divisions in the region could do little in a conflict with the superior French forces. The command of the Wehrmacht felt that the western fortifications served at best to block cooperation and mutual assistance between the French, the British, and their allies.

By early summer of 1939, plans for the invasion of Poland had approached the final stage. Hitler was not to be deterred from his vision of a rapid attack in the east and a counteroffensive in the west. From his perspective, the West Wall would serve as a powerful buffer between Germany and the west in the event that France and Britain decided to honor their pact with Poland by invading Germany on its western border as it engaged Poland. In August, Hitler ordered a special massive program to fortify the West Wall line. Steel and armaments production was briefly directed to this effort. Hitler, who predicted a speedy victory in Poland, expected this defensive line to hold until there could be a rapid redeployment of troops from the Polish front to the Western Front.

Fritz Graebe represented one of nearly a dozen German contractors who were assigned to hasten the work and strengthen the line. Since the summer of 1939, Graebe and his colleagues had labored. By late August 1939, the work on the West Wall was almost finished, and it appeared to be able to withstand any strike by the French or British armies. The beginning of the war on September 1, 1939, followed by an attempt to assassinate Hitler on November 8 in Munich and the widely disseminated assertion that this plot was the work of the British

Secret Service, only redoubled the resolve of most of the workers.

Between 1939 and August 1941, Fritz Graebe served at his engineering post in Kronenburg at the West Wall, planning and implementing designs from Berlin, supervising, and traveling extensively for his employer, the Josef Jung construction firm of Solingen. Graebe had already distinguished himself for his ability to coordinate and manage very large labor columns. His hard work and the distinctions he had earned on the vital western fortifications project enabled him to avoid the war and the general muster.

August 1941 was a fateful month for Graebe. In that month, Hermann Goering appointed the director of the Reich Security Service, Reinhard Heydrich, to be the chief designer of the "Final Solution." Though they would never meet face to face, Fritz Graebe and Heydrich would soon be locked in a private war: one would devise the means of mass murder while the other would work tirelessly to protect the sanctity of human life. But in August 1941, Graebe was pondering the implications of a telegram that would signal a critical change in his life. The young engineer read and reread the telegram from the Todt engineering headquarters in Berlin as he stood in the cool shade of a tree near the West Wall staging area in Kronenburg. The wire directed him to report to the Ukraine, first to Lvov and then to a city farther east, where he was to serve as the manager of a railroad engineering project for the Reich Railroad Administration.

For Graebe, the Ukraine was a distant, unknown place. Yet the task to be done was important, even if it was dangerously close to the war. It would mean an even longer absence from his family than this one, but it also would mean an unparalleled opportunity to advance himself and to improve his skills in the field. Graebe packed for his trip and planned a brief stopover in Solingen and nearby Grafrath, his home town, to visit his family and to interview and hire ten additional workers to help open the project. By now, his wife Elisabeth was accustomed to her husband's travel schedule and long absences, but she secretly hoped that he would refuse the call to work in the Ukraine. Fear for her husband's safety was combined with concern about the distance that would separate them and for their nine-year-old son, Friedel, whose time spent with his father was already too limited. Fritz had made his decision, however, and he left Grafrath for the Ukraine on schedule.

At this time in the course of the war, there was as yet little general knowledge of the atrocities being suffered by the Jews. Few people were even aware of the law that had been passed on November 29, 1939, requiring all Jews in occupied areas to wear distinctive armbands and either yellow patches (as was the custom in the Ukraine) or yellow Stars of David. News traveled slowly from the Eastern Front, and the Reich's extermination plans also were still secret. Early in 1941, the *Einsatzgruppen* had been formed, transported, and deployed throughout the eastern countries, and the final three months of 1941 silently witnessed the establishment of camps such as Theresienstadt and Chelmno and the massacre of nearly twenty thousand Jews in the Odessa region of the Black Sea.

While Fritz Graebe was making arrangements to obey his orders, *Einsatzgruppe* C was preparing to move against the Jews of that same small city in the Ukraine to which his work was taking him, a city then completely unknown to Graebe, but whose name would soon be etched indelibly in his mind: Sdolbonov.

2. Terror in the Streets

It is essential to understand some of the models and forces that shaped and influenced Fritz Graebe to become an altruistic person and later a rescuer of Jews and peasants.

By the autumn of 1941, Fritz was already forty-one years old, a husband and father, and a successful construction engineer. Though small in stature, the bespectacled Graebe was trim and muscled from his labors. His businesslike demeanor was softened by an easy smile that warmed his usually stern face. He was a German, and his upbringing, education, and experience were substantially similar to those of an entire generation of Germans born in the years preceding World War I. Clearly, Fritz Graebe possessed a sense of responsibility for others that was to develop in surprising ways, but that moral empathy did not spring into being out of nothing. There were deep roots from which his feelings and actions rose, roots developing early in his childhood and nurtured by a variety of later events and relationships. But these roots were subtle and diverse, and their full effect did not become evident until Graebe, a German official, found himself face to face with the Nazi atrocities in the Ukraine.

Herman Friedrich Graebe was born on June 19, 1900, in Grafrath, a small town near Solingen in the Rhineland region in northwestern Germany. He was the eldest of two boys, his brother Erich having been born in 1902. His father, Friedrich Graebe, was a weaver who worked long hours and then gave much of his free time to serving on the local volunteer fire brigade, which he had helped to found. His mother, Louise Kinkel Graebe, worked as a domestic to help support the family, but much of her energy was reserved for her children. To Fritz, her presence and example were the major influences on his later life.

Louise Graebe was a deeply religious woman with strong convictions about right and wrong. Her faith and defined moral values were by no means unusual for her time, but she was known both for her personal warmth and for the very genuine ecumenism of her beliefs. For her, all people were children of God, and she related to them on that basis. The doors of her home were quite literally open to all. The Graebes themselves were Protestants, a minority in predominantly Roman Catholic Grafrath, and Frau Graebe was a staunch member of her local Lutheran parish. She counted a number of Jews in her community as personal friends, and she also frequently gave aid to the charities of the local Catholic church. Sister Angelica and the other nuns were always welcome, and they, along with people from nearly every walk of life in Grafrath, always found a warm welcoming embrace at Louise Graebe's door. One measure of just how profoundly her love and fellowship had affected the town came at her funeral in 1938. Fritz Graebe remembers:

> There were so many flowers for her and the newspapers carried a detailed story about the funeral. There had never been such a large funeral procession in the region. The procession was so long, nearly one kilometer, that the first people arrived at the cemetery just as the last ones were leaving the house. . . . It was so moving to see so many people come to pay respects for my mother.

While Louise Graebe was lovingly remembered by many, she may have had her greatest influence upon her own sons. Fritz grew up in a world of distinct right and wrong, but that sense of righteousness was always tempered by an equally strong sense of charity, a willingness to understand and appreciate the position of the other person. Louise Graebe instilled both of these values by her personal example. Morally, she neither feared nor hesitated to speak out against what she perceived to be wrong, and she encouraged the boys to do the same. Ethically, she often combined her sense of empathy and understanding with her moral values and taught them in the same lesson.

One vivid example involved Fritz's younger brother Erich, who had been born with a crippling, and later disfiguring, spinal deformity. Physicians had initially thought that he would never either walk or be able to participate in normal activities. His mother, however, insisted on treating him as normally as possible, expecting from him the same things that she expected from Fritz. Erich was eventually able to attend school. His classmates, though, had no sense of how difficult this feat had been for him, and one afternoon Fritz and his mother happened upon a group of boys who were ridiculing Erich for his deformity.

Stung by their cruelty, Frau Graebe scolded the boys for their thoughtlessness. Then, as if catching herself, she paused and looked each boy squarely in the eyes while she softly asked how he would feel if others made fun of him for something he could not help. Her gentle firmness made its point. The teasing ended, and Erich was accepted by the other children. Taken as a single incident, Frau Graebe's lesson was not remarkable. Many a parent has asked a child to consider how a thoughtless action makes another person feel. For Fritz Graebe, however, there were literally scores of times when his mother would call his attention to a difficult or confusing situation and ask softly, ". . . and you, Fritz, what would you do?" He was repeatedly called upon to imagine himself in another's place:

> I always put myself in the place of small people. . . . When my aunt Anna killed her husband she was shunned by the family, all except my mother, her sister. While others ignored her and failed to visit her in prison, my mother would go out of her way to be with her sister. Their mother was critical of her for this, but later my mother would say to me, Fritz, what would you do?—Support my aunt, of course.

Another value strongly emphasized in the Graebe household was the virtue of hard work and diligence. Fritz's family was poor but respected, and he learned early on that he would have to depend upon himself to achieve his potentials. Just how seriously he took this belief is shown by his response to a difficult problem that he encountered late in his teenage years. Fritz was attending a technical college in a nearby town when he suddenly and inexplicably developed a debilitating stutter. Almost overnight, the once-popular Fritz withdrew from his normal social activities, and soon his studies began to suffer as well. He felt almost paralyzed, unable to speak without the humiliating stutter.

In a time long before behavior modification psychology became popular, Fritz had virtually no one to help him with this profound problem. How he finally overcame the stuttering reveals much about the values he learned growing up in his family, and it also helps to account for the determined and focused energy that was to play such an important part in his later efforts in the Ukraine. Put simply, Fritz Graebe decided that the stutter had to stop. He bought a self-help book and practiced reading aloud daily in front of a mirror in the privacy of his room for almost four years until he could speak without a trace of hesitation. During those years he continued to go to school part time, but because of his embarrassment over the stutter, he was forced to teach himself much of what he needed to learn in order to become a licensed engineer. He succeeded at the task of passing the state licensing examinations, just as he had overcome the stuttering. His faith in his own abilities and his capacity for difficult, sustained work would serve him well later.

One of Fritz Graebe's abiding interests was the theater, particularly the light opera. He admired the ability of the actors to take on the range and dimensions of their roles: strong and powerful in one instance, crafty in another, modest and reserved in still another. He also thrilled to the music and the spectacle of the performances. As he neared the end of his engineering training—having only recently cured his stuttering problem—Graebe began socializing with his friends again, and one of their favorite places to go was the nearby town of Wuppertal, where a light opera company performed regularly. One evening at a performance of that company, Fritz caught the eye of an attractive young woman, but he was shy and afraid to approach the group of young women she was seated with. Fortunately, one of his friends was bolder, went over to the young women, and invited them to join Graebe and his friends. This proved to be the beginning of a formal two-year courtship between Fritz and Elisabeth Stader, the young woman who had caught his eye. The romance developed slowly because Elisabeth lived near Wald, and because Fritz's studies and work commanded most of his time.

By 1923, Fritz was in his final year of schooling and was working on the side, maintaining machinery at a steel factory in Grafrath. One night, while he was repairing a damaged belt on one of the machines, the belt suddenly snapped and hurled him to the ground, causing him to strike his head. When he was taken to the local hospital, the doctors were pessimistic about his chances for recovery because he was bleeding from his ears and had double vision. A friend soon contacted Elisabeth, and she arrived just after the attending physician had informed Graebe that his vision had been irreparably damaged. The nurses were equally bleak about his prospects. One confidentially informed Elisabeth that Graebe "would not make it." Elisabeth, however, understood Fritz and knew what he needed. After visiting a few moments with him, she announced that she would marry him as soon as he recovered!

The intercranial pressure gradually subsided, and Fritz began to recover enough to go home. The main problem was the persistence of the double vision, which meant that he could not return to his work and would again have to slow down his studies. He did not return to work, but instead concentrated his energies on the task of completing his education. Elisabeth, true to her word, set about planning for their wedding.

The wedding took place on July 24, 1924, in the village church at Ketzberg, near Grafrath, but it was no simple accomplishment. Fritz felt that his pastor in Grafrath had behaved unethically in an earlier incident, and the highly principled young man refused to permit that pastor to marry them. Elisabeth agreed, and together they finally found a distinguished minister and scholar to perform the service. This seemingly minor incident confirms the strong commitment to a system of life-directing values that both Elisabeth and Fritz shared.

After their wedding the couple continued to live in Grafrath. Fritz worked haltingly on the completion of his studies and on his licensing examinations. Elisabeth was employed as a weaver in a factory in the neighboring city of Haan. As his eyes healed and corrected themselves, Fritz completed his studies and began working as an engineer. It was not a prosperous time in Germany. The armistice following World War I was a heavy burden on the economy and spirit of the nation. With the persistent economic depression, Elisabeth worked until November 1931, when she took a leave of absence to give birth to their son.

Also in 1931, Fritz Graebe made a decision that he would soon come to regret. He joined the increasingly popular National Socialist Party over the strenuous objections of his wife and against his own best judgment. The membership was, for him, an informal and meaningless association which he took out at the urging of a business associate who convinced him that the membership would be good for his future. Fritz disapproved of Hitler and the racial policies, but his associate encouraged him to overlook the leadership's brassy style and those policies that were a reflection of a naïve political group. The businessman was certain the naïveté would disappear as the Party assumed power and began working for the best interests of all German people. Fritz recalls what motivated him:

> Hitler said he would rebuild Germany. I was a builder so it might be good for me. A better economy meant more work for me, and in my own field. Isn't that what everyone in Germany believed? I think we all needed to believe it—I was no exception.

By early 1932, however, Graebe was beginning to have his doubts. Brownshirted men paraded around in small groups, often soliciting funds to aid the cause of the National Socialist movement. Posters were going

up on virtually every wall and fence, proclaiming that National Socialism was the will of the people, the destiny of the nation. Public parades
created the impression of great support for a renewed and spirited Germany, but the streets told another story. Fights regularly broke out between the Nazi Party faithfuls and their adversaries.

The frequency of these clashes and their escalating violence soon made
clear that they were far more than youthful exuberance. Germany was
being divided into factions, and the Nazis were revealing an unantici-
pated ugliness. As these things continued, whatever vague enthusiasm
Graebe had had for Hitler and his programs was lost, and both Fritz
and Elisabeth became powerless observers of the deteriorating political
situation. They could no longer foresee a future under Hitler or National Socialism that would lead to a resurgence of pride and greatness.
So they remained aloof and expressed their criticism in caustic jokes
shared with a few trusted acquaintances. On occasion, though, it was
impossible to remain indifferent. Fritz remembers:

> I recall one time when I was particularly fed up with all the
> propaganda, all of the pressures to join the Party. A young man
> was passing through the neighborhoods putting six or ten flyers
> in every post box. The flyer had a picture of Adolf Hitler and a
> call to patriotism. They had been around the streets with marches
> and bands. It was too much. I took the flyers and threw them
> out into the street. My neighbor saw me and warned me. I don't
> think it was a bad thing to do. I saved one flyer, read it, and
> threw it away; it was trash. I doubt if my neighbor reported me;
> there was not a mood for that kind of thing, yet.

Not until their infant son became ill and in need of medical attention
in 1933 did they begin to realize how dangerous the changes taking
place around them were. As she left their home in Grafrath to take her
sick child to the family physician, Dr. Jacob Markus, Elisabeth Graebe
passed signs announcing the enforcement of boycott laws directed against
Jewish-owned businesses. She did not make a connection between the
signs and her mission at that time.

But when she arrived at the office, which also served as Dr. Markus's
residence, a burly SA guard forcefully blocked her way and snapped,
"There is a boycott against Jews. You may not go in there."

Clutching her feverish son in her arms, she tried to push past the
guard, who continued to block her and arrogantly announced, "Aryans
go to Aryan doctors."

She protested, but the guard persisted. "How can you let a Jew touch your boy? He's such a good-looking German boy."

That was enough for Elisabeth. "You lay one hand on me and I will tell the world exactly what kind of an Aryan you are," she snapped, then pushed past the guard and went inside. But this was to be her last visit to Dr. Markus. Everything was changing.

By mid-1933 Germany was a churning cauldron of political activity. Chancellor Adolf Hitler was traveling from town to town campaigning for the National Socialists. Every evening huge Nazi rallies spilled out from auditoriums and stadiums, and the streets were crammed with snaking parades of chanting people, illuminated by the eerie light of burning torches. These awesome scenes, frightening but compelling, evoked the most primal rituals.

Adolf Hitler's famous "Peace Speech" on May 7, 1933, gave world leaders a false sense of security in the face of a resurgent German nationalism. This period of apparent conciliation was short-lived, ending abruptly on October 14, 1933, when Adolf Hitler announced to a stunned world that Germany was withdrawing both from the League of Nations Disarmament Conference and from the League of Nations.

Shrewdly, Hitler announced a plebiscite, which would essentially be a vote of confidence, on his League of Nations decisions. The date for the plebiscite, which was to substitute for a democratic election, was set for November 12, 1933, fifteen years and one day after the signing of the fateful World War I armistice—an infamous date that symbolized defeat and dishonor to most Germans. Two weeks before the November plebiscite, in a large pre-election rally, Hitler linked past defeats with the call for a national resurgence:

> See to it that this day [November 12, 1933] shall later be recorded in the history of our people as a day of salvation—that the record shall run: On an eleventh day of November the German people formally lost its honor; fifteen years later came a twelfth of November and then the German people restored its honor to itself.

So astute was Hitler's election strategy that he was able to attain better than ninety-six percent of the votes cast. The plebiscite was, on the surface, a clear vote of confidence for Hitler and the Reich. The decisions to leave the Disarmament Conference and to withdraw from the League of Nations, and the election of a single-party Nazi slate for the Reichstag, consolidated Hitler's power and redirected the energies of the nation. To the outside world it looked like a peaceful, if troubling, transition: a legal transfer of power by the vote of a majority of the populace. A witness to the plebiscite of 1933 referred to it as a "revolution by amateurs and bullies," ruthlessly complete in scope, legal, but not necessarily the free will of the German people.

Grafrath was not particularly supportive of the Nazi movement. Like that of most small towns, its life-style was simple and placid. Everyone knew everyone else; it was a place where folk could complain about or reflect on current events, share gossip, discuss family matters, or express their fears about the subtle changes that were becoming evident in their city and in Solingen, the seat of the regional government. However, the small size of the close-knit community made it difficult for the people to take a definitive public stand against the Nazi government. Yet it also made it impossible to miss the signs of the Nazification of Germany.

Since January 30, 1933, when Hitler became chancellor, there had been an increasing number of small parades, diminutive marches, boring speeches, and heated arguments in the taverns. In the neighboring city of Cologne, where Konrad Adenauer and his Catholic Center Party had presided for sixteen years, the Nazis had gone quickly from a small minority to a position of control in the city council. Street names were speedily changed to reflect the shift in power and to honor the regional Party faithful and the high-ranking members of the Reich. Even before the elections it was not uncommon to see armed Nazi guards stationed in or near public buildings. In Cologne, after the November election the flags of the Nazi movement appeared outside the city halls, railroad stations, and district offices.

Because of its small size and close-knit character, Grafrath was initially spared most of the house searches, beatings, street fighting, and turmoil in town council meetings. Other than at the marches, parades, and rallies, there were not even Nazi flags in Grafrath until long after the November election. Yet the people in Grafrath, like those in towns and villages throughout Germany, could not really resist the attraction of Hitler and his followers. The Brownshirts may have been a romantic, undisciplined army, but they were impressive when they marched and sang, the seasoned veterans and the new visionaries, young and old together. Their commanding presence was a warning, a preview of the trouble that could come to anyone who resisted. The pomp, the raw numbers, the mystique, the shows of force in one town and then the next, all combined to minimize dissent and keep people fearfully insecure—even in small, intimate towns like Grafrath. Resistance and disapproval were beaten down; they were never ignored. Nazi culture, form of government, and life-style quickly became the order of the day, even for those who had not voted for Adolf Hitler. It was a time when conformity to a system, to a way of life, took precedence over everything else. Loyalty to the movement, no matter how strong or weak that loyalty, took precedence even over friendships, associations, and family ties.

That point was brought home to Grafrath on November 12, 1933, the day of the plebiscite itself. Fritz Graebe remembers the day as starting out gray and damp. There had been a virtual bombardment of propaganda, culminating on the night before the election with a call by President von Hindenburg for the unity and solidarity of the German people. Though it was not widely publicized, people knew by word of mouth that they would have great troubles if they did not vote or if they voted the wrong way. Therefore, the majority of eligible voters arrived at the polls to perform their "civic duty."

When Fritz and Elisabeth arrived at their precinct voting station on Schulstrasse, they found the procedures for voting to be different from those of the past. People were lined up waiting to enter the room with the curtained voting booths. The crowd was unusually quiet—even the most opinionated were remarkably reserved—and somber. As they entered the room, Fritz and Elisabeth saw the usual four or five curtained booths standing empty while the queue formed in front of a simple open desk. Standing behind the desk was a neighbor, Reinhard Bertram. Bertram was a "little Hitler" who wielded a good deal of power locally now that Adolf Hitler was in command of the national government. The voting set-up itself sent a clear message: Everyone was free to vote in a booth, but such an action could be interpreted as opposition to the Party. The cautious and the wise stayed in the line and awaited their opportunity to make an X on the paper in Bertram's sight.

As the Graebes approached the voting table, there was a small commotion from the back of the room where a man was pushing his way through the bottleneck at the doorway. A ripple of noise moved through the line. Emerging from the mass of faces and breaking ranks with them was Adolf Stöcker, a highly respected member of the community and an important man in the economic circles of Solingen. The sixty-year-old manufacturer carried himself with the dignity of an aristocratic baron. Rather than stand in a line and be accountable to a hooligan like Bertram, Stöcker strode to one of the booths, nodded to the awestruck crowd, took off his hat, entered the polling booth, ceremoniously closed the curtain, and cast his vote. Emerging within seconds, he carefully replaced his hat, shot a disdainful glance at Bertram, and walked out of the room.

At six o'clock the polling stations closed and by eight the results were in. Across the land the vote was declared "a Hitler vote!" In Grafrath there was only one "no" vote and there was no doubt about who had cast it. Elisabeth Graebe was preparing the evening meal when the first shouts wafted through their kitchen window. Across the small, narrow valley that separated them from Stöcker's house, Elisabeth could see a thin line of torches snaking up the hillside.

The night had brought an end to the earlier damp; it was now clear and crisp, and a wind blowing across the valley carried the shouts of the marchers. Adolf Stöcker had a home that befit his high status in the manufacturing community. The beautiful residence had large windows and a sumptuous view of the valley and Grafrath. As the first marchers reached the Stöcker house, Fritz could see by the torchlight that the windows were closed and boarded. The Graebes watched the crowd grow in numbers, the sky glowing with the light of the kerosene torches.

Soon a chant could be heard filling the air. At first it was hard for Elisabeth and Fritz to make out the words. Then someone began chanting into a loudspeaker, shouting over and over, "What should we do with Stöcker? What should we do with Stöcker?" and the crowd roared back a rhythmic response: *"Aufhängen! Aufhängen!"* ("Hang him! Hang him!") For half an hour the crowd chanted at the doorstep of the town's most respected civic leader, until all that could be heard was the phrase *"Aufhängen!"* Then, unexpectedly, the chanting stopped and the crowd dispersed. The carefully staged event had made its point. Others would hesitate to imitate the independent Stöcker.

Fritz Graebe remembers just how great the power of the crowd was:

> Adolf Stöcker had two sons. The great tragedy of the voting affair was the widely believed rumor that his sons were present in the crowd. One was an SS and the other was an SA. Rumor had it that both sons had been required to climb the hill with torches in their hands shouting "Hang him! Hang him!" Can you imagine that? Those bastards! What a tragedy for Stöcker. They made his sons do something terrible like that. Can you imagine that poor man in his house knowing that his sons were outside shouting such words?

The Nazis did not hang Adolf Stöcker; instead, the Gestapo arrested him the next day while he was walking down one of the town streets.

He spent the next six months in prison. The terrible lessons of November 1933 were beginning to become apparent even in Grafrath: There were no more free elections, there were no more independent parties, there was no longer room for divergent points of view, and, if the Nazis could do such a thing to Herr Stöcker, the distinguished businessman, imagine what they might do to lesser citizens who did not cooperate. Soon rumors were spread by the Nazis that Stöcker was a Social Democrat. (The Reich had banned all opposition parties because they were a threat to the reunification efforts.) Somehow this was meant to explain or justify the imprisonment of a prominent member of the community. The Nazi leaders attempted to refute those who charged that Stöcker was arrested because he voted against the Nazi measures in the plebiscite. The refutations fell on deaf, powerless ears, as Graebe recalls:

> These were not free elections. It makes me so mad, so bitter to hear people say that the German people wanted Hitler and got what they deserved. Americans say to me, "You voted for him." Yes, we voted for him, but we did not have a choice. I chose the easy way. I went in the line, made the cross, and left the room. Stöcker was stupid, but very principled. He was an honorable man, but couldn't he see that no one could do anything to stop the party? Maybe he had to do what he did. On November 12 I did it the other way.

In the months that followed Hitler's plebiscite, the Nazis had intensified their anti-Jewish activities. Militant Nazi Brownshirts blocked the entrances to Jewish stores, markets, and offices. Anti-Jewish boycotts and blockades became more aggressive as vicious anti-Jewish slogans appeared on walls, were splashed on windows, and paraded on placards. Each day it became less and less safe for Jews to appear in public. Curfews were violently enforced, while Jewish businesses were closed and their inventories expropriated. Hitler's Reichstag speech following the plebiscite, accepting "the will of the people," was an ominous sign for the Jews and others who opposed Adolf Hitler and his plans for National Socialism.

The parades, the swastika flags and armbands, and all the action in the streets signaled the massive changes that were coming. The Nazi salute was replacing the handshake while the militant *"Heil Hitler"* became a more common form of greeting than the familiar *"Guten Tag."* The newsreels featured endless shots of Hitler standing in an open car being driven through throngs of seemingly adoring people. Street brawls continued between youthful Communists and National Socialists, and the inflammatory rhetoric and the persecution of Jews increased at an alarming rate.

3. The Essen Jail

In the spring of 1934, barely six months after Adolf Hitler's triumphant election victory, Fritz Graebe was working as a building contractor, constructing small homes with adjacent garages. It was not the sort of engineering work that he preferred, but he was grateful for the chance to work at all. Adolf Stöcker was released from prison; but something else Graebe learned one morning, however, deeply disturbed him. He had gone, as he often did, to buy building supplies from his friend Cronbach. But when he arrived he found Cronbach agitated and almost incoherent. Finally Cronbach managed to stammer out his story. One of his suppliers, who was also a friend and colleague of Graebe's, was a Jewish businessman named Leon Kirschbaum. Together with his wife Avivah and their daughter Sarah, Kirschbaum had managed to keep his business together in spite of the poor economy with its scarce goods and inflated prices and in spite of the Aryanization laws that were beginning to be enforced.

Several weeks before, Cronbach had gone to Kirschbaum's large store—it had fifteen to twenty showcase windows and large double-entry doors—and placed an order, even though Kirschbaum himself could not be certain of a delivery date or even about his own ability to obtain the materials. As they transacted their business, the two men talked, and Kirschbaum reminisced about how things had been before Hitler, when materials had been plentiful and when Jews had not had to live in such fear, blamed for every problem in German society. "Cronbach," he finally asked, "what is going to happen to us?"

The next week Cronbach had returned to Kirschbaum's establishment with another order. Kirschbaum seemed preoccupied, however, and his wife left abruptly as Cronbach approached the counter. When Cronbach asked what was the matter, Kirschbaum told him that representatives from the Party had come to see him.

"They are buying me out," he said. "I must prepare an inventory for them."

"But, Kirschbaum," Cronbach protested, "you don't want to sell—least of all to them!"

"I have no choice, Herr Cronbach," Kirschbaum sighed. "I am a Jew. My family is Jewish. I want no trouble, no pain."

Cronbach nodded numbly and left with his order in his hand.

Now, telling Graebe his story, Cronbach paused and stared into Fritz's eyes. Finally he continued.

"Yesterday I went back to Kirschbaum's store. You wouldn't believe it! All of the doors and windows are covered with slogans—obscene, anti-Semitic. . . . I could hardly move. I stood there in shock. When I finally went inside the place was practically empty, and a couple of men I'd never seen before were crating and loading up what was left."

Cronbach caught his breath. "The worst thing, Fritz, was that Avivah was there, watching them. I went up to her and she was so choked up she could hardly talk. Her eyes were red from strain and fatigue and tears that had cut a soft pathway down her dusty cheeks. She told me that Kirschbaum had disappeared."

"Disappeared!" shouted Graebe.

"She said the Party men had told him to come to their office and bring his inventory. The exact prices—the buying prices, not the selling prices. Even before he went there, a man came from the Party, looked around, and told them the Party would buy everything and give them a one-way ticket to Jerusalem. So Kirschbaum went to the Party office with his buying-price list of 800,000 Reichmarks. The Party official had given Kirschbaum a sealed envelope, but when he tried to open it there, the official told him he had to do that at home. When he got home, he opened it and found a check for 80,000 marks. He went back to the office because he thought they had misplaced a decimal point, but he never came back. Now I've learned from a friend that he was sent to a concentration camp."

Cronbach's story ended with a gesture of futility as if he knew their friend would never return.

Graebe subsequently made discreet inquiries about Kirschbaum, but could learn nothing further. He even went to the store, but could not go in. The hateful slogans still covered those windows that had not been shattered, and the store itself was empty and padlocked. Kirschbaum was gone, presumably dead, and his business destroyed, all for the "crime" of being a Jew. Like Cronbach, Graebe was horrified.

Several weeks later Fritz went to a meeting at the request of Cronbach. The two men sat together in a large hall surrounded by nearly a thousand other businessmen from various parts of Germany. The purpose of the evening meeting was to provide information about the new regulations that would now govern business practices in the Reich. The hall was decked out in the manner customary for meeting places in Germany at that time: Reich flags adorned the walls and platform, and posters and Nazi emblems filled the remaining spaces on the walls. Proud, well-dressed members of the Party were in attendance, and the local Party leader was on the platform preparing to speak from a lectern guarded on the front and sides by a phalanx of brownshirted storm troopers. The crowd stirred with excitement.

Then suddenly, as if at an unseen command, the room fell silent. The Party leader, a *Gauleiter*, approached the microphone and launched into a harangue about how the Jews were sapping the lifeblood of the great German nation. Soon he was well into the now-familiar rhetoric, calling for one-way tickets to Jerusalem for all Jews.

"But," the Gauleiter affirmed piously, "no Jewish businesses will be taken without adequate compensation. We will pay fair prices for businesses and speed the Yids out of Germany!"

The crowd loved it, but Graebe knew what had happened to Kirschbaum and began whispering to Cronbach about it. Cronbach was frightened and tried to shut him up, but he was unsuccessful. The guards quickly noticed the disturbance at the end of the hall and called the two men to the Gauleiter's attention. He demanded to know if there was a question.

Fritz stood up and sheepishly said, "I have heard of a case—"

Before he could finish the words the Gauleiter was calling him forward. Nervous and not wanting the attention, Graebe was trapped. He began moving awkwardly through the rows of chairs to the platform where they demanded to know his name.

As he identified himself he explained that he had a question about fair compensation for businesses. The Gauleiter interrupted. "You do business with a Jew?"

The crowd laughed in response. His arrogance angered Graebe, who stood and spoke back: "Yes, yes I do. One of my suppliers who was forced to sell his life's work and prepare an inventory—an inventory which he made and which was approved by the authorities. But just a few weeks ago when my friend collected the check for that inventory, it was only one-tenth of what it should have been—80,000 marks instead of 800,000 marks. He went back to complain because he thought it was a mistake, but he disappeared and no one has heard . . ."

"Oh, Herr Graebe"—the Gauleiter had remembered his name—"Herr Graebe! You're the victim of this Yiddish propaganda." The Party leader began to play to the crowd. "We know those Jews! They inflate their prices because they have an innate hunger for our money. That Jew's greed was seen, that's all. That's how he got himself into trouble."

"That's not true!" By now Graebe was outraged. "My friend was good and honest—"

The Gauleiter interrupted, wagging his finger. "Don't let those Jews fool you, Herr Graebe!" Then he smoothly changed the subject. "Now let's get on with the meeting. I want to discuss the ways in which good Aryan businessmen can acquire abandoned Jewish concerns and property."

When Graebe attempted to return to his seat in the audience, he saw that Cronbach was gone and that a man sitting in the aisle was effectively blocking him. So he left the auditorium and walked back toward his automobile.

Looking back on the incident that followed, Graebe remembers his fear at leaving the auditorium, realizing how much he had underestimated the Party. But he remembers too how angry he had been, and how strongly he had felt the need to defend his associate Kirschbaum:

> My maternal grandfather had many Jewish friends and associates in the nearby city of Marburg an der Lahn. He took my mother there to live and work with a Jewish family for one year. She was a good worker—they paid her double for her work at their butcher shop. This entire procedure was most unusual at that time—a Christian rarely did such a thing with a Jew. My grandfather liked these friends very much because they were kind and very honest. They would say "yes" or "no"—this was very important to my mother and it has been important in my life, as well. To me "yes" must be yes and "no" must be no. When Grandfather took Mother to the Jewish family, she did not know they were Jews. Only later did my grandfather tell her that they were Jewish people. She did not know the difference. That was not important to her, nor is it to me.

It made no sense to Graebe to persecute people simply because they were Jewish; and he knew, because of what had happened to Kirschbaum, that the Gauleiter was a liar. The Reich's well-publicized policy of sending Jews to Jerusalem was a coverup for other, darker activities in concentration camps.

Walking down the darkened street back to his car, Graebe began to sense that he was being watched from a distance. Increasing his pace, he did not turn his head. He walked on, listening for a telltale sound. Soon he heard the scuff of leather against the cobblestone street and chanced a quick glance over his shoulder as he rounded a corner. Two Brownshirts were running down the darkened street after him.

Fritz fought the surge of fear that rushed through his slight frame. Quickening his pace, he cut through alleys and circled around the side streets, stopping only briefly in shadowed doorways, his ears filling with the sound of his heart pounding violently, echoing the distant rhythmic sounds of the heavy jackboots pounding along the bricked streets. After a few minutes he found a place to rest for a short moment, in a small grove of trees in the town square. He could hear voices now and again, lost in the darkness. Finally, when it seemed safe enough, he began to trace his way back to his car. Cautiously, slowly, Graebe took a circuitous path back to his car, certain that he had successfully eluded the pursuers by his meandering race through the sinuous maze of streets.

As he rounded the corner near his car, however, the dim streetlights silhouetted two figures in the shadows. Then suddenly, two more Brownshirts quietly materialized behind the young engineer, and he heard the dreaded words, "Herr Graebe, Gestapo!" The words reverberated from the still walls and down the empty street. The voice was all-knowing, confident, and resonant.

Graebe was taken to the jail in Essen. He was never beaten or physically mistreated, but neither was he formally charged nor ever told the nature of his offense. There were only two clues to what he had done. One was a plaque that hung on the wall of his cell. On it was a printed code, a sequence of letters and numerals that had meaning only to the prison authorities. While Graebe was told during his confinement that this code explained his offense, he was never able to crack it.

The second clue was even more elusive. Fritz's cell was small and contained a bed, a stool, a toilet, and a dirty, narrow window that was too small and too high up the wall to be useful. The cell also contained two books. One was a Bible, which Graebe read only infrequently. When he did read it, he turned to the Psalter to find personal strength and direction during his ordeal. The words of David's psalms, with their carefully measured meter, relieved his mind of the dulling seclusion of his prison cell.

The second book was a copy of a treatise by Martin Luther, *Against the Robbing and Murdering Hordes of Peasants*, a polemic written in response to the violence of the Peasants' Revolt in southwestern Germany in 1525. Clearly this book had been placed in his cell for a specific reason; obscure sixteenth-century tracts were hardly available in libraries, let alone in a Spartan cell in an Essen jail. Yet the meaning was far from clear at first.

Luther's treatise was exactly what its title implies: a vicious polemic that blamed the savage bloodshed of the Peasants' Revolt upon the peasants themselves. His major point was that the peasants had forsaken their loyalty to their rulers and that, since they had done this under the banner of Christ, they were guilty of blasphemy. This meant, Luther argued, that the rulers were entitled to quell this revolt of "mad dogs and the devil." Luther called, in effect, for a holy war of the German princes against the blasphemous peasantry for the sake of a united German nation. He exhorted, "Let anyone who can, smite, slay, and stab, secretly or openly, remembering that nothing can be more poisonous, hurtful, or devilish than a rebel." The well-armed gentry quickly heeded his advice and the Peasants' Revolt was snuffed out by the superior forces of the rulers.

Knowing this, Graebe pondered why the Nazis had chosen Luther's hateful treatise as one of the few adornments in his cell. Reading the tract, he quickly grasped the point: loyalty to the state was paramount. Either one supported the authorities or—like the Swabian peasants of the early sixteenth century—one died in rebellion. And as Luther had so vigorously assured, rebels were damned as well. Luther's treatise had a definite message, then; it showed what would happen to those who performed acts of opposition or sedition. The Nazis wanted to make sure that Graebe got the message. As Martin Luther himself had suggested, rebels would be punished without mercy. It had happened to Kirschbaum, and the Nazis made very clear that it could happen to Fritz, too.

Throughout his imprisonment, always during each night but often during the day as well, Fritz heard other prisoners crying out, begging for mercy. Often there would be a sharp crack, a dull thud, or even the report of a gun, followed by silence. The lesson of Luther's treatise was being acted out before him. But Fritz knew that cooperation was not right:

> I read that book by Luther and it made me bitter, very bitter.
> That is how I came to oppose Luther. He should have stopped

the landlords from harming the peasants. The peasants had supported him from the days of Worms. But maybe . . . maybe he felt that it was more important to save himself. I could not stand with Luther because he unfairly sided with the greedy power class and justified their excesses. That is evil.

One pivotal event that crystallized Fritz's anger at Luther, as well as at those who had planted Luther's tract in his cell, came on the day that Fritz received his first and only pastoral visit. The prison chaplain was a Lutheran, and it is reasonable to believe that he was associated with the "German Christians' Faith Movement," founded in 1932 by Ludwig Mueller, an army chaplain. Mueller was a close friend and supporter of Adolf Hitler and, after the Fuehrer's rise to power, Mueller was rewarded for his loyalty by being the first to be "elected" to the office of Reich Bishop. Fortunately, Mueller's election owed little to the desires of the Lutheran church itself. The government, bent on electing Hitler's ally, intervened heavily. A number of regional church groups were forcibly disbanded, isolating their clergy and forcing Mueller's only opponent, Pastor Friedrich von Bodelschwingh, to withdraw from candidacy. Thus in 1933 the "German Christians' Faith Movement" and Ludwig Mueller were overwhelmingly elected, and he in turn assigned Party loyalists to key pastoral positions. These functionaries then did the bidding of the Reich in various settings and institutions, including, apparently, in the Essen jail where Graebe was imprisoned.

Because of the blatantly political interests of Reich Bishop Mueller, pastors loyal to him were expected to fulfill both religious and secular missions. When the prison chaplain came calling at Fritz Graebe's cell, it was probably less out of concern for his spiritual welfare than it was from desire to bring this recalcitrant German back into the flock loyal to Adolf Hitler. This political intent became clear to Fritz very quickly after the pastor arrived unexpectedly, entered his cell, greeted him, and immediately turned his attention to the mysterious coded plaque that hung on the wall.

"So," he said firmly, "you've offended the Fuehrer! Spoken out against him." Pointing to the plaque, he continued. "So that's what you are. . . . That's what you are!"

Fritz had been lying on his bed when the chaplain arrived and, as he began to sit up, the pastor pulled up the stool and sat down without missing a word.

"Herr Graebe," he intoned piously, "you should be ashamed of yourself. A man like you in jail—it is a disgrace to your family."

Graebe did not trust the man and said nothing. The minister, however, was undaunted and continued sermonizing. "They tell me that you don't cooperate, don't exercise, don't talk with others, don't eat much, or have visitors, or even go to church."

Fritz liked him even less and remained silent. The chaplain tried another approach.

"The Third Reich needs you. It needs men of character with skills and commitment."

Still silence.

"Too much stubbornness can lead to trouble—perhaps even twenty or thirty years of it. After all, you have an obligation to the Fatherland, to your family, to the world. It is your Christian duty."

I can wait, Fritz thought to himself and, as if to distract himself from the chaplain, he began to thumb absently through his Bible, whispering almost inaudibly that he would wait and things would change. This continued for a few moments, with the pastor preaching at him and Graebe muttering to himself his opposition as his fingers turned the pages of his Bible.

Finally, Graebe had had enough. He turned and looked directly at the chaplain, wagged his finger at him, and growled, "Pastor, even for you, things will change. As for me, I can wait."

The minister was surprised and reacted with threats. "I will report all of this," he sputtered, "you could pay for this!"

Fritz, for his part, lapsed back into silence, wondering if he had pressed his luck too far. The minister railed on about how Fritz could suffer for the trouble he was causing.

Finally, Fritz had heard enough. "Listen," he said, "do yourself a favor and get out of here." Fritz snatched up the stool that the chaplain had earlier been sitting on and cocked his arm. "I said to get out . . . otherwise . . . "

The pastor scurried out the door, leaving the cell silent once again. After his exit, Fritz picked up Luther's treatise and read until he found the line he had been looking for: *But if the ruler is a Christian and tolerates the gospel, so that the peasants have no appearance of a case against him . . .*

"That's it," Fritz realized. "They are not established by God. They use God to punish us, to trick us, and to hurt people. They are wrong—and I know it!"

Luther's words now took on an ironic counterpoint, just the opposite of what had been intended by Graebe's Nazi jailers. Now Fritz was certain that he knew what Luther's treatise was all about and how dangerous and worthless it was: "It was trash. I threw it where one always throws trash. I became bitter, so bitterly opposed to Luther and, thanks to Luther, opposed to Hitler."

The chaplain never returned, and Fritz was relieved several months later when a Party official casually informed him that he had been stripped of his Party membership. He had been expelled for a serious "breach of Party discipline" as a result of his vocal support of Kirschbaum. During his imprisonment Fritz had already decided that he would drop his membership after his release if it had not already been revoked.

Oddly enough, in spite of the official's announcement, Graebe's name was not removed from the Party's membership list immediately. This oversight would be used against him many years later when attorneys for *Gebietskommissar* Marschall—who was being tried in 1960 for the murder of a Jewish carpenter—would seek to introduce Graebe's Party membership as a way to discredit him before the German courts.

4. From Kronenburg to Sdolbonov

Fritz Graebe never learned who authorized his release from the Essen jail. The reason for his release was also unclear because he had not complied with or given in to the demands of the jailers and Party officials. One morning a guard opened the cell door and told Graebe to gather his personal effects and leave. Nothing further was said as Graebe walked out of the building.

In the years following his imprisonment, Fritz Graebe worked hard on his engineering skills and continued building houses, garages, and whatever anyone was willing to pay him to build. Throughout those years, Fritz watched the buildup: war talk, parades, military training, armaments construction, and a tidal-wave resurgence of national patriotism symbolized by the ever-present swastika flags and the incessant singing of *"Deutschland über Alles."* He carefully avoided political discussions by throwing himself into managing construction projects and working hard on his engineering texts in order to stay current with his profession.

He was ordered to report for military service in 1938. Fritz was adamantly opposed to serving this particular government and the kind of people who had put him in the Essen jail. His private values conflicted with what he was witnessing on the streets and reading in the newspapers. Moreover, his family and career meant far more to him than a languishing stint in the service would. But in spite of his preferences, Fritz was in a quandary. He dared not risk his reputation by further confrontations with the authorities or by willfully disobeying the law.

One sleepless night as he lay in bed brooding over his dilemma, a plan began to emerge in his imagination, a plan that could enable him to avoid the call to arms and still preserve his reputation in Grafrath. On the day when he was to report for induction, he left home early in the morning. At a carefully selected site along the nearly deserted highway, Fritz pulled off the road, removed two nail-studded boards from the trunk, and drove his car over them, flattening all the tires. Stranded, he waited beside the road until a police unit happened by—almost an hour after the appointed time for reporting to military headquarters. He protested to the police that he would be too late for the muster and that that would be an embarrassment and cause him great distress because he was a patriotic German citizen. The police asked why he had not seen and avoided the boards.

His response, typical of the bravado that would characterize his later rescue efforts, was, "It was so dark outside and I wanted to be the first to sign up, so I left home very early in the morning and I must have been so tired that I didn't see the boards."

The police, impressed by his earnest sincerity, bought the story and gave him a note, signed on the back of a citation, that explained his tardiness. By the time he repaired his tires and arrived at the address, he had missed the sign-up. He banged on the doors and finally raised an understanding office worker. Feigning despair and frustrated patriotism, he got the old man to give him another note indicating that he had been present to sign up but that the military staff had departed.

He took his two notes and his pretended nationalistic fervor to the local military recruiter, who told him that they would call him up at a later time. In this way Graebe was able to avoid military service and seek some civilian employment that would keep him out of the war effort and away from political intrigues.

After having artfully manipulated the German bureaucracy by eluding the call to military service, Fritz decided to make himself available to the government as a civilian engineer. In this way he was able to avoid dealing with the Party, even though it meant a brief absence from his family. Late in 1938 he was directed to report to the city of Aix-la-Chapelle to work in the construction team that was building the West Wall. His friend Max Jung asked him to help use his influence there to secure work for his family firm, the Josef Jung construction firm. Using his engaging personality and his assertive style, Fritz was able to win a construction project for Max and his father. They would build major bunkers designed to block the progress of advancing armored units. Fritz himself was then transferred to their detail as a field manager.

By the autumn of 1938, Fritz was consulting in Düsseldorf and living with his family in Grafrath. The events that took place that fall were to change the direction of German internal and foreign policy and the fate of the Jews under German command. During the last days of October

1938, Jews from a number of German cities were rounded up and transported to concentration camps in Poland. The family of seventeen-year-
old Herschel Grynszpan were among the Jews forcibly removed from
their homes in Hanover and taken to the Polish camp at Zbonszyn
(Benschen), near Lodz. Grynszpan himself was at that time a Jewish
refugee living in Paris. A letter from his interned relatives near Lodz
alerted him to their plight and drove him into a very deep depression.

His tenuous refugee status, the extreme danger facing his family, and
his rage at the Nazis' treatment of the Jewish population drove him to
seek revenge. On November 7, 1938, he purchased a small pistol, entered the offices of the German Embassy in Paris, encountered Ernst
vom Rath, the third secretary of the legation, shouted his protest, and
shot him. (Ironically, vom Rath had not been a dedicated Nazi.) Hitler
seized on the opportunity, promoting vom Rath to the position of embassy counselor. Hitler then disclosed a "serious Jewish plot against the
highest officials of the Reich." Vom Rath's death on November 9 led to
a night of the most violent and destructive actions yet to be taken against
the Jews of Germany, *Kristallnacht*, "The Night of Broken Glass" (so named
for the tremendous amount of shattered glass left in the streets following
the actions taken against synagogues and Jewish businesses).

In what were described by the Party as "spontaneous demonstrations,"
the German people, particularly Party members, flooded into the streets,
broke windows, and desecrated and burned synagogues, Jewish homes,
and Jewish businesses. There is ample postwar evidence to disprove the
propagandistic assertion that the nationwide pogroms were spontaneous.
In fact, the local expressions of the pogrom were carefully orchestrated
and controlled by police and the highest officials of the Reich.

Photographs of *Kristallnacht* are gruesome and devastatingly the same:
streets full of shattered glass; smoke pouring out of synagogues in every
German town, village, and city with a Jewish population; littered streets;
groups of Jewish elders paraded through the streets surrounded by Gestapo and Party loyalists; eerie midnight scenes of burning synagogues
casting shadows behind stained glass windows bearing the Star of David.
The scenes in Düsseldorf, where vom Rath's funeral was to to be held
on November 16, were unbelievable.

Fritz Graebe left his home by auto for Düsseldorf on the morning
after *Kristallnacht*, unaware of the events that had taken place. As he
drove along he found the streets filled with broken glass and furniture.
In front of an apartment building he paused to stare at the remains of
smashed porcelain figurines and at a once-ornate frame now buckled,

with its canvas torn and hanging like a parched tongue. Stunned, Graebe drove his car slowly down the street. Beyond the intersection he saw a cluster of people looking at the old synagogue. Fritz parked his car across from the smoldering ruins. On the sidewalk in front of the crushed doors were ruined books and desecrated Torah scrolls; a twisted menorah lay on the steps, and the sides of a jeweled spice box were scattered from impact with a brick wall. The crazed participants had entered the burning synagogue to carry out the *bema*, the platform from which the rabbi spoke, which they then cast onto the spiked arms of the iron fence. A phylactery moved slightly in the breeze, caught on a small branch of a tree near the door. Fritz drove off, only to stop again in front of a store across whose walls were smeared the words "punishment for Paris." Lurching through the smashed plate-glass front, two men dragged the proprietor's lifeless body.

A passerby stopped to watch. Fritz rolled down his car window to inquire of the man what had inspired all this destruction. It was then that he learned of the assassination and the scope of the bloody vengeance. With a strange pride the pedestrian looked first at the dead Jewish merchant and then at the rubble before he began to boast about the deaths of certain "Jewish renegades." Disgusted, Graebe stepped on his accelerator and left the man midsentence. Fritz was determined to escape the vile scenes, but he only went a few hundred yards before he again stopped, this time to watch three SA men who were reading from what appeared to be an official list and gesturing toward some apartments. They looked around, confused, and then compared their list to an address plate on the door. Their confusion ended, they burst into the flat. Within moments they threw open a sash and started throwing things out of the window. A small sculpture crashed to the ground, and china exploded on the sidewalk. Books and paintings flew out, followed by a mirror and a crystal chandelier. Suddenly, the neck of a grand piano protruded through the window. Graebe could hear the loud, frantic voices of the men, then the piano was pulled back in and lustily hacked apart with axes. Within minutes pieces of the instrument fell heavily from the window into the growing, ignominious pile of debris in the street. Finally, the three men appeared at the window arguing about a very stylized menorah. They did not know what it was, but one man finally grabbed it and threw it to the ground. Graebe recognized the man who threw it as an employee of the Mercedes-Benz repair shop where Fritz took his car. Fritz recalls, "The paper reported the story the next day as a 'Spontaneous Action of the German People.' It could not have been so spontaneous—the three of them had lists and were looking around to find where they were to go. It was a joke—a spontaneous action."

Much later, ironically, while working on war crimes for the International Military Tribunal, Graebe read and translated many of Hermann Goering's communiqués and directives ordering the destruction of synagogues, businesses, and homes following "the Night of Broken Glass." From Solingen to Düsseldorf to Mülheim, the street scenes were the same that day. The vista was broken by wispy plumes of gray-black smoke rising to the heavens like the beseeching arms of a dying man, haunting testaments to yet another burned synagogue or business. Later that day in a Mülheim cafe, Fritz listened as several of his Jewish business acquaintances complained about the damages and the new Reich directive that would keep them from collecting their insurance money and requiring them to clean up the communities after the *Kristallnacht* pogroms. However, even worse directives and events were still to come. The warning came in a news communiqué issued by Dr. Josef Goebbels at five in the afternoon on November 10, 1938:

> The natural and fully justified outrage felt by the German people at the brutal Jewish assassination in Paris has been expressed this evening in reprisals against Jewish shops and businesses. I now appeal to the entire population to desist at once from any further demonstrations or actions against the Jews. The last word on the Paris assassination will be spoken by legislation.[3]

This well-tempered circumlocution masked Goebbels's opportunism and rage and signaled the beginning of a long-sought redirection of German policy toward the Jews. *Kristallnacht* was the climax of an era of legislation that had given "Aryans" the right to expropriate Jewish enterprises and to burn synagogues and Jewish-owned businesses. The dawn of the new era ushered in laws that directed the burning of Jewish women, children, and men.

In August 1941, when Fritz Graebe received the wire from the Todt organization headquarters in Berlin directing him to report to the offices of the Reich Railroad Administration in Lvov, Max Jung succeeded in persuading Fritz to remain under contract with the Josef Jung firm and to seek railroad contracts for the company in the distant Ukraine. Fritz agreed and, within a short time after his arrival there, he succeeded in winning a significant contract.

Fritz arrived in Sdolbonov in September 1941. He set up the Jung firm's regional office in Sdolbonov. With him was a team of twelve foremen and four engineers from the home office in Solingen. The necessary office and field equipment and the machinery required for resetting the tracks and for the construction work did not begin to arrive for several months. This gap in time allowed Fritz to find staff, to compete for additional contracts, and to establish his office.

His assignment for the Reich Railroad Administration contract was to establish an engineering office and recruit construction teams that would design and build communications facilities and the various structures necessary for the maintenance of trains and the storage of parts and supplies. Because the German and Ukrainian railroad tracks were differently gauged, Graebe's crews also had to reset the tracks to receive the German trains. Projects for the Reich Railroad Administration were given top priority in the war effort. If the drive to secure an Eastern Front were to succeed, workers had to be deployed and the most responsible firms employed. The Jung firm was one of the best.

One of the bitter ironies about the railroad projects in the Ukraine was that, in spite of the methodical murders of the *Einsatzgruppen,* many of the laborers working on the railroad lines were Jewish. In spite of the fact that most of the skilled Jewish workers had already been exterminated, Graebe found a ready supply of skilled Jewish carpenters, masons, joiners, and draftsmen. Many Jews had left their homes to travel in search of work, but a sizable contingent had found themselves trapped in Sdolbonov, behind the lines of the *Einsatzgruppen,* unable to move elsewhere. This skilled group was ready to work; and because there was little competition, and because the Reich demanded that rail lines and facilities be completed without delay, Graebe was able to secure contracts for work throughout the region.

Several months earlier, Maria Warchiwker, a secondary school teacher, had left her home in Lodz, Poland, with her husband in search of a place far from the war. They traveled southeast to Sdolbonov, hoping to escape the anti-Semitic attitudes and the frequent beatings, harassments, and pogroms the Jews of central Poland experienced. They also thought mistakenly that it would be easy to find work and to blend into the new environment anonymously. Shortly after their arrival in Sdolbonov, Maria chanced to meet a refugee who seemed to have lost his mind. He warned her about an unusual military group that went from city to city killing Jews, mostly the men. At first Maria discounted the story as the imaginings of a raving man. She went on with her life, seeking whatever work was available to her. She insisted, however, that

her husband remain in their small flat. She had heard snide, racist remarks in the marketplace and knew what the local people thought about
Jews. She believed that her husband's very "Jewish-appearing features"
made him unusually vulnerable. She would take no chances, even if they
had to live in isolation and poverty. Then, on August 6, 1941, word
spread through Sdolbonov that a German army unit had just encamped
at the outskirts of the city. Maria pictured the mad eyes of the refugee,
and the whispered words of his warning echoed in her memory. Frantically, she tried to think of a way out. If they were going to kill only
the men, then she would hide her husband. She went to a family for
whom she had worked, but they were unwilling to help. She finally
found a basement and hid her husband for the night, but following the
gray dawn his hiding place was discovered. He was dragged and kicked
from the small earthen room and shot to death that August 7. *Einsatzgruppe* C threw his body along with the rest into the rough-hewn grave
behind the cement factory.

In the traumatic six weeks that followed the murder of her husband,
Maria was interrogated, processed, moved from her home, and included
in an official German census of the Jews. She vowed to avenge her
husband's death by doing everything possible to save other Jews—she
would find a way. Because she both spoke and read German, the German regional worker procurement office sent her to be interviewed by
the managers of several German firms that were opening in the city.
Her first interview was at the office of the Josef Jung construction firm
of Solingen, Germany.

The scene was chaotic when Maria arrived at the office of Fritz Graebe.
Carpenters were adding walls, rooms, and storage areas. Others were
carrying desks or assembling drafting tables. The cacophony of saws,
hammers, and the shouts of the workers added to the confusion. Trying
to escape the chaos and the deafening noise, Graebe escorted Maria to
his private office. The yellow patches on the front and back of her coat
identified her as a Jew. Ignoring the patches, he inquired about her
previous work experience and seemed genuinely perplexed when she
told him that because she was Jewish she was not allowed to pursue her
profession as a teacher. Pleased with her ability to handle German, Fritz
hired her and set her to work translating the difficult technical German
engineering forms into Polish. Another Jewish woman, Claire, was also
hired to assist in this work. Claire's husband too had been murdered in
the August 7 *Einsatzgruppe* Action. Her eight-year-old daughter sat daily
under a tree outside the office, watching Claire's every move.

As an administrator, Graebe was cordial to his Jewish workers—behavior quite unusual among Germans in similar positions who would not otherwise have engaged their employees in anything beyond the necessary official conversation. He often did something as unheard of as assisting a Jewish woman with her coat. At first, Maria suspected his motives: "I was convinced that he was being nice to us in order to trick us. I was nearly convinced that he was a Gestapo, waiting to trap us and send us away." The longer she observed him, though, the more she began to believe that his behavior might be genuine. This impression was strengthened when one of the Polish draftsmen in the office told her how Graebe had recently asked him about his family. When the draftsman had told Graebe that his daughter was ill, Graebe had recommended milk and sugar for the child. The draftsman had shaken his head in resignation. Milk was easy to come by most of the time, he had said, but sugar was a rare and precious commodity. Later that afternoon, the German engineer stopped by the man's work table and left a carton of sugar. Nevertheless, despite her inkling that he might be trustworthy, Maria and the other Jewish workers had no choice but to remain reserved in their relationship with Graebe. The consequences could be fatal if he were a spy.

One afternoon several months after his arrival in Sdolbonov, Graebe went to meet with Regional Commissioner (*Gebietskommissar*) Georg Marschall. A major item on Graebe's agenda was a request for increased rations for his Jewish workers. When Graebe brought this issue up, Marschall was cordial and understanding, promising to discuss the matter with his staff. Graebe was pleased by Marschall's willingness to help, and the conversation soon drifted off into social pleasantries. After a few minutes of such chatting, Marschall casually asked Graebe if he had been aware of the operations of an *Einsatzgruppe* in Sdolbonov the previous August. When Graebe indicated he knew nothing, Marschall continued, "You didn't know they killed nearly two hundred fifty Jews behind the cement factory?"

The question caught Graebe completely off guard. Like most Germans, he had been unaware of the systematic murder of the Jews by the *Einsatzgruppen*, and he was horrified to learn that such an atrocity had taken place in Sdolbonov so recently. But his shock was tempered by an even more urgent reaction: a sudden, cold wariness. *Why*, he thought after a moment's reflection, *is Marschall telling me this?*

"This deed was not given proper thought," Marschall was continuing, oblivious to Graebe's silence. "It was barbarous, inhuman. Such a thing should not happen again."

As Marschall paused, Graebe began to feel relieved. Apparently Marschall was telling him of this horrible incident to inform him of it and of the Reich's official policy against such killings. But Marschall was not finished speaking.

"In the future we shall do it differently, more humanely. We shall not shoot men only, but also the women and children. It is the only correct method." Graebe stared in disbelief. "This is the only possible solution of the Jewish problem—remove them all. Yes, Herr Graebe"—Marschall smiled—"we must make things the way the Fuehrer wants them."

Graebe's earlier relief turned to dread. He stared at the smug *Gebietskommissar*, knowing that he could never again ask for increased salaries or more rations for his Jewish workers. They would have to work longer, harder, for less pay, and with even less food. Graebe would find no support from Marschall, the Reich's official representative in Sdolbonov, nor from any other German officials. Things would be done "the way the Fuehrer wants them."

Graebe left his meeting with Marschall far warier than he had come to it. After all, he thought as he walked back to his office, he'd seen men like Marschall before.

There were many kinds of disruptions of the orderly schedule that Graebe created for himself and his staff. The humanitarian side of the engineer was always concerned about the well-being of his workers. On November 6, 1941, unknown to Graebe, *Einsatzgruppe* C was preparing to enter the city of Rovno, twelve miles north of Sdolbonov. The Jewish citizens, who constituted more than half of Rovno's population, had been advised to pack their belongings and prepare for a mandatory relocation to an area some distance from the zone of military activity. On the appointed day the Jews were to report to the Rovno town square with whatever belongings they could hold in a single suitcase.

Word of the planned relocation reached one of Fritz's most valued workers, Franz Rosenzwieg, a Jewish carpenter who had left his wife and infant daughter behind in Rovno while he worked for the Jung firm in Sdolbonov. Rosenzwieg came to his manager and announced that he could not go to work. "I must go to Rovno. My wife and child are to be sent away."

"What do you mean, sent away?"

"They are to be deported—I must save them."

"You work for me," said Graebe. "I'll go to Rovno and bring your family back here."

"How can you do that?"

"Because you have a work permit," Graebe assured him, "they will be safe here."

Fritz's response was typical of his concern for his workers and of his willingness to extend himself on their behalf. His plan was to take the firm's automobile, drive to Rovno that very evening, locate the family, and bring them to Sdolbonov before any harm could befall them.

Graebe was not prepared for what he found in Rovno when he arrived at nine that evening. The town had been sealed off by the militia. He tried every tactic to gain entry, but he was kept out. In the distance he could hear the guns being fired and people screaming. The *Einsatzgruppe* was in the process of murdering nearly five thousand Jewish men, women, and children. In stunned silence the defeated Samaritan returned to Sdolbonov. Deeply troubled and unable to sleep, Fritz drove back to Rovno once again the next morning and again he was barred from the city, but now the consequences of the previous evening's activities were clear. Maria remembers that "when he came back to the office from Rovno that morning he was so distressed. [Claire and] I had never seen him like that—so enraged. He cried out, 'Maria! They have killed the Jews in Rovno!' "

As he said this, Maria thought about this complex and contradictory man. *How can he not know about the things that are happening to the Jews in the entire Ukraine—is he really that sheltered?*

Maria's thoughts were interrupted by Graebe's demanding voice.

"Did you know?"

"Yes, I knew. Why shouldn't I know? After all, my husband was killed by them right here."

"Why didn't you tell me?" he cried. "You are worse than Hitler. You knew!"

In the brief silence, Maria thought, *If he was with the Gestapo how could he say something like that about Hitler? He is so mad that I am afraid for my life.* "Why should I tell you?" Maria snarled back. "You are a German!"

Graebe slammed his coat to the floor and stormed out of the office, leaving Maria and Claire confused and frightened. It took a great deal of persuasion to keep Claire in the room after Graebe's outburst.

Shortly after this episode the office janitor, a Jewish man named Witelson, came into the office, ostensibly to stoke the fire, and talked with Maria and Claire. Witelson, who would later fall victim to the final extermination of Jews in Sdolbonov on October 13, 1942, explained to the two women what had happened when Graebe had arrived in Rovno the previous night. After Graebe returned to Sdolbonov, Witelson had observed Graebe going to Marschall's office. Witelson slipped unnoticed

behind a door where he could overhear part of the conversation between the two men. Graebe had demanded that Marschall give him a
permit to retrieve Rosenzweig's family. Marschall coldly refused.

While Witelson was briefing Maria and Claire, Graebe went to the
office of Marschall's chief deputy, *Stabsleiter* Erich Habenicht. SS Lieutenant Beck was also present in the room when Graebe spoke.

"What happened last night in Rovno cannot happen here in Sdolbonov. My orders come from the highest authorities in Berlin—I report
directly to the Army and the Railroad Administration—"

Graebe's anger was betrayed by his voice as Beck interrupted, "You
must really learn to calm yourself, Herr Graebe. The solution to the
Jewish problem has been carefully planned and no one, not even you,
can stand in the way."

"I have my deadlines," responded Graebe, "and if I do not make them
I will be court-martialed, not you or Marschall—*me!* Do not disturb my
labor column—I don't care if they are Jewish."

Habenicht joined the conversation hoping to calm the two men. "We
all have our orders; besides only half of the Jews were killed. You have
plenty left, Herr Graebe."

Deliberately, carefully, Graebe shook his index finger in the direction
of the men. "If I fall behind, by even just one day, because your people
are killing my Jews—I will go directly to Berlin. Then the burden will
be on you."

Dripping with sweat, Graebe spun on his heels and slammed the door
as he retreated to his quarters. As the shaken engineer rounded the corner of his building he saw Rosenzweig standing in a daze near the front
door. Their eyes met and no words could express the pain, the futility,
the anguish of the two. His own impotence in the face of the killers
and the grief of the husband and father transformed Graebe, giving him
the resolve to take his stand in the face of the monstrous and speading
evil that he had witnessed from a distance in Rovno.

Walking quietly into his office, Graebe picked up his coat and collapsed into his chair. Maria's and Claire's eyes carefully darted from the
engineering texts and met. They did not move or say anything. Graebe
slowly moved from his chair, and he wearily shuffled to the door to
throw the bolt. Turning to the two women he said, "Something must
be done—I cannot do it alone. You have to help me; I cannot even talk
to people."

The terror that he had experienced indirectly at Rovno that November deeply affected Graebe. The senseless inhumanity, the thoughtless
obedience to authority, and the awareness that it would happen again

and again unless he intervened inspired Graebe to plan and implement rescue efforts. Whatever considerations he had for his own safety were lost to the haunting gaze of his valued carpenter and to the trauma of the Jewish women in Sdolbonov.

There were other disruptions to the carefully planned days, company disruptions that were impersonal and uncontrollable and that created unique problems. Frequently, construction deadlines were impossibly short and incredibly labor intensive. These abbreviated deadlines, the severe weather conditions, and inadequate food supplies for his workers meant delays; and with the delays, the threat of a court-martial hung ever more heavily over the Jung regional office manager. After a mid-December 1941 meeting in Berlin with Dr. Dorpmueller, the director-general of the Reich Railroad Administration, Fritz's crews began a twenty-four-hour work cycle in order to meet the demands of a contract. However, the severe winter and the overworking of the crew significantly delayed the completion of the project. In January 1942, Graebe was ordered to report to Kiev to stand trial for the delay. Six railroad engineers served as judges in a court-martial proceeding that did not permit a defense attorney to be present. As he stood before the court of his peers, Graebe realized that both his newly developed concern for the safety of the Jews and his vocational reputation would be critically jeopardized by the outcome of the trial. As the trial proceeded, Graebe worked himself into a theatrical, carefully planned rage. When he was finally allowed to speak, he methodically outlined the procedures that had been followed on the project and the reasons for the unavoidable and uncontrollable delays, and he reasserted his own loyalty to this work and to the Reich. Turning the tables on the court, he became their judge.

"I have worked my ass off out there and this is what you do to me! You drag me all the way from Sdolbonov; you keep me from supervising my workers—no wonder there are such delays. It will not be because of me that the war effort is jeopardized."

His stunned colleagues sat in silence as the lecture reached a crescendo. With his voice lowered, and calmly shaking his finger at his peers, Fritz warned, "It is because of you—you are the ones who delay the completion of the work, you are the traitors."

The shaken engineers, unaccustomed to judicial proceedings and anxious to do their work with a minimum of the kind of attention that would invite intervention from Berlin, beat a hasty conciliatory retreat from their assertive colleague. To save face they issued a reprimand and admonished Graebe to be diligent in his work. He was never bothered in this way again.

After his unsuccessful attempt to save Rosenzwieg's wife and child in Rovno in November, Fritz had vowed to protect Jews from the marauding soldiers. Maria's and Claire's descriptions of the Actions of the *Einsatzgruppen* convinced Graebe that the attacks were not at all random. It also was clear that he would need the help of the two women if he were to develop an effective plan to save lives. He also would need to recruit more substantial contracts in outlying areas, establish other small Jung field offices, and requisition more Jewish workers. Any other procedure was certain to arouse the suspicions and interest of Marschall, Beck, Habenicht, and ultimately the commanders of the *Einsatzgruppen*. Maria was convinced that nothing could alter the savage fury of the murderers. It was Graebe's persistence and his vision that convinced her of his sincerity and of his ability to subvert the mechanisms of mass execution.

The first major assignment away from the "mother house"—the name given by Fritz, Maria, and Claire to the main Jung office in Sdolbonov—was in Kiverce, to the northwest. Because Claire had become increasingly nervous about being recognized and about endangering her daughter, Fritz assigned her to start the small new office. He arranged for their travel documents, false identification papers, and an excuse for Claire's absence from the Sdolbonov office, and they were gone. The first mission of the mother house was founded, and a construction office was secretly turned into a rescue network headquarters.

In order to minimize the danger to those being rescued and to prevent an accidental betrayal of the effort, Fritz had to carefully foresee the situations and interpersonal dynamics that would confront him in the rescue efforts. The actual situations were nearly unpredictable. Spies, soldiers, collaborators, and the war itself magnified the risks in every move. It was one thing to work with those Germans who held power as agents of the regional occupational government and with the minor but troublesome German civil servants, but yet another matter altogether when one had to face the SS. It required still other skills and patience to meet panicked Jews and Polish peasants who would do nearly anything to protect themselves and their families. These trapped, defenseless people were nearly as unpredictable as the war itself. Working in this environment, with these complex and demanding human dynamics, greatly taxed Graebe's strength and imagination.

Communications quickly became the primary concern in the rescue effort. A switchboard was brought in so that Maria could maintain constant contact with each office or construction site and with the home office back in Solingen. She monitored the movement of people, supplies, and the progress of the projects, and in this capacity Maria became the mainstay of the total effort. Because she was multilingual and a familiar face in the Jung office, she could supervise the construction work as well as nearly every aspect of the rescue effort. Her presence and skills enabled Fritz to maintain the necessary critical balance between his roles as construction manager and prime mover behind the rescues.

The entire effort might have died, however, in the sea of paperwork that was required by the ever-efficient German bureaucracy. The standard forms and papers had to be located, stolen, forged, falsified, validated, and carefully distributed. These papers included work permits, travel visas, office site requisitions, birth certificates, and Aryanization forms. Every time someone was to be relocated, Fritz had to get the forms and have them validated without raising suspicions. Everything had to appear to be routine and pleasant. Without ever revealing the true nature of his mission, Fritz cultivated friendly, reciprocal relationships with low-level government employees who could help him relocate people.

One such connection was with the officer who stamped the permits and forms from army headquarters in Sdolbonov. A lonely, gregarious fellow, the soldier looked forward to Fritz's visits, to a shared drink, to a few stories, and to a gift—usually a cigarette or a cigar. His ability to share these rare, highly prized favors gave Graebe status and mystique beyond his station—but this too was part of his plan. Whenever he needed a form stamped, he would take it to that officer and engage in friendly banter while complaining lightheartedly about all the forms and requirements. If questions came forth from the officer, Fritz would casually offer a cigarette, which in turn led to the offer of a drink and then to further conversation. The diversion always succeeded, and Fritz was never denied his requested authorizations. As he recalls those encounters:

> I knew the mind and the experiences of the German civil servant—I had been around them for years in Solingen and . . . Aix-la-Chapelle. I had to be sympathetic, polish the apple, provide small favors or a bribe—it never failed to work.

Graebe took certain special precautions that seem minor in retrospect, but that may cumulatively have protected his efforts and saved lives. Whenever Fritz planned to relocate someone to a distant office, he had them hide overnight in his car, which was parked in his garage. At the appointed time, Fritz drove the carefully hidden person away from Sdolbonov. Once they were clear of the city, Fritz had the person sit up, and they would proceed in a routine way to the train station in the neighboring city of Schepetowka, which lay to the southeast of Sdolbonov. Fritz correctly reasoned that departing from another city would reduce the likelihood that the person being sent away from Sdolbonov might be recognized and challenged and the escape foiled by an arrest or investigation.

Whenever someone was traveling in this way, Maria, sitting at the switchboard, would send a carefully coded message, such as, "The joiner you requested will be arriving on the evening train" or some similar announcement. When the person arrived safely at the distant Jung office, a coded message was sent back to the Sdolbonov office. It was this careful attention to the smallest details that kept Graebe's adversaries off guard. Certainly they had their suspicions, but the thorough procedures and trusted secretary kept Graebe's enemies from getting the solid evidence they needed to eliminate him. This careful attention to every detail, combined with the effects of what he had learned about the fate of the Jews, was changing Graebe. His vibrancy began to fade, worry lines etched his brow, and his smile was no longer so quick and easy. Once so straight, his shoulders took on a slight but discernible stoop.

Word of Graebe's compassion spread quickly and discreetly through Sdolbonov's Jewish population. "If you need a small favor, a transit visa, anything—go see the German engineer." Every day, literally hundreds of fleeing Jews and displaced Polish peasants coursed through the cluster of cities and villages around Sdolbonov. The Jewish refugees kept moving, hiding, and scavenging for scraps of food, for shelter, for any respite from the exhausting, debilitating struggle to exist. Because they had nowhere to go and because they either lacked papers or held poorly disguised false papers, some Jews were quickly and easily exposed and placed either in ghettos or with forced labor columns. Many fell victim to atrocities at the hands of civilians, partisans, or military units.

The non-Jewish civilian populations in the Ukraine quickly learned the attitude of the occupying powers toward Jews. Large painted signs appeared warning all people against hiding or in any way providing aid or comfort to Jews. The warning continued with the threat of summary punishment—usually execution—for activities that in other times and places would have been considered humanitarian, Christian, and altruistic. Other signs offered cash rewards to those who either exposed the location of Jews or "patriotically" informed the authorities about people who were aiding Jews. In a wartime economy, cash incentives were sufficient motivation to turn people against neighbors and needy strangers.

No one could miss the explicit message that came from the rifle butts and bullets of the mobile killing units. Jews were personae non gratae everywhere. Any Jew without a yellow star or a yellow patch and a place on the census list was a candidate for merciless pursuit and brutal treatment. As the months passed, even the star or patch were of little protective value. Berlin's policies were gradually implemented in the eastern zones, depriving Jews first of social positions and civil rights, and then of employment in any of the skilled or public jobs. Between any of these steps could come a beating, an imprisonment, a deportation order, or a bullet.

It was against this backdrop that one Jewish family, Tadeuz, Irene, and Romak Glass, sought help from Fritz Graebe. Tadeuz was working as a conservation engineer at the time when he entered the Jung office in Sdolbonov. With reserved dignity he delicately asked Graebe to help his family.

"I must escape from this place or my wife and son will be killed."

"Where will you go?" asked Fritz Graebe.

"I don't know, but I will need papers to show that I am an Aryan."

Maria, who had been observing this cautious give-and-take from her seat at the switchboard, interrupted, speaking to Glass in Polish, "Play the open cards—you can trust him."

Only then did Glass let down his guard and explain his plight. He described his skills and repeated his request for help. Fritz intoned his standard question. "Are you ready to take off those yellow patches? If you are not, then I cannot be of any help to you."

Glass neither hesitated nor flinched in answering affirmatively. This encounter was the beginning of an important and trusted friendship between the two men.

Fritz considered himself a competent judge of character and took an immediate liking to Glass. He asked him to help them in their rescue efforts. Glass was a sensible man whose courage and professional skills made him an invaluable asset to the rescue effort. Fritz was about to open another construction site and requisition Jews and others to fill the labor force. The office was to be in Rovno, where Glass felt he would be reasonably safe. But Graebe felt that Rovno was geographically too close for Glass and that someone might recognize him or his wife. Too many Germans who were regularly in Sdolbonov also spent time in Rovno. The risk was simply too great. The decision was made to send the Glass family to the small village of Slawuta, which was southeast of Sdolbonov. There was as yet no work in this area, but a small local office might increase the prospects for a contract. It also was farther from the grasp of the authorities.

The strategy was to send Tadeuz to be the resident Jung agent there, and Irene was to be represented as the bookkeeper. There were several major problems that troubled Fritz and Maria: Tadeuz's features were decidedly Jewish, and the accents of the two adults might betray both their ancestry and the region from which they came. Romak, their young son, also would be a problem. He could easily divulge their plight without realizing what he was doing. His circumcision also could arouse suspicions, if it were detected. Fritz remembers how common such a situation was:

> The danger in this sort of situation was well established for us. A short time before the arrival of the Glass family the identity of one of Marschall's secretaries, Frau Pater, had been accidentally discovered when someone questioned her young daughter. One question led to another, then to hidden family pictures and finally to the disclosure that the child's parents were Jewish. Until that moment Frau Pater had been able to hide her identity. By the end of the day Frau Pater and her daughter both were dead.

Considering everything, Slawuta still seemed the wisest, if not the only, course of action; the Glass family would go there by train, fill out the forms necessary to open an office, and begin soliciting contracts for the Jung firm.

As Jung offices were opened in Kiverce and Rovno, they were required to conform to occupation policy directives that required German site foremen to supervise the daily progress. Meanwhile, Jewish workers were being saved by Graebe's requisitioning them for work details. Under Graebe, any foreman who zealously applied Nazi policies to the Jewish workers was either reassigned or threatened with transfer and induction into the regular army. This had to be done with great care; reasons other than harsh treatment and anti-Semitism had to be listed in order to justify the reassignment. Though completely unaware of their manager's sympathies and activities, several of Graebe's foremen themselves were sympathetic and concerned about the plight of the Jews. These foremen treated the Jews with respect.

During this entire time Maria continued to monitor carefully the movements of the firm's German staff. If an engineer or foreman were scheduled to travel between Jung offices or construction sites where he might know or recognize one of the disguised and resettled Jewish workers, a coded warning was sent ahead from Sdolbonov by Maria. As more people were relocated to distant Jung projects, the monitoring and traffic flow problems became increasingly complex and risky. One day, quite coincidentally, a German worker offhandedly mentioned to Maria that he was going on a holiday to visit a friend in Kiverce and asked if he could carry anything to the Jung office. He had known Claire while Claire was working in the Sdolbonov office and wearing yellow patches. A frantic series of coded calls went between the mother house and the mission in Kiverce. For one week the office was closed due to illness among the staff.

Working in close cooperation with her employer and co-conspirator, Maria succeeded in preventing all the thirty or forty German staff from "accidentally" making contact with those who had been given false papers, who had removed their patches, and who now managed or worked at one of the regional offices. This task had been complicated because of telltale physical appearances and dialects. Fortunately, Maria spoke several languages and was sensitive to these potential sources of betrayal. Once again, attention to the smallest details prevented encounters that would have compromised the rescue effort.

All this time there had been no diminution of the number of Jewish refugees streaming through the region. If anything, the flow had increased. Likewise, there was an ever-increasing river of regulations, policies, and procedures flooding from Berlin to all the occupied zones. It was now routine to inform on Jews and those who aided them. Indiscriminate brutality and harsh punishments were daily occurrences. Rumors of the existence of death camps arrived, carried by the transient Jews from the interior of Poland. People were understandably frightened and suspicious. Whenever there was an incident, a wave of panic ran through all of Graebe's workers holding false papers. The anti-Jewish pressures and the policies that mandated tightening discrimination increased the risks of rescue and greatly concerned Graebe. It was clear that he simply lacked contracts and offices in locations that were sufficiently distant from the places where the Nazi policies were enforced.

But in February 1942, Fritz Graebe nearly danced into the office at Sdolbonov. Maria remembered the day: "He was all sunshine and very happy—a rare mood for him." He had managed to locate a place far to the east, in Poltava. He also was close to being awarded a contract in that region. Immediately, plans were formulated and set in motion. Tadeuz and Irene Glass would be relocated so that they could open and manage the office. There would be major problems with the start-up of the project: it would be difficult to procure and transport supplies to the Poltava region, situated as it was so far in the interior; workers would be slow in arriving owing to the winter conditions and the great distances; and suitable staff would need to be chosen and sent from Germany. But the main problem was that, for many important reasons, it would be necessary to hide the existence of the Poltava site from officials at the Jung home office in Solingen. Awareness of the project meant audits, visits, and possible detection of the rescue efforts. Also, it was not possible to formulate quickly an economically sound justification for such a risky venture and to receive approval from Solingen in time to save endangered Jews. The venture in Poltava, although under the Jung banner, would be required to survive on its own—though it would receive major contributions from Fritz Graebe's personal financial resources in difficult times. To accomplish this risky feat, a separate accounting system was developed and maintained by Frau Glass with reports going directly to Graebe. The office in Solingen was told that a foreman was needed for another project that was to start in the near future. So the mandatory German foreman was brought in fresh from Solingen. He knew no one and had no idea what was happening around him.

As the Poltava office was opening, Claire, in Kiverce, was becoming increasingly alarmed by the new Reich policies and by the horror stories being told by refugees who stopped in Kiverce—any one of whom she feared might recognize her. Rather than risk discovery and live in constant fear, Claire asked to be moved. Fritz drove to Kiverce, loaded her few family possessions, and under the cover of night took Claire and her daughter to the train station in a nearby city. Maria called Tadeuz in Poltava to announce that his new cook would arrive several days later on the eastbound train.

This left the Kiverce office without a "cooperative" resident manager. At about the same time Alojzy Dutkowski, a Christian married to a Jewish woman, came to visit Fritz at the suggestion of the Judenrat. Alex, as he was known to the Germans who could not pronounce his Polish name, and his wife Lydia were living in one of the Nazi-established ghettos. He had witnessed acts of atrocity carried out against innocent Jews. German authorities had frequently questioned him, first suggesting and later demanding that he separate from his Jewish wife. One bold officer made Alex an offer. "We'll arrange a divorce for you in just a few minutes. Then you are free of that Jewish beast."

Alex's volatile temper exploded in a defense of the woman he loved. "How dare you! You bastard! Get out of my house before I break you in pieces. She has done nothing to you and she is my wife—get out, now!"

"Herr Dutkowski, if you don't get rid of her, you'll suffer her fate as well."

Alex reasoned that Lydia would soon be taken from the ghetto to a worse fate. But Maria talked with Alex before this happened. As she talked, she was considering how Alex might be helpful in the effort.

"Herr Dutkowski, you are faced with three options: first, you could go to the same fate as your wife; second, you could resist, and obviously you have the capability to kill several of your attackers before they kill you and your wife; third, you could go underground or relocate. If you are willing to relocate we can use you in our project."

Maria presented her evaluation to Fritz, who then interviewed Alex. Fritz recognized, as Maria had, the strength of character, the courage, and the potential in Alex. As a Christian he would not attract undue attention; he needed no forged papers; he was knowledgeable in engineering; and he was highly motivated. He was respected among the Jews of the ghetto and was obviously not an informer or double agent.

Fritz decided to take him on. He told him, "You will be in the office in Kiverce, but your wife must be completely invisible there. The dangers are very great for her. You seem the sort of man I need to run an office and to provide cover for the rescue effort."

Alex agreed; arrangements were quietly completed, the Dutkowskis were taken to the train station in Schepetowka, and soon they were residing in Kiverce. For the time being, all the regional offices were secure, and both the construction and rescue operations could proceed without unusual problems.

The halting, disorganized Aryanization process, begun in 1938, was slowly excising Jews from economic, political, and social life. Supplementary decrees streamed from Berlin, and one in particular, which was being stringently enforced at this time in early 1942, threatened to radically alter the staffing patterns of the Sdolbonov mother house: Jews were forbidden to hold positions of importance or prominence; they were only to be assigned to labor groups. The German government had been using the majority of the two and one-half million Jews of Poland in labor columns, factories, and camps for several months. There was nothing Fritz Graebe could do to delay or ignore the enforcement of this policy. All Jews now wore the yellow patches on their fronts and backs, and they were recorded by name, date of birth, and residence in a separate Jewish census. (Jews in Berlin and other metropolitan German areas wore yellow stars, but in the provinces simple yellow patches of cloth were the norm.) Failure to register or to wear the patches invited a severe beating or, more likely in most cities in the Ukraine, either deportation or summary execution. Any proprietor who continued to keep Jews in prominent positions risked jail or worse.

After receiving the memorandum from *Gebietskommissar* Marschall, issued by the Reich Labor Service, Graebe called his trusted colleague Maria into his office one morning.

"You cannot remain Jewish and be my secretary. But you cannot leave because I need you at the switchboard."

"It's an impossible situation, Herr Graebe."

"You can't wear those patches any longer."

"How can I suddenly not be Jewish in a town where everyone knows me? I would be killed the minute I showed up on the street without the patches, and claiming to be Aryan."

Fritz knew that Maria was correct, but he had a plan:

> I was terribly reluctant to pursue the matter with Maria. After all, the poor woman had been through so much already. Now I was coming to her and directing her to become something that she was not. They had murdered her husband because he was Jewish and there I was telling her to pretend to take on the religion of the killers. It was very hard for me to do that, to ask this of her, but I had no choice—it was for her safety and for the future of the rescues.

Fritz Graebe had a flair for the theatrical. With his creative mind and his commonsense awareness of "the way Germans think," combined with his dramatic skills, he gave birth to a plot that would enable him to circumvent the new policy. The day after his talk with Maria, the speaking lines for the drama were ready and the strategy was set: the two actors rehearsed their roles for the next several days. The simple but risky plan required falsified papers and a "consultation" with *Gebietskommissar* Marschall. The story was to be that Maria, whose name sounded vaguely Christian, was actually a Catholic who had never formally converted to the Jewish faith. She believed that she had become Jewish when she had married a Jewish man, and by now she felt that she owed it to his memory to remain a Jew.

It was a perfectly credible story, one that Marschall would easily understand. Many non-Jews were married to Jews. They went wherever their spouses went, including to the ghettos. At the time when the anti-Jewish policies were being promulgated and the strategy with Maria was being planned, Fritz was living in the same house with Marschall. Marschall had wanted to have senior managers from German firms living in or near his house. Graebe suspected that his living quarters were arranged to allow Marschall to monitor his movements. Eventually, in order to avoid Marschall, Graebe moved to a house adjacent to his office. Marschall did not protest or try to block the move. One evening after dinner, Graebe described the "crazy situation with my secretary." Marschall told him to come to his office the next morning to discuss the matter in detail. The next morning, after a final review of roles and lines, Fritz was at Marschall's door with Maria and her "new" baptismal certificate. She waited in the anteroom while Graebe talked with the *Gebietskommissar*, whose door Graebe had deliberately left ajar.

"I am so fed up with this dumb woman! I told her she had to take off that stupid patch if she was going to work for me. It's that stupid patch, that's what is behind this whole wild story."

Maria sat straining to hear the conversation. So much rested on the success of this strategy. Her heart began to race as she anticipated the confrontation with the hated Nazi. Fear welled up: Would she remember the carefully rehearsed argument, the denial, the submission? Would she be able to hold her tongue in front of the murderer? Could she follow the lines and not betray herself with unconscious actions? In the other room Graebe ranted on about something to do with Maria's late husband being a Jew. Suddenly Maria felt weak and faint as she remembered the man she had loved and married, and his brutal death behind the cement factory. A gentle serenity filled Maria at that moment as she remembered too the vow she had taken in those numbed days after the *Einsatzgruppen* had left Sdolbonov: She would exact her revenge by saving others. Now she had the means to honor her covenant. For her husband, and for the others who were now bound for a similar fate, for her Jews, she would deliver her lines with conviction and confidence.

Marschall had ordered his desk officer to bring Maria into his office. Fritz seized the initiative.

"*Herr Gebietskommissar.*" He used the formal title to make Marschall feel important. "This woman is a Catholic. Her husband was a Jew and now she wears the patch of the Jews."

Marschall interrupted Graebe and in warm, condescending tones he spoke to Maria. "Where is your husband?"

"He did not return, sir."

Her short, placating response was carefully planned so that it would neither challenge nor offend Marschall in the event that he might be trying to trap her or assess her attitude. Graebe, feigning angry displeasure and impatience, shouted at Maria, "You are so stubborn—you make me sick."

Marschall ignored Graebe's outburst and continued to question Maria. He then examined Maria's baptismal certificate, but failed to ask for her marriage certificate. (It would have listed her as Jewish.) When he was finally satisfied, he issued her a direct order.

"You will immediately remove the yellow patches and never again appear publicly with them on your clothing. You are an Aryan! Do you understand me?"

"Excuse me, sir, but people will think I am abusing the law and they will kill me for not having the patches."

Marschall again summoned his desk officer, directing him to remove Maria's name from the Jewish census and to include it in the Aryan census. Furthermore, he directed the officer to publish a suitable notice of this discovery and change in status.

The ploy had succeeded! At Marschall's order, she could now move freely and continue her work without fear of arrest and deportation. It had been a terrifying experience for her, but it gave her a new confidence that freed her to push limits whenever it became necessary for the rescue efforts. Maria's commitment to the task was renewed by the memory of her husband and by her desire to vindicate his death by protecting others from a similar fate. This encounter with the Nazi hierarchy was the turning point in the rescue efforts because Maria now had access to the innermost circles of the regional government.

As the Poltava operation was getting off the ground, it was clear that funds had to be found or diverted in order to maintain it. The contracts were slow in coming through, so Poltava could not be self-supporting. But Graebe dared not turn to the home office in Solingen. His personal standards, the risk to the total effort, and a very precise accounting system in Solingen all made any diversion of funds or embezzlement out of the question.

Fritz had deposited nearly one half million Reichmarks in his personal and business accounts in a Solingen bank before leaving for work in the Ukraine. By the end of the war, he had spent more than three hundred thousand Reichmarks from those accounts to maintain the activities of the regional rescue centers. If funds were needed, Tadeuz would wire from Poltava or Alex would send a "special requisition" from Kiverce. The funds that they received came from the private accounts of the German engineer. As more people received the false papers and were relocated to construction sites, particularly in Poltava, funds had to be secured to meet their living needs. The demands for relocation had become less discreet and were escalating rapidly.

Symcha Scheifstein was the leader of the Judenrat, the council of Jews, in Sdolbonov. A conscientious man, he now found himself acting as an arbiter of death. His leadership was necessarily a compromise with the army of occupation, and he was restricted to choosing between lesser and greater evils. Graebe appreciated the tremendous burden that Scheifstein carried. Whenever he needed to see Fritz, he was greeted warmly and every attempt was made to accommodate his requests.

On one particular day, Scheifstein was desperate. Actions against the Jews were increasingly frequent, nothing seemed to stem the floodtide of refugees streaming into the region, collaborators were everywhere and profiting from the suffering of others, and now word of the death camps had reached the Judenrat. To Scheifstein, there seemed to be but one practical solution.

"Herr Graebe, you must open new projects. Jews with work cards live. Those without, die. Please, you must open more sites, call more people, issue the cards."

Fritz already knew about the camps, but he could do no more than assure his friend that his concern was real. He promised to do all in his power to help, provided he could do so without jeopardizing the entire rescue effort. Scheifstein knew that he could ask no more than that. Both men knew that there was no guarantee that Graebe could save anyone; the best he could do was buy time and delay death; this might, ultimately, save lives.

5. The Moses of Rovno: July 13, 1942

A crucial incident took place in Rovno in July 1942, less than a year after Graebe's arrival in the Ukraine. The incident shows the complexities and severe dangers that faced the Jews and their protector in the Ukraine, Fritz Graebe. Graebe and Otto Koeller, the Reich Commissioner for Jewish Affairs, wasted no time in becoming adversaries, working for exactly opposite purposes. Their displeasure with each other was rarely masked, but because he outranked Graebe, Koeller was a very real threat.

On July 11, 1942, Fritz Graebe paid one of his regular visits to the Jung office in Rovno. While visiting one of the building projects, the site foreman for the Jung interests in Rovno, Fritz Einsporn, confided to Graebe that word had reached him of a "Jewish Action" scheduled for July 13. The Action, planned and promoted by SS Major Dr. Puetz, was to eliminate all the Jews in the Rovno region, including the nearly one hundred twenty Jews working for Jung. Einsporn had received his information from a loose-tongued officer in the Wehrmacht. When Graebe heard the names of those associated with the Action, he knew that he had to act quickly.

Recognizing the great risk in what he was about to do to delay the Action, Graebe directed Einsporn to "order our Jewish workers and the women to travel to Sdolbonov today, at noon, and have them bring all of their belongings."

"We can't do that without causing trouble in the ghetto" was the foreman's reply. But the order stood, and the Rovno Jews began packing. Rumors of an Action had been flying around the Rovno ghetto for several days, and the departure of the one hundred twenty workers in the Rovno Jung labor column threw the ghetto into hysteria. The Jung workers arrived at Mizocz the first night. Their departure led to an explosive confrontation between the Judenrat and Dr. Puetz.

"We must know," they demanded. "Is there an Action planned?"

Puetz, who knew nothing of Graebe's order or of the departure of the column, demanded an explanation. "Why do you come to me with this idiotic question?"

"Because the engineer Graebe, of the Jung firm, has withdrawn all of his workers and taken them to Sdolbonov," the Judenrat members replied.

Puetz adamantly denied to the Jewish leaders that there would be an Action, and sent them away. He then ordered the immediate arrest of the foreman, the business manager, and all of Graebe's Polish personnel. The business manager, who was able to escape arrest, made his way by night to Sdolbonov, where Graebe now was, and reported the arrests. In spite of the arrests, Graebe relied on normally well-informed sources that he had among the police; they had not heard of a planned Action, and Graebe was soon convinced that the Action had really been only a rumor. He knew that fear spread quickly in the ghetto and that these rumors regularly rushed like wildfire through the oppressed people. After consulting with Maria, it was decided that Graebe would drive to Mizocz and explain the situation to the Rovno workers, who were still there.

The frightened workers were very reluctant to believe their boss and return to Rovno. Graebe calmed his younger workers by promising them that he would protect them and their parents if their lives were endangered by an Action. The next morning the entire Jung column returned to the work site in Rovno; their arrival was as clearly noted as their departure had been. After the column arrived in Rovno, Fritz paid a visit there to Dr. Puetz.

Pretending to be confused and inconvenienced by the arrest of his senior staff, Graebe explained to Puetz that all his workers had returned to their home base for the routinely scheduled delousing.

"I can't have a typhus outbreak. Last year, as you know, thousands of people died in the typhus epidemic. I must have all of my workers if I am to complete my assignments for the Reich, so I schedule regular treatments for them."

Puetz's response was comforting to the worried engineer. "Herr Graebe, really! An Action now would be absurd. You need your people, the railways need people, the military needs people; that sort of Action just now would be foolishly contrary to the best interests of the Reich."

Graebe was in fact being misled by the smooth, diplomatic comments of the SS major. Still in Rovno, he returned to his local office there, to

find another SS man waiting with an order for him to appear immediately before the regional commissioner for Rovno, Dr. Behr (who was
not with the SS). When Fritz arrived at the SS headquarters, he was
taken not to Behr, but to his deputy, Lieutenant *(Stabsleiter)* Beck, whom
Graebe remembered from the Rovno Action the previous November.
The engineer repeated his story about scheduled delousings and expressed his concern over an outbreak of typhus. Graebe explained, "I
cannot stress enough that we are on a tight time schedule, regulated by
direct orders from Berlin. Any disease or Action will cause delays, and
delays will mean investigations by Berlin and trouble for us all."

"Herr Graebe, who issued your orders from Berlin? May I see them,
please?" Beck requested. He thereafter repeatedly interrupted Graebe's
argument, attempting to learn the office or the names of those in Berlin
who had issued the engineer's orders.

Fritz's response was always the same. "It is not possible for me to
divulge the source of my orders—they are confidential and come from
the highest authorities. . . ." Then with a knowing glance and a wave
of his finger, he warned, "Besides, it is better for you that you not know
about Berlin."

Beck persisted with his inquiry, asking Graebe what unit in Berlin had
issued his orders and to whom in Berlin he was responsible. Graebe
again evaded him. Then, for inexplicable reasons, Beck leaned over the
table and in tones of whispered confidence warned Fritz, "Tonight at
ten there will be an Action, but you may not do anything at all."

"I'll withdraw all of my people, now, and return them to Sdolbonov,"
said Graebe.

"You must not do that!" replied the now-frightened officer, "you'll
create a panic and then everyone will die. I'll give you a signed document that will safeguard your employees. You may come back in two
hours and pick up your people. Believe me, they will be safe."

Beck gave Fritz the signed document and asked him to leave Rovno
immediately. He did not trust the document now that he had discovered
Puetz's duplicity, but Graebe complied, leaving Rovno for a hasty consultation with Maria at the Sdolbonov office.

Maria and Fritz considered the document, the consuming violence an
Action would involve, and the dishonesty of the Reich command. There
was no choice for Graebe. "I am going back to Rovno tonight," he said.

"What? You can't do that!"

"I must. I promised our workers that I would protect them. They
might panic and all be killed by the militia, who don't give a damn
anyway."

"You're mad!" Maria cried. "Do you hear me? You're mad! They are already shooting people and they won't hesitate to shoot you, too."

Maria's response did not faze the highly principled German, who nevertheless knew that his secretary was correct.

Word of Graebe's decision raced through the Jewish workers in the Sdolbonov office. They fully appreciated the severe risk that their employer was about to take. A few stopped him to express their concern for him and for his safety. Mixed with their expressions of compassion were reasonable concerns for the safety of the Sdolbonov staff and the overall rescue effort. "What if they shoot the engineer?" they asked themselves. "What if he dies—what will happen to us and to the others? He cannot go there and risk everything."

For his part, Graebe would have none of that fear and hysteria. He had given his word to the workers, and he would be there to protect them. If he feared anything at all, it was the possibility that the Action would move from Rovno to Sdolbonov. He directed Maria to stay in the office by the phone and to avoid the city, warning her, "If the shooting starts here, there will be no protection for anyone and I must have someone on the switchboard."

Graebe's decision was further complicated by the fact that Elisabeth and Friedel were visiting Sdolbonov at that time on a specially arranged family holiday. When she had arrived two months earlier in May, Elisabeth had witnessed the results of the hanging of a Jewish carpenter. Otherwise, she knew little about the mistreatment of the Jewish people. Fritz had intentionally withheld the full scope of the suffering from Elisabeth because he did not want her to be implicated if his efforts were discovered. He wanted no accidental slips of the tongue that might later betray his work. But now he had to tell her nearly everything, in large part because he feared that he might die, and he did not want to leave his family ignorant of his mission. Fritz explained to Elisabeth the plight of his workers in Rovno and the promise that he had made to them when they left from Mizocz to return to Rovno. Her response was typical of her: "Fritz, you have no choice to make. You gave your word to those poor, suffering people, and now you must keep your promise. I ask only that you arrange safe passage to Solingen for Friedel and me."

The long-awaited family reunion was ending prematurely, but somehow no excuses or justifications seemed necessary. Graebe went back to his office to complete some details, and in the pressured moments before his departure for Rovno, he retreated from his worried staff to the quiet of his study and drafting room. There he wrote a rough copy of a letter authorizing the safe passage of his family. He also drafted a note to his wife, a note that Maria would type and hold until the results of his efforts were known:

> My dear Elisabeth, if you receive this letter, fate will have caught up with me. Maria has the letter authorizing the train trip for you and Friedel. God bless you—I love you and Friedel. I am thankful that you told me that I could not forsake the people— so I did not desert them in their time of need.

Fritz Graebe walked out of his office renewed and ready. With his coat under his arm, he gave several orders to the office staff and left the letters on Maria's desk. A deep silence fell over the office; all eyes moved with each step of the engineer as he resolutely strode toward the door and an uncertain destiny in Rovno. Those who were present recall that the eyes of nearly everyone in the office were clouded with tears. Absentmindedly, Maria picked up his letters as his hand pulled the door shut. Her eyes scanned the page and her sobs broke the silence. "Oh, no!" she cried out.

This released the cries of the others. Graebe walked to the house where Friedel and Elisabeth were waiting. Graebe and his wife went into the bedroom, leaving Friedel in the darkened living room. A soft ray of light seeped into the room from a crack in the bedroom door. Friedel strained to hear a word, any word, that might reveal the situation, but he could detect only the urgency and tension in the hushed voices. A bag was packed, then the two adults emerged from the bedroom. Almost oblivious to their son, they continued talking and making preparations for Graebe's departure. Finally, the moment arrived. Motionless and silhouetted against the dark window, Graebe slowly removed Beck's paper from his billfold and held it before his wife.

"My head hangs on this," he said solemnly.

A warm, gentle embrace, tears, and the fragile prospects for the future were all placed in perspective by Frau Graebe's deeply held religious values.

"You must go to them now," she said. "Try everything and God will protect you."

Friedel quietly watched as his mother paced the floor. Then his father's parting words created a blended emotion of fear and hope.

"I will be careful—for you and for Friedel. I love you."

Later that night Friedel was cradled in his mother's arms. Pretending to be asleep, he rested in her arms, recalling, over and over, the ominous words that his father had spoken.

Maria and Fritz had devised a plan. He would go to Rovno with his coachman and two horses. He would send back a message with the coachman if there was danger, and Maria would then dispatch trucks for the workers and their belongings. But if the driver failed to return or returned without news, it was to be the signal to commence a larger effort. Contrary to his normal style, Fritz decided to take an automatic pistol with him. He knew the Ukrainian militiamen were brutal and unpredictable. The superior firepower of an automatic weapon might prove to be the one thing that could change the situation in his favor, although he had no intention of firing it unless lives hung in the balance.

From the time he arrived in Rovno that evening until nearly six o'clock the next morning, Fritz stood in the street at a spot where his workers could see him from their hiding places in two separate houses. He reasoned that if there were trouble, the desperate refugees might take flight and further risk their lives. His presence at that location would calm them. A symphony of slaughter echoed through the city all night: Bullets whistled and ricocheted off brick walls; grenades flew like wingless bats, exploding and sending fragments smashing against glass and splintering wood; trucks filled with guards darted in and out of alleys, careening frantically, tires screaming; and people howled, the final human sound in this, their requiem.

The "Jewish Actions" were studies in mayhem and chaos. People who in normal circumstances might never harm anyone suddenly succumbed to bloodlust and hatred. The Ukrainian militiamen went from house to house, smashing doors, breaking windows, carelessly trampling on furniture and personal things, while indiscriminately beating children, women, and old men with the butts of rifles. Once a group of militiamen came to the door of one of the houses where Graebe's Jews were hidden. Graebe dashed toward the house shouting at them, but because he spoke no Ukrainian none of them understood him.

Fritz has never forgotten that horrifying scene:

It was a terrible moment before the confrontation with them. What was I to do—I spoke no Ukrainian and they spoke no German. As they prepared to bash in the barricaded doors I decided I had no other alternative. I pulled the automatic pistol from my coat and made it very clear to them that I would shoot unless they went away. They seemed to understand the universal language of violence, but I was terribly frightened. I was

certain I would be forced to fire the gun and people would be
hurt. The Ukrainians had the same fear because they saw that
mine was an automatic weapon and theirs were not.

This confrontation occurred at about three in the morning. It was the
impetus that caused Graebe finally to scribble a note to Maria and send
it off with the coachman. The militia group had rushed the next house,
smashing doors and throwing a grenade through a window. No one
survived that raid. It was now only a matter of time before Maria would
have the trucks en route to Rovno.

Many of the militiamen behaved like sadists. It was more than bloodlust that led them to seek out the youngest children. They seemed almost gleeful whenever they found a mother with an infant. Ripping the
child from its mother's arms, they would rush from the house, holding
the screaming infant by a leg. Then they ritualistically would whirl the
child several times overhead and smash it against a pillar. From his vantage point Graebe saw such acts of terror repeated again and again in
front of terror-stricken mothers. There was no way that one man could
stop the carnage. Graebe watched everything, recording in his methodical memory the incidents and the identities of the instigators and the
perpetrators.

Fritz Graebe was well known among the Jews. As he stood guard at
his street corner station, hundreds of them passed, prodded by militia
and police. Those who recognized the engineer called out to him, pleading
for his intervention. To save one in this column would have been to
jeopardize the one hundred and twenty in hiding. The dilemma was
worse than that faced by King Solomon when two women claimed to
be the mother of the same child. But wisdom in Rovno, dispensed in
front of machine guns, was not wisdom from a throne. Hundreds marched
past Graebe en route to the collection point and on to death.

By five in the morning, Fritz was physically and emotionally exhausted. The confrontations with the militiamen, the incomprehensible
brutalities, and the futile pleading had drained him of energy. For the
victims, death was an escape from the terror. Mysteriously narcotized
by their own violence, the guards too escaped the trauma of their actions. Only the engineer could not forget the horrifying scenes. In a
state of foggy exhaustion he took a vow never to forget, and to seek
justice for the murdered. The images of that night remained with him
for the rest of his life.

By six o'clock, two of Graebe's workers and the foreman, Einsporn, from the Rovno office slipped past guards into the ghetto. They hardly recognized the exhausted engineer.

"Herr Graebe, you look terrible. You must rest. Go to the office and have some coffee."

"You are right," he replied. "Stand here! Whatever happens, don't move away, not even for a minute! One of you come get me immediately if the militia comes."

The office, which was four or five hundred yards from the corner, provided a momentary sanctuary for the engineer. He collapsed into a chair and quickly dozed in a fitful nap. His mind raced through the scenes of devastation, but he could not wake himself to escape the dreams. He was startled awake as a German worker burst through the door. The Action had begun at the house where Graebe's Jews were hiding.

"Come quickly! Some of the Jews were looking out of the slatted windows on the first floor. The militia spotted them. They have been dragged out and taken to the collection point!"

Seven of the Jewish workers were being taken to the center of town. Graebe flew out the door and threw a revolver taken from the office to the foreman, shouting, "I command you to shoot anyone who tries to break into this house again! My people are not to be touched. You are responsible for everything." With that he ran in the direction of the town square, hoping to stop the militia before they arrived.

Nothing was the same in Rovno. The familiar landmarks had been reduced to rubble. Broken windows and smashed doors, broken furniture, and bodies in bloodstained nightshirts all littered the streets. And at the base of the stained lamppost lay a child whose blood heralded the arrival of the angel of death.

At the collection point near the fountain were hundreds of Jews, mostly men, squatting with their hands behind their heads. It was a macabre scene, with the hunched shadows of the victims, and Dr. Puetz, like a devil in one of Dante's scenes, standing with one hand on his holstered revolver and a whip darting carelessly about from the other. His raised eyebrows signaled his astonishment as the interloping engineer shouted, "Dr. Puetz!" Graebe stressed the title, hoping to control the dangerous situation.

"I must remind you of what you told me yesterday! Exactly the opposite has happened."

"Why are you here, Graebe?"

"Why did you lie to me, Dr. Puetz? I tell you now what I told you before. I need all of my workers. I want them back, now!"

Puetz's response was almost inaudible. "No."

When the soul of a man has been brutalized by such scenes of slaughter, when every muscle is exhausted, when death alone prevails, when there is no help, no compassion, and no end in sight—where does a person find the strength to go on?

From some untapped reserve of energy, Fritz Graebe centered himself on this dusty, public stage, commanding the situation. With a firm, stately gesture, Graebe took out Lieutenant·Beck's signed document and handed it to Puetz. It was cold water in the face of a raging man.

Puetz trembled and screamed, "No! No! I cannot release anyone who is here. I start Actions, but I am powerless to stop them. These people shall be transferred to another location."

Graebe stood motionless, silent. He stared straight at Puetz, his mind racing: *Another lie. Transfers mean death. I must have my people.*

Puetz could not stand the silence. As if he were reading Graebe's mind, he shouted, "No, damn it! Get away from me."

Then, as if his personality had been transformed, Puetz smiled. Slowly he began pulling his revolver from its holster. Graebe cautiously mimicked Puetz, allowing his automatic to rest visibly at his hip.

The gun hung limp in Puetz's hand at his side; his finger inched slowly toward the trigger. For several minutes, the silent confrontation continued, observed by the squatting victims, many of whom understood German. But Graebe and Puetz waged a silent battle. For uncounted seconds that lasted as long as hours, they stood face to face, still as statues. Puetz was attracted to death as much as Graebe was attracted to life. For Puetz, these Jews were merely things, objects of inconvenience and derision. Puetz lived, thrived because of his unlimited hate and his insatiable appetite for homicide.

Almost imperceptibly Puetz's finger moved into the trigger guard. Graebe's eye caught the subtle motion, and he began to move his automatic weapon up from his side. His voice filled with madness, Puetz ripped at the silence.

"Nobody gets out of here!"

Puetz spotted motion in Graebe's arm and began to level his gun.

Graebe thought to himself, *What a damn fool I am. One of us must die. There is too much tension. Too many guns. I know that if he shoots me, I can take him with me, too.*

Whether intimidated by his opponent's weapon, or anxious to get on with the killing, or convinced of Graebe's will, Puetz dropped the gun to his side, leaving his finger in the trigger.

"Graebe! Go get the rest of your Jews; take them with you and leave."

"Puetz, I want my craftsmen—there, these seven men."

The ploy failed. The choice before Graebe had once been Solomon's: seven men or more than one hundred? Graebe's mind raced; there was no choice, again. Then he made a final counterdemand.

"I'll go, but you must send with me an SS guard, because the Ukrainians don't understand me; they are drunk with killing and I cannot protect myself and my workers from them."

The demand was honored but not without a condition. "You have your people," said Puetz. "Get out of Rovno by eight o'clock this morning. If you are not gone, my men will bring you and your workers back here."

The whip, which had rested inertly in Puetz's left hand, suddenly leaped to life, slicing the air and pointing to the victims who were squatting, as Puetz snarled, "By eight o'clock, Graebe, or it will be your problem."

The two adversaries parted, one to kill, the other to search for the strength and the means to escape. Graebe turned and slowly walked over to his seven workers. Now, at this moment, the fast-approaching deadline was less important than the momentary visual embrace that was to come. Graebe's eyes must have shown the pain and powerlessness that he felt so intensely. Every other memory of that night—the bloodied infants, the beaten women, the pillaged city—was pushed back as Graebe's eyes settled on each man, making a covenant with each of the seven: *I will never forget. Never!*

Their eyes caught his unspoken message, and there was no recrimination. The men seemed to understand, to accept. Slowly, intentionally, Graebe walked away, pausing near each man. Not one protested. Never had Graebe known such silence, such pathos, such fear. No one moved, no one spoke, as the German engineer walked away.

He felt that perhaps this was the quietest moment in the Holocaust.

It was already seven o'clock in the morning. Fritz ran back looking for the coachman whom he had dispatched to Sdolbonov with the note for Maria hours earlier. When he arrived back at the safe house, there was no truck, no coach, only his German staff standing guard on the corner. Time was now critical, with less than an hour remaining before Dr. Puetz sent his SS goons to clear the house. The engineer's usually clear mind was clouded by exhaustion and the encounter with Puetz. Fighting his sense of impotence and emptiness, Graebe stopped to think, to formulate a new strategy. He decided to march his Jews on foot out of Rovno and on to Sdolbonov, in the hope of meeting the trucks and coach en route. The Jung workers began lining up outside as Fritz explained the urgent situation to them. Suddenly fear-struck, one of the men hurled a challenge.

"I thought you promised to protect us. Have you forgotten your word already?"

There was not time to argue, and no energy to waste. "Shut up! Don't make me lose my nerve."

A number of women who had been hidden in the other house arrived, and their presence seemed to break the tension, allowing Graebe to reassert his purpose. The twelve-mile march began without further incident.

Maria, stationed at the Jung switchboard in Sdolbonov, had not received a phone communication since seven o'clock the previous evening. All had seemed well at the time, so the engineer had promised to call again at eight. Worried that the call might not come across the line, Maria began calling Rovno at seven-thirty. When she finally managed to get a line through, she was informed that all communications were suspended on the order of the *Gebietskommissar*. This was the dreaded signal that an Action had started. Throughout the night Maria maintained a silent, fearful vigil. She was poised to act quickly, but the catalytic call never came, nor did a coachman bearing instructions arrive. Throughout the night she imagined the scenes at Rovno, and then she imagined herself delivering the letter and papers to Frau Graebe.

It also was a sleepless night for Elisabeth Graebe. All night long she paced the floor of the house, trying not to disturb her son. She feared for her husband's safety, but also for the well-being of the Jews whom he loved.

At seven o'clock in the morning a delivery man stopped briefly and confirmed Maria's worst fear: The Jews in the Rovno ghetto were being killed. The Action had started hours earlier. By eight, she was frantic. What could have happened to Herr Graebe and to the one hundred twenty workers? Finally the familiar sound of the wagon and horse team brought Maria out of her worried imaginings. She raced out of the office to meet the coach.

"Where are they? What has happened to the engineer?" she asked.

The mumbling driver fussed over the harness and reins as he described the scenes in Rovno. "They are killing the Jews, even the children, in the streets," he said.

As the coachman went on detailing the horror in Rovno, Maria noted that his horses were neither lathered nor panting.

"When did you leave Rovno?" she demanded.

"Oh, maybe it was about three or four this morning. I don't really recall."

Maria exploded at the revelation. "Where have you been? It takes little more than an hour to get here. Why didn't you come directly here? What did Herr Graebe say to you?" Her questions flew at the bewildered and cowering driver.

"All Graebe said was, 'Quick! Quick!' But what does he know?"

"Where have you been all these hours?"

"Herr Graebe doesn't know horses. You can't wake them in the middle of the night and expect them to work. When I got out of the sound of the shooting in Rovno, I let them graze and water. They need good care or they don't work."

Only at that moment did the coachman reach into his pocket and deliver to Maria the letter from her boss.

Maria could not contain her rage as she ripped open the note. It was already two hours late. Her screams startled the horses.

"Oh, my God! We must go get them before it's too late. How could you do this?" She imagined the plight of Graebe and the Jewish workers. *His mission may have succeeded only to fail because of these stupid horses—I must get to them.* By the time she had received the note, all the trucks that could have been used to rescue the people in Rovno were out on the road projects five miles north. Worse, the trucks could have gone off on any of three different roads. Maria jumped on the wagon.

"Let's go, we must find the trucks now."

The driver balked because he felt that his horses had labored enough for one day. Maria grabbed the reins and threatened to go on without him. Cursing her, he finally started the beasts on the search for the trucks.

Maria attributes it to an act of God that they turned onto the first road and within a few miles located the convoy of trucks. When they reached them, a surly foreman proved to be uncooperative. Maria told him that he must obey Herr Graebe's orders, to which the foreman retorted that his orders came from another division and not from the Railroad Administration. With patience spent and time racing to a potentially awesome end, Maria called out, "Who drives this truck? Come forward, now!"

A Jewish boy with yellow patches on his coat jumped out of a ditch and volunteered to drive.

"Take off that jacket and hide it under something in the truck."

As Maria and the boy drove toward Rovno, they passed Ukrainian farmers carrying their loads to market. The fresh morning air and the tall corn reminded Maria of prewar Poland. It was a rare but momentary escape from the reality of war and the urgency of her mission. Behind the truck came the coachman and horse team moving almost as fast as the dilapidated truck.

While the coachman had been meandering into Sdolbonov with the urgent message, Graebe had arranged his workers into a column. An SS sergeant with four militiamen had been assigned by Puetz to escort the column to the city limits. Women were placed at the center in case an SS patrol stopped the group and caused trouble. During an Action it was common practice for the SS units to range around an area looking for Jews who had escaped or who traveled unwittingly through an area without papers. Graebe anticipated a confrontation between the column and such a unit. For the moment, though, Fritz had to worry about the Ukrainian militiamen blocking his exit from the Rovno ghetto. It was obvious that Puetz's escort would do no good; they found the entire spectacle amusing. At about seven-thirty, with no sign of the truck, Graebe placed his German staff at the rear of the column and he took the lead position. The march began with Graebe holding his automatic pistol in front of himself at shoulder level, pointing the way to freedom and warning any marauders. Ukrainians were killing every Jew that passed their rifle sights. The automatic pistol was a clear enough warning for these murderers. Carefully, quickly, the column scurried down streets filled with rubble from the Action. Finally, the column reached the intersection of the road to Kwasilow. Fritz could lower his weary, trembling arm and holster his weapon. They marched as fast as they could— really a slow walk, because people were exhausted and starved—toward Kwasilow, the westernmost boundary of the Rovno region, and on to Sdolbonov and immunity from Dr. Puetz.

Graebe's group trudged through the morning heat under the beautiful skies that went unnoticed, past rows of tall cornstalks. The cornfields seemed to be teeming with life, shaking, moving, cracking in the warm, windless morning. Hidden Jews moved through the corn like swarms of grasshoppers. Whenever it was safe, a signal was given and one or two people would jump from the cornfield into the safety of the column. They all wore patches and were emaciated. As each new person joined the line, they were sent back into the middle of the column, where they could remain hidden in the event of an encounter with the SS.

On the horizon, a large dustcloud created by the truck and wagon alerted the refugees to the arrival of their rescuers. As Maria and the boy drove past the tall cornfields, she suddenly saw the column. She remembers the scene with incredible clarity:

It was a sight: there they were, twice the total number in our group, all walking, struggling behind Herr Graebe. He was totally spent—I do not think I had ever seen him so completely fatigued. He was wearing his leather hat and long coat, leading the Jews. Women huddled in the middle; flashes of yellow darted from the corn into the center of the line. When we arrived I fell crying into Herr Graebe's arms—I tried to explain to him about the grazing horses and the coachman's wonderful compassion for his horses. Herr Graebe managed a small grin.

Fritz ordered the people with personal belongings to place them on the wagon. Then he climbed aboard and the column set out for Sdolbonov. The truck brought up the rear of the line, providing a sort of flank guard.

Word had reached Frau Graebe that her husband was returning. She awaited him on the porch of the house, and when she saw him she rushed weeping into his arms. Once back in Sdolbonov, those people without papers were issued papers, everyone was fed, and Graebe retired to a tavern frequented by German soldiers and workers. Because the area is so close-knit, word of the march had spread through Sdolbonov, and everyone was talking about Graebe leading the column of his Jews. When he walked into the lounge, one of the German officers lightheartedly teased, but for Fritz the title conferred in jest was, in truth, a great honor:

"Here is the leader of those Jews, the Moses of Rovno."

Graebe was relieved to have his workers back safely in Sdolbonov, but the loss of the seven men was a heavy burden. The Moses of Rovno wondered to himself how the Moses in Egypt would have felt and acted if Pharaoh had commanded him to leave seven Israelites behind.

The anguish over the seven who were left behind was compounded one night, a short time after the rescue, when a Wehrmacht officer confided to Graebe that the only reason there had been an Action that night was a visit to the area by the senior Reich commissar for the Ukraine, Erich Koch. Drs. Puetz and Behr had wanted to give him a gift. When Koch arrived, the Rovno ghetto had been gift-wrapped in blood and rubble; it was *Judenrein*, empty of Jews. To gratify murderous egos and to nourish a ravenous, diseased political system, thousands of Jews had been murdered. But the eyes of the seven skilled Jewish craftsmen had sealed their covenant with one German witness, who promised never to forget and who kept that promise.

6. Dubno, The Land That Trembled: October 5, 1942

In 1941, German military forces had made significant advances, invading Yugoslavia, attacking the Soviet Union, and forcing the partial evacuation of Moscow as German Panzer units approached that city. Late 1941 through 1942 was a critical period for the progress of the war and for the Reich's efforts to eradicate the Jewish populations on the European continent. The Wannsee Conference, on January 20, 1942, detailed the plans to murder the more than eleven million Jews believed by the Nazis to be living in Central and Eastern Europe. By June, exterminations had begun at Sibibor, Belsec, and Treblinka, and Jews were being detained and deported to Auschwitz and Majdanek. By August, Actions against the Jews had been conducted in the Warsaw and Lvov ghettos. The war effort was not allowed to interfere with the extermination camps, even when the Soviet Army launched a major counterattack near Stalingrad on November 19.

The partisan movements, facing the overwhelming manpower and weaponry of the Germans, had to rely on either stealth or lightning raids. Throughout Byelorussia, Poland, and the Ukraine, a few small Jewish resistance groups formed in the ghettos and forests as Jews were deported or shot. The partisans and Jewish resistance groups were vital forces in disrupting Hitler's armies, but were not able to reduce the flow of victims to the extermination sites.

The main local partisan groups rarely participated in actual rescues unless the effort afforded them an opportunity to sabotage or significantly inconvenience some part of the Nazi war machine. While a few groups did help with rescues, most were notably as anti-Jewish as their German adversaries. Jews could not expect much help from them; indeed, there were many verified incidents where the partisan underground murdered Jewish refugees. The civilian populations often actively cooperated with the invasion forces by revealing the presence of hidden or fleeing Jews. German soldiers were deployed to hunt the Jews; virtually no group or country was willing to offer sanctuary to the refugees. Those few Jews who could find weapons to aid in their own resistance movements found the weapons to be in poor condition and inadequately supplied.

In the Ukraine, there were strong pockets of resistance, and partisan groups worked to subvert the efforts of the Reich. But few did anything to help rescue Jews. Fritz Graebe's strategies, originating in Sdolbonov, were the most successful in the region. The Jews under his care were generally safe or were provided the necessary documents for escape. A subculture of compassion was thriving, almost unnoticed, in the area.

Three essential services remained unavailable to Graebe's workers, however. Without these services, the severe winter weather or the slightest disease could spell the death of many of them. Using the authority of his official position and some of his personal funds, Graebe requisitioned the buildings necessary to open a clinic, a tailor shop, and a shoe repair station. Shortly after the buildings became available, a woman doctor, two nurses, five tailors, and a cobbler were busy serving the Jews and Polish peasants from the work columns, ghettos, and forests.

As far as the Nazi administration was concerned, the German engineer had simply requisitioned additional space for his firm in order to provide services for his German staff. Somehow, the actual purpose of the services was overlooked by the authorities. Bronka had been able to obtain the services of the medical team, but there was no medicine. Much later, after she returned to Solingen, Elisabeth would prepare packages that contained aspirin and whatever else she could find. A courier for the Jung firm, Paul Krilow, regularly traveled between Solingen and the Ukraine. He would stop at the Jung office in Solingen for the packages. In two years Krilow made twenty-five runs with the only basic medicines and supplies available to the doctor and nurse.

In the meantime, four small sewing machines clattered along repairing clothing, while ten pairs of shoes each day received the attention of the lone cobbler. Later, after the October 1942 Action that decimated the Jewish population of Sdolbonov, a kitchen was opened to feed a large group of displaced Polish peasants that had settled in the forest near Sdolbonov. Graebe's concern for his workers did not stop with the details or mechanisms of rescue, but extended to their dignity and well-being. He was willing to go to any length and to any expense to create a hospitable and secure environment for the victims of Nazi oppression.

Hospitality was the central motif in Graebe's conception of his rescue efforts. He provided food, rest, shelter, protection, and friendship to the sojourners. As time went on, he was able to provide work, clothing, and medical attention. In a murderously hostile environment, he was an oasis of compassion.

The year 1942 also saw pivotal changes for both the Reich and the Graebe network. For Graebe, the establishment of basic services and the increasing number of contracts kept the network viable. Other changes in the situation, however, beyond Graebe's control, began to pose a very real threat to all of those concerned with the efforts. *Gebietskommissar* Georg Marschall continued in office, but his deputy, Erich Habenicht, was transferred to the Eastern Front as a lieutenant in the Wehrmacht. The person responsible for the changes was the man who replaced him, Otto Koeller. Marschall had known Koeller during the period when Marschall was the commander of and a teacher at the Reich school for Party indoctrination at Vogelsang. As Reich Commissioner of Jewish Affairs for Sdolbonov, Ostrog, and Mizocz, Koeller used his office to vigorously prosecute Reich regulations, to expropriate Jewish property, to deport Jews, and to arrange for the liquidation of the Jewish ghettos. For this effort, Koeller came to be known as "the Butcher of Sdolbonov." Koeller, radically anti-Semitic, and Graebe frequently found themselves in conflict over the treatment of the Jewish workers in the region.

Where Habenicht had been humane and helpful to Graebe, Koeller was the opposite. One example from among many will illustrate. Before the arrival of Koeller, Graebe had arranged with Habenicht to provide the refugees in the labor column with a special felt shoe that was unwanted elsewhere. The shoe afforded a small measure of warmth and comfort to the nearly frozen workers. After a vigorous argument over the appropriateness of the allocation, Graebe prevailed and Marschall released the shoes. When Koeller arrived, he was shocked and infuriated to discover that the Jews were wearing the shoes. He snapped at his superior, Marschall, "Let their toes freeze off!"

As Fritz remembers it,

> I soon noticed that Koeller had a strong influence on Marschall, much stronger than I had. When he realized that Marschall showed himself somewhat soft toward Jews, Koeller turned on him violently. He succeeded in changing Marschall's opinion and convinced him to send Habenicht to the Eastern Front.

In spite of these factors, Graebe succeeded in saving people from the Nazi executioners and the Ukrainian militia because he thoroughly planned for his rescue efforts. He anticipated circumstances, interactions, and likely outcomes. He avoided the bravado, the gambles, and panicked thinking characteristic of reactive responses. The rescue in the Rovno ghetto on July 13, 1942, was a necessary violation of his own wise principles. Those forty-eight hours had embodied all the threats that might endanger his mission.

The July 13 Action in Rovno grew out of a secret plan devised by men who represented a system that was daily becoming more fascinated with the mechanics of mass death. With the increased fascination came efficiency. In a predictably bureaucratic way, the officials—Koeller, Puetz, Behr, Beck, and Marschall—wanted to appease and satisfy their superiors and, in so doing, secure their own positions in the hierarchy. Each exhibited a clear and profound attraction to death. They seemed excited by the Actions. These executioners lived under the illusion that their involvement with mass death was indeed benefiting society and enhancing human existence. One may recall the accusations of "parasitism," leveled against Jews and gypsies, that was the Reich's theoretical justification for the Actions and the extermination camps. Extermination of "parasites" would produce a superior breed and race—or so the argument went. Hitler is recorded in the annals of the International Military Tribunal as having said that "the Jew is a parasite. . . . Elimination of the Jew from our community is to be regarded as an emergency measure." Similarly, Heinrich Himmler remarked to a meeting of death camp officers, "Most of you will know what it means to see a hundred corpses— five hundred, one thousand—lying there. . . . This is a never-recorded and never-to-be-recorded page of glory in our history." His delusion was even more visible in another remark: "We can say that we have completed this painful task [the annihilation of the Jewish population] out of love for our people. In our own selves, in our own souls, and in our character we have suffered no damage therefrom."

Persons like Fritz Graebe perceived the contempt for life in this rhetoric of death, but Graebe went further than merely perceiving evil. In Rovno, he spoiled the aura of excitement surrounding the Action. He challenged and frustrated the authority of the bureaucrats who sought to please their superiors and protect their privileged positions. He placed his body between the executioners and the victims.

Because he interfered with their still-secret ritual of death, Graebe placed himself and his ongoing rescue efforts in extreme danger. The long sleepless nights and the intense pressures of the Action brought him to the point of physical collapse. The insane, repetitive acts of brutality in the Action drained his emotional strength, numbing him and undermining his commitment to the sanctity of life. The marauding militiamen posed a constant danger to his own safety and demanded a vigilance that strained his weary mind and exhausted his body. His threatening, assertive presence at the Rovno town square aroused the suspicions of his adversaries. Once they had believed the ruse that he was obeying orders from highly placed, secret sources in Berlin. Now they had reason to question his credibility, his loyalty to the Nazi cause, and his real purpose. Those who had not dared to question the origin of Graebe's orders now saw him as a threat because he had challenged with impunity their territory and their private prerogatives.

The days and weeks immediately following the July 13 Action in Rovno afforded little opportunity for the engineer to recoup his strength. Graebe would have been very relieved if, on his return to Sdolbonov, he had found that his family had departed for Solingen. They had not; the trains were all delayed by various war-related disruptions. Elisabeth's response to her husband's telling of the incidents in the Rovno ghetto was deeply emotional. For days she cried with her head in her hands. Fritz was distracted and irritable. Two weeks passed before the train connections to Solingen were complete. Fritz had tried his best to keep his family uninformed about what was happening. But he did not want to risk their lives, and now he needed the freedom to take whatever risks he deemed necessary without having to consider the safety of his family.

In the days remaining before the train came, Fritz had Herr Praschko, one of his most loyal Jewish workers, give Friedel riding lessons and take him around in a horsedrawn wagon. With Friedel thus occupied, Elisabeth and Fritz had the opportunity to make plans for any contingencies that might occur when the family returned to Solingen. It was agreed that she would return to their home and resume as normal a life as possible. She would pretend to be ignorant of her husband's whereabouts and his dealings. Fritz promised to write whenever it was safe, but he warned that the contents of his letters would be routine. She should also expect that there would be times when he could not write, long blocks of time when she really would know nothing. Graebe was in a position in which he could occasionally send his family a small parcel of meat or fruit without endangering the health of his workers. He introduced Frau Graebe to Paul Krilow, the Jung courier who would stop at the Jung offices whenever he was in Germany. If there were messages or packages going in either direction, he would deliver them.

Elisabeth was willing to go along with this strategy. She knew that certain things would be needed: medicine, bandages, aspirin. She promised to have parcels ready to go whenever Krilow called. In this way she felt she was a part of what her husband was doing. She too could manipulate the very system that her husband sought to thwart. Elisabeth Graebe had hitherto never said or done anything that would divert her husband from his mission. Now she herself could have a role in helping save lives. For herself and their son, she secretly wanted her husband away from the dangerous intrigues in the Ukraine. For the Jewish victims of the war, however, she would give up her husband for the duration of the war.

The day of departure finally arrived. In the morning, Friedel insisted on just one more wagon trip with Herr Praschko, who had become his friend. When the two returned, Graebe held the reins as Praschko respectfully removed his hat and with great affection embraced the boy, saying, "God bless you, dear Friedel." Elisabeth walked to the Jung office to bid farewell to Maria. During the short holiday they had had many occasions to talk and become friends. Elisabeth knew that Maria would contact her if anything happened. As they embraced, one of the Jewish secretaries, Frau Lerner, handed Elisabeth some freshly cut flowers wrapped in a wet handkerchief and a dry newspaper.

At the passenger dock of the train station, the scene was full of sadness: a gentle embrace, a few tears, the usual fatherly admonishments from Fritz to Friedel, an extra-long glance to cement a fragile memory. The knowledge that the future was tenuous at best restrained the farewell. A sharp whistle heralded the departure.

Graebe watched the train until the last car had disappeared around the stand of poplar trees, whose leaves were turning to welcome the approaching autumn. The pensive engineer walked slowly back to his car, aware now that every moment had to be devoted to the work and the rescues. He wondered if there would be a future for his family.

The horror at Rovno caused Fritz to redouble his rescue efforts. A trait commonly found among the Nazi-era rescuers was their ability to place themselves in the role of the injured or endangered party. The Rovno rescue and massacre gave Graebe a vivid picture of the horrors faced by those who were not rescued. It heightened his empathy for the Jews and the Polish peasants whose suffering confronted the German engineer daily. Graebe could exchange roles with the Jews in his imagination and envision himself in their place. He saw the face of his young son in the smashed and lifeless faces of battered Jewish infants or in the innocent terror-stricken faces lining the pits at the outskirts of the cities. His mother's empathic question would haunt and empower him. "And what would you do?"

Gradually, the days resumed a semblance of normality. Fritz and Maria listened intently for any signals that would indicate that his adversaries were monitoring his activities or plotting against him or compiling a dossier that would be submitted to the SS in Warsaw or Berlin. Graebe knew that at Rovno he had pushed himself and the Nazis to the furthest limits of tolerance and that everything could be lost. It was a time for him to keep a low profile and appear more involved in his work. After all, if he was going to argue that his work was vital and secret to the Reich, he should appear to be involved intently in its progress. He pursued contracts, supervised building sites, regularly visited construction projects, and, it seems likely, sidetracked any infiltrators or observers who might have been gathering information. Yet in spite of this extra attention to the details of engineering, in spite of the fears and precautions, Graebe's rescue network never missed a beat. People still came for and received work cards, false papers, and travel permits. Whenever possible, people were sent to one of the work projects. He now says:

> Having seen such things [as Rovno] I had no other choice than
> to work harder to save the Jews who came to me. One cannot
> see so much death and remain unaffected. I had to do some-
> thing, I had to protect as many people as I could.

One of the rescues involved a very bright woman, Barbara Faust, a Jew with false papers whom Graebe sent to Dubno in order to save her from the death squads. She arrived there in September and began working in various capacities at the Jung Dubno office. At least once or twice each week, Fritz visited the Dubno projects. His visits enabled him to check on the security of his staff and to be certain that their papers and identities were not compromised; he could also supervise the progress of his contracts. To the bureaucrats and his staff in Dubno, Graebe gave the impression of being a stern, task-oriented manager of a German engineering company. His attention to detail, the small gifts he left for the minor civil servants stationed in this forgotten wilderness, and his simple human courtesy won him the confidence of these workers in Dubno.

On October 5, 1942, as was his weekly custom, Fritz left the Jung headquarters in Sdolbonov to drive to his regional offices; first he went to Dubno. There had been no word of an impending Action; indeed, the rumor mill had been unusually quiet. As he arrived in Dubno, he found the entrances to the town completely blockaded by police and heavily armed militiamen, the now commonly recognized sign of an Action in progress. During an Action, no one from the outside was allowed to enter the town and no one from the inside could leave. Spotting one of the officials he had befriended, Graebe offered the excuse of a cramped schedule and the importance of clearing some papers with his office manager, Barbara Faust, in order to gain entry to the city. Since the Action was nearly over and had been virtually restricted to the ghetto, the official cleared the way for Fritz to enter the town and go directly to his office.

Barbara Faust, who had been living illegally outside the ghetto, was nearly hysterical when Graebe arrived. The shooting had been going on for a full day and night. Communication with the rest of the world had been halted without warning, and she had not even been able to leave the town to alert her employer. Jews were still being rounded up and killed when Graebe arrived. Not even the Jung workers were exempted from the horror. Though Barbara Faust was safe, she was helpless and frightened. Nothing could calm her. Graebe promised to go to the building site to determine what had happened to the many people who had worked for him.

When he arrived at the project, he was met by his site foreman, Herbert Moennikes, a man of about sixty and an active Party member. Moennikes, who always wore his Party badge and emblems, was very agitated. He immediately recounted, at a spitfire rate, what had transpired during the preceding two days. The experience had been a revelation for the foreman. Never before had he been through anything even remotely like an Action. "If I had not seen it with my own eyes, Herr Graebe, I would never have believed that such a thing was possible," he said.

On the first day, the SS, the militia, and the local police had surrounded the city without warning. The SS were from the Rovno District Brigade and obviously knew their task. The nearly five thousand Jewish inhabitants of the city and the refugees were rounded up and marched out of the city to the airport, some eight miles away. The airport was no longer in use and was less than a hundred feet from a Jung construction site. At the edge of the abandoned airstrip was an earthen mound ten feet high, one hundred feet long, and behind it was a pit that would soon become a mass grave.

Moennikes watched, horrified, as the SS and the Ukrainian militiamen murdered fifteen hundred Jews the first day. Each Jew received one bullet, and in many cases a parent was forced to hold a child so that two persons could be dispatched with one bullet, a perverse practice in this economy of death that otherwise seemed willing to spare no expense or inconvenience when it came to killing Jews. Moennikes was shocked by the killings and the obvious indifference of the soldiers. They seemed to participate willingly in such inhumanity. "How could they do such things and not be completely disgusted with themselves? How could they ever look their own wives and children in the face, knowing what they had done to these children and women?"

To the stunned Moennikes, the SS symbol, the "death's head," took on new meaning and relevance. These soldiers had surrendered their reverence for life in order to become murderers. They did not even hate the people they killed; they simply obeyed orders and performed the functions of the system that controlled their lives. Moennikes, who previously must have lived in a very sheltered ambience, was overwhelmed by the behavior of his own people—behavior that was, to his thinking, blatantly inconsistent with the values of German culture and religion. Moennikes was nearly broken when on the second morning nearly fifteen hundred more Jews were murdered.

As the two men stood near the great mound of earth that had been excavated for the mass grave, Moennikes began describing the ritual of death that was by now familiar to Graebe. The Jews had been forced to line up in family groups. As they neared the site, armed guards brutally ordered everyone to undress, to neatly fold and stack their clothing, and to proceed in the line. Moennikes interrupted his narrative:

"Look over there, Herr Graebe. There, there a heap of shoes, hundreds of shoes, and there a stack of shirts, another of pants, dresses, and jackets. Everything is so neat and orderly, even to the piles for men and women and children."

So vivid was Moennikes's recollection that, as he talked and waved his finger from pile to pile, it was as if the Jews were again present, standing naked in family units, waiting for the German guards to call them to take their places at the edge of the mass grave.

On the first day, when Moennikes had walked toward the mass grave, he was not stopped. Bodies were piled helter-skelter in the pit. Many were still alive, moving, but unconscious and unable to escape.

"You cannot imagine it, Herr Graebe. The three SS guards just stood there smoking, nonchalantly, as if they were watching crews unload coal." Moennikes began to cry. "Another guard, with a rifle yesterday and a pistol this morning, sat with his feet dangling over the edge of the pit—ten or twelve people brought in a truck, undressed, ordered to lay down in the pit, and the guard sitting on the ledge shot them. He didn't care if his shots were accurate or fatal."

On the second morning, another pit appeared; it too was twenty feet wide by one hundred feet long.

"In one day they filled the first pit and now the second one is half full and it is just ten o'clock. Do you have any idea, Herr Graebe, what it takes to fill such a pit?"

As Moennikes continued, his voice became increasingly hysterical. Graebe reached out to comfort him but Moennikes kept on talking, oblivious to the gesture. There were long gaps between his bursts of words; his eyes remained fixed on the mounds of earth beyond them.

"It's all right, Herbert," Fritz comforted. "There is nothing you or I could have done. These bastards would have stripped and killed you, too, and for that matter, me."

But Graebe's words fell on deaf ears; they offered little solace to Moennikes, a man destroyed by lost innocence. In a deep, somber tone of voice that seemed to come from somewhere other than the old man came words of despair:

"They did it to me, they've stripped me and killed me. My own people."

As Moennikes was speaking, a truck noisily lumbered up the airport road and stopped near the two men. The Ukrainian militia jumped from the truck and began pushing people from it. Fritz Graebe watched as the people were ordered to undress. As he later recounted,

> I wanted to avert my eyes, but I couldn't; they were riveted on the people. They put their clothes in neat piles arranged by type of clothing and segregated further by the sex of the person, and with all the children's clothing in still separate piles. It was so cold, so methodical. Soon all of the Jews from the truck, perhaps twenty-five of them, were standing naked behind the mound of dirt. Moennikes and I walked toward the pit—it was like a magnetic attraction, I could not draw away from the place. I don't know what compelled me to go there and watch—whatever it was, it was stronger than my will.

As Graebe approached the truck and the mound, his eyes fell on a family of eight people. They were already naked, waiting for the call to take their places beside the pit. This specific scene would haunt Graebe for the rest of his life; forty years later it had the power to wrest tears from his eyes and wrack his body with sobs. His mind reversed the roles, and he saw himself and his beloved Friedel and Elisabeth standing there. He could not take his eyes from the innocent family. The covenant of Rovno now included the Jews of Dubno: "I will never forget."

There was the father and next to him was a boy, perhaps ten years old—Friedel's age. The father was a kindly appearing man who sought to still the fear and anguish of his son by placing his hand on the boy's shoulder. In a soft, inaudible voice the father said something to his son which caused the boy to look toward heaven. The father's hand moved gently to the boy's head. The other hand pointed to heaven as the father again spoke. The boy was fighting his tears and trying to maintain his dignity. They were so brave.

Beyond these two stood the man's wife and an older, white-haired lady who was cradling and singing to a small child. She too gently stroked and comforted the child in her charge, gently taking their own minds off the remaining minutes, the last minutes of life. Suddenly a raucous voice shattered the spell: "Next ten! Move! Quickly! Quickly!" The family moved as a unit around the truck, past the speechless engineer and foreman. The boy held his father's hand while the smaller child nestled in the grandmother's arms.

"Herr Engineer."

The words, in an unfamiliar feminine voice, shattered Graebe's consciousness. He had seen no familiar faces in the area. Indeed, he assumed that all his workers had either escaped or been killed. Who knew him now, in this terrible moment? Graebe was recognized by a young woman, a member of the family he had been observing. She may have been one of the many whose papers he had signed without ever meeting the person. As she passed by him she ran her hand in front of her small breasts and past her slight, demure body.

"Herr Engineer. Twenty-three, only twenty-three." She pointed beyond to the grave.

> She passed by me, as close as I am to you. Do you understand? Only twenty-three and going to her death. It was too much for me.

Graebe did not, could not, watch the shooting. Another ten came forward, and the ritual repeated itself. By now, Moennikes had ripped off his Party badges and was raving about the murderers.

"Why are they letting us watch?" Graebe asked Moennikes.

"Why not?" Moennikes answered. "Yesterday the postal workers came and viewed everything. It was like a circus. No one gives a damn about the Jews and their dignity. These guards are proud of what they are doing—they want an audience."

With that, Fritz walked around the mound to the pit. People were still moving. The SS guard fired one bullet at a time, one bullet for each person.

> The lucky ones died quickly from the shot. I turned and yelled at the other SS man, "Look, they still move!" One of the guards shouted back, "We don't have enough ammunition to please every single Jew. Why waste more than one bullet on them?" Moennikes walked up behind me, and in that strange, frightening voice said, "Herr Graebe, I've watched mothers and fathers hold their children up high so they would take the first shot and not suffer." Out of the corner of my eye I saw a very purposeful movement in the pit. It was the sister of the young woman who had recognized me. She was stroking the body of the one next to her. I cried out to the SS man who sat on the edge of the pit, "Do something, she is suffering—she's not dead." To which he replied to me, "Forget it! Tonight this grave will be covered with garbage and dirt and everything will be finished."

Fritz Graebe was in no condition to travel, and he was deeply concerned for the well-being of his traumatized foreman. He took Moennikes from the scene and sat with him through the night. The next morning Graebe returned to the construction site. Walking over to the mounds, he discovered that the pit had not been covered over and that five or six women had pulled themselves out of the tangle of bodies. Another fifteen or twenty men had escaped, but the chilled night, the loss of blood, and the injuries had claimed their victims forty or fifty feet from the pit. Several other wounded Jews were sitting naked on the ground. Some of them huddled together to protect and warm themselves. One rushed to Graebe, begging for help, for clothing. Fritz was about to gather them and lead them to a spot in the nearby clump of trees to hide while he would try to locate one of his trucks to move them to safety. Suddenly, however, a fast-moving car and several trucks rounded a corner and sped toward the site. The less severely wounded Jews began stumbling toward the woods. The car screeched to a stop behind one of the trucks while the other truck, filled with soldiers, raced after the wounded. Shots were fired everywhere without hitting anyone. But they stopped the flight of the Jews, and all were returned to the pit. The SS officer in charge, Major Braun, stepped from the car, ordered the area cleared, and because he was the one commanding the Action, the order was obeyed. From the area next to the nearby Jung construction site, Graebe heard more shots, and then silence. For the rest of the day cars and trucks came and went from the pit. Each vehicle disgorged a small number of Jews who had managed to hide briefly, or who had just been betrayed by informers, or who were unwitting refugees moving through the area in search of safety and had been caught in the SS dragnet. Every player observed the same routine—executioner and victim—to the end, with one shot.

There was nothing that Graebe could do. All communications were stopped. No one could enter or leave the area. There was no one with whom he could plead for his missing workers. It was simply too late. Though helpless, he was not sightless or without memory. That day the Rovno covenant was renewed again and again.

Graebe stayed at the Jung construction site at the airport. This enabled him to keep track of the Action. Finally, a large truck arrived. It was full of people in hospital gowns. They were weak, and many were bleeding from the face and head. They had been overlooked until just moments earlier. The militiamen, obviously embarrassed by their mistake and now annoyed and inconvenienced, vented their wrath on the hapless sick. They were tossed to the ground, much as one tosses a lifeless bale of hay from a wagon. One man was pulled by his feet from the bed of the truck. As he dropped to the ground his head bumped hard against the side of the truck and then against the fender.

> Those vicious militiamen made even the sick people strip naked. All they had on were their hospital gowns. They made them suffer so. They piled their gowns in a particular spot. Several people were badly infirmed and slow to remove their clothing. Each one of these received a kick or a blow from a rifle butt. This simply slowed things more and further enraged the guards. I left—I couldn't bear any more. My heart ached. Everything in me hurt. Shots rang out and I knew it was over. There were no more Jews in Dubno. Even my workers were dead. I had received no warning of the Action or I would have found a way to protect them. Later I learned that a few, who had forged papers and false identities, had been saved. There was one thing that struck me about this Action. As I looked back it was true of every Action. Not one of the victims protested, not one really resisted. Four guards, six militia, but no resistance. Why? Why? Why? Then I realized what had happened. It had nothing to do with numbers or weapons. At that moment I realized what the father had said to his son as he pointed to heaven. It is what I would say to my son in such a circumstance. I believe that these

people had suffered enough—that is why they did not resist. I too would comfort my son, point to heaven, and say to him that there was a better future there than here. In heaven, at least, there will be not even one SS or militia or police. That is what I would tell my son. Unbelievable. That is exactly what it was, unbelievable. The civilized German people, my people, were doing these things. It was better to be in heaven with a loving God than be at the hands of the unworthy who sought to rule the world. How would you feel? What would you do?

Fritz Graebe turned and walked slowly away from the pits. As he passed the mountain of shoes, the piles of clothing and underlinens, a surge of adrenaline coursed through his body. He could see the covered earth of the first mass grave quaking slightly but unmistakably. The not-yet-dead struggled against the dead, and the mound moved. Perhaps this was the fulfillment of the prophet Jeremiah's vision of a world wracked by slaughter and trying to hide it from itself:

> I beheld the earth, and look, it was formless and void, and the heavens held no light. I saw the mountains and look, they were quaking, and all the hills moved to and fro—they trembled. And lo, there were no human beings and all the birds had fled. Lo, the fruitful land was a wilderness, and all its cities were broken down. (Jeremiah 4:23–26)

Fritz was exhausted, weary to the very center of his being. He wanted to be alone to ponder why he had heard nothing of the plans for the Action before it had occurred. He returned to Sdolbonov to sign more work permits and travel papers, and to forge more certificates. He would try to save even a few more lives as long as his strength held out.

7. Death in the Ukraine: The Sdolbonov District is Judenrein

The Jung Sdolbonov office as well as Graebe's rescue efforts were dealt an incalculable blow in the early days of October 1942. A Frau Pater had held a position in the regional government that was as public as Maria's with the Jung firm. But Frau Pater's identity as a Jew was accidentally discovered, and she and her daughter were killed. Maria became increasingly frightened as the discovery of Pater's status led to suspicions about other persons in sensitive positions. As severe new Aryanization laws arrived from Berlin, they were vigorously enforced by the regional authorities. Maria had sensed danger in the new laws, and the executions confirmed her worst fears. Believing that her papers would be suspect and that she would be discovered, Maria convinced the reluctant Graebe to send her on to work with the Poltava group. She followed the ritual that she had prepared so carefully for so many others: hiding overnight in Fritz Graebe's car in a garage under the German officers' quarters, then a quick early morning ride to a train station in another area. The phone signal to Tadeuz Glass for Maria was, "The cook is arriving tomorrow." Maria's departure saved her from the terrors that were to engulf the region.

For two days, rumors had been moving quietly among the Jews, but the rumors had seemed far less urgent than usual, except to one group of Jews who had come to Graebe with information and a question. It seemed that several people happened upon an army crew near Nowo-Mylsk as they were preparing two large trenches that obviously were to be used as mass graves. The trenches were a considerable distance from Sdolbonov, which confused the witnesses. Why would the Nazis place mass graves at such an inconvenient distance? Were they indeed mass graves, or had these huge pits some other disguised purpose, perhaps as antitank trenches? Those who had seen the preparations reported them to the Judenrat, who went to Fritz with their question: "Is an Action being planned? What shall we do?"

Because he could not be certain of his status with the regional officials, Fritz was forced to take a slower, more conservative approach in the face of this possible Action. Graebe had sensed that he was being watched by the authorities and that the July Rovno intervention had been the catalyst for their suspicion and distrust of him. He was certain that the SS was monitoring him, but the fact that they had not moved against him indicated that he had his enemies off guard. Yet the situation was perilous, because Graebe could not yet determine the extent to which they were spying on him. The motivation for this clandestine activity of the SS was vitally important to him, because it would indicate the sort of responses that Graebe could expect from them. Did the bureaucrats suspect his rescue efforts and believe him to be a shrewd "Jew-lover" subverting the Reich administration in the Ukraine? Or were they resentful of his alleged "secret orders from Berlin," of his brazen displays of power? Or did they believe him to be simply an eccentric professional who failed to see the larger picture of the war effort? If they believed the first, then Graebe had to assume that communiqués were racing between the Ukraine and Berlin and that he and his efforts were in extreme danger. If the SS resented his "secret orders," then they would not dare to bring their challenge to Berlin, for fear that Graebe really was who he claimed to be. Graebe used his knowledge of the way the Nazis thought:

> It was simple. I knew how the German mind worked. They always bowed to higher authorities. No questions. No challenges. If I could be theatrical enough in my presentations, the SS and the government men would not risk confronting me or reporting me to Berlin for fear of their own safety. It was a risk I had to take.

The risks needed to be shared and spread. This burden would fall to Heinrich Zimmerer, a sympathetic colleague managing the German construction firm Poehner-auf-Bayreuth. Several months earlier, Zimmerer had shared with Fritz his disgust with Nazi atrocities and his disillusionment with National Socialism and the Party. On October 12, 1942, a week after the Dubno Action, Zimmerer and Graebe met at a café to discuss their problems. They concluded that a frontal approach was necessary: a visit to *Gebietskommissar* Marschall to complain that the war effort would be hindered by the further loss of skilled labor. Moreover, previous Actions had led to the loss or destruction of tools and precision instruments. These losses, it would be argued, were a serious setback for the construction projects.

Their strategy carefully mapped, the two went to the office of the *Gebietskommissar*. The guard at the reception desk called Marschall to announce the visitors, but he refused to meet with the engineers. In spite of this bad beginning, the two persisted, but ultimately they were rebuffed by the guard. Determined, they set out for the office of his deputy, Otto Koeller. Koeller, the cynical, argumentative killer, agreed to meet with them and, in fact, relished a confrontation on his own turf.

Koeller received the two civilian engineers as one would receive a problem child about to be disciplined. An armed guard ushered the two men into Koeller's large office, while the Party leader remained seated behind his huge, ornate wooden desk. He offered no seats for the comfort of his adversaries. As they entered he carefully shifted his weight backward in the large leather chair and stretched out his arms in such a way that the elbows locked and the palms of his hands rested flat on his desk. His air of authority and arrogance signaled problems.

Zimmerer was quiet while Graebe presented their questions and concerns:

"Is there to be an Action? If there is, you must know that the loss of personnel, laborers, and the danger to the equipment will jeopardize the work of the construction projects and, therefore, the interests of the Reich."

There was a private war going on between the "Butcher of Sdolbonov" and the "Moses of Rovno." The stakes were much more personal than they appeared. Because of this fact, it was probably poor strategy to have Fritz speak.

Affecting a wise and thoughtful mien, Koeller responded. "I don't answer to you. Gentlemen, we are not political children, you know. The orders here originate with me."

"What is this, 'political children'? Either yes or no. Is there an Action planned?" Graebe's impudence was shocking, but the power was behind the desk with Koeller.

"I don't answer to either one of you. I have no more time for you. Get out of here, now!"

Zimmerer and Graebe were quickly ushered out of the office. They retreated to assess and review the incident. There was scant evidence of an impending Action. Although angered by the confrontation, Zimmerer, a relatively quiet man, was not convinced that anything was planned. The two men resolved to check all their sources and to have their scouts look for signs of an impending mass murder. It was too late.

The Action commenced just hours after the two engineers had left each other that evening.

At three in the morning, Graebe was awakened by pounding and shouting at his front door. The sound of semiautomatic weapons fire shocked him from his drowsiness. As he approached the front door, the police burst through. Fritz blocked their path down the hall, demanding to know the purpose of their intrusion. They pushed past him, ignoring his presence, his demands, and his threats, and set about searching the entire house. They opened closets; banged on walls, floors, and ceilings in search of hidden passages and spaces; they looked under beds and behind doors. A policeman grimly pronounced his final verdict to an SS officer standing nearby: "No Jews." They departed. The Action that would establish Sdolbonov as *Judenrein*, "Free of Jews," had begun.

By the time the search of Graebe's house was completed, the Jewish section of Sdolbonov had been completely surrounded by two or three hundred Ukrainian militiamen and local police. Graebe left his house for the ghetto, planning to search for his workers. The problem was that there were nearly fifteen hundred Jews from the ghetto working for Jung. There were more than double that number of Jews in the entire ghetto. How would he get them out? To whom could he turn for help? There was no one else; Maria was far away in Poltava. It would not have mattered. Graebe was blocked at every entrance to the area. The brutal guards ignored his threats and arguments.

Graebe then set out for the Jung office. When he arrived there, he found a woman waiting for him. Rosa Schachter had lived in Ostrog until June 1942, but had fled when the first Actions began. She then settled in Ozenin, but soon that area too was engulfed in the terror. After three Actions, she was afraid that she could no longer continue to hide. Rumor had reached Ozenin that a German engineer was employing Jews and helping them to escape the terrors. For three months she had cautiously worked her way to Sdolbonov in the hope that she would find the German. It was a cruel trick of fate that she should arrive at the "safe haven" just as an Action was beginning.

Graebe, recognizing her plight and realizing that the SS might at any moment raid his office as they had his home, did not wait for her full story. He called for one of his trucks, argued heatedly with the driver, and convinced him to take Frau Schachter to the only safe place in the area: the living quarters of the German Jung staff. There was no time for an explanation or for the niceties of Prussian hospitality. She was locked in a dark, empty room, and there spent the night crying and frightened as the slaughter raged noisily around her. Early the next

morning, the same driver arrived, bearing permits, papers, and intro-
ductions for the "newly arrived" Jung worker. He took Frau Schachter
in the truck to the Jung office in Rovno, where the foreman, Einsporn,
welcomed her and set her to work in the employees' canteen. Graebe
sent her to Rovno because he was certain that there would be no further
Actions in an area already considered by the Germans to be "free of
Jews," *Judenrein*.

> Puetz and Koeller and Marschall had made themselves ready for
> me. They prepared everything so that I could not interfere with
> the Action. Rosa Schachter was the only person that I was able
> to help directly—can you imagine that out of fifteen hundred
> people I only saved one? Puetz must have warned the guards
> and officers, because they very effectively kept me out of the
> ghetto. All I could do was stand opposite the ghetto on the
> steps of the post office and watch their shameless acts. Koeller
> or Marschall played a very mean trick to confuse my workers
> and make them believe that I was able to protect them. SS men
> went around the streets with a bullhorn, calling out, 'All labor-
> ers from the Jung firm, present yourselves at the backyard of the
> high school.' They repeated this message throughout the ghetto,
> causing my workers to think that they were safe and could ap-
> pear at the school. But I no longer had a position of power in
> Sdolbonov. I lost all of my Jewish workers except for a few who
> I believe may have escaped.

From his vantage point at the post office, Graebe watched Koeller,
armed with a pistol, move in and out of the streets. The Sdolbonov
Action had the quality of a free-for-all. Railroad workers and postal employees joined in the hunt for Jews in the ghetto. After it was over,
Fritz was talking with the head of the police and asked him if these
other civil servants had been commanded to assist in the grisly work.

"Oh, no!" the man replied. "This was completely a voluntary thing.
Some people, like myself, do not have the stomach for such things."
The railroad workers had asked permission to join in the Action, and it
had been granted by the local head of the administration and by the
police.

Graebe witnessed a particularly brutal display by a policeman named
Wacker. Wacker had rushed out of the front door of a house with a
Jewish infant in his hands and had smashed it against the doorpost. The
family followed through the door shortly after, and Wacker dangled the
bloody, lifeless form in front of its parents before taking them to the

collection point. Later, Fritz happened to overhear this officer bragging about his "exceptional courage" in breaking down doors to get into houses in order to rout the Jews. Wacker concluded his account of his "war heroism" by noting his indebtedness to the "SS, who showed me this especially effective method."

Jews were pushed through the streets of Sdolbonov; many were shot, beaten, or killed by hand before they reached the collection point at the school. Those who made it there were loaded on trucks, driven to the prepared mass graves in the distant village of Nowo-Mylsk, forced to undress and climb into the graves, and were then killed, each with a single rifle shot.

An unusual thing happened during all three October 1942 Actions in the Sdolbonov district (Dubno, Mizocz, and Sdolbonov). Volunteers from the local police backed the heavy concentration of militiamen. These police volunteers frequently were more brutal than even the most sadistic of the SS. One volunteer was a low-ranking officer named Attinger.

Attinger seemed to be consumed by an insatiable desire to be an executioner. This bloodlust made him one of the most feared men in the District. He seemed to move unrestrained from massacre to atrocity, from ghetto to mass grave. At one point, Attinger had a special celebration to recognize the occasion of his killing two thousand Jews. Attinger enjoyed his reputation as a killer of Jewish children, often taking them out of shops and shooting them in the streets or catching them in the sight of his weapon, following them, and then shooting. During the Sdolbonov Action, from his vantage point at the post office, Graebe could see Attinger taking people to the school, beating some and shooting others whenever the fancy struck him. Later reports indicated that Attinger went to the mass graves and acted as the executioner throughout the day and night.

Late in the day of the Action, Fritz was sitting in his office when Attinger walked in. It was not uncommon for Attinger to order materials for himself or the police. But on this occasion Attinger had an agenda other than business. Graebe's secretary Bronka stood to greet him, offering her hand to him. With a certain serene dignity, he begged her pardon and declined the courtesy.

"I cannot. My hands are full of Jewish blood. Perhaps another time." He turned to Graebe, who noted that Attinger's boots were covered with the powdery dust common in the area around the mass grave, and said, "I have a message for you from a Jewess named Zolotow."

Frau Zolotow had worked for Graebe in the front office of the Jung firm. The shock registered on Graebe's face, but he pretended to be confused and uncertain about the point of the conversation.

"She told me to tell you thank you. She's gone now."

With the message delivered, Attinger turned smartly on his heels and left the office.

Fritz recalls:

> Attinger was a pathological man. He was so proud that he could deliver Frau Zolotow's message to me. I do not think he fully realized what he was doing. It was the same evening as the Action. Attinger had killed two thousand Jews and was having his beer party to celebrate the distinction. As the party was going on a messenger arrived and handed Attinger a telegram. I watched him become very quiet and then tearful. It seemed that his son had been killed at the front. The party immediately cooled off. Attinger became inconsolable. Finally, he and some of the others left to "find more Jews to kill." Watching Attinger, I concluded that it was his private war. He wanted to round up Jews, beat them, put them in trucks, strip them, and personally shoot each one. To me, he was the complete physical embodiment of the Final Solution. He was the sort that the Reich was looking for—a cool, mindless predator.

When the authorities left the ghetto, Graebe went in: to see, to fuel his memory, to try to locate any signs of survivors. As Fritz came to the school, he saw a man picking up money and stuffing it in his pockets. The Jews had dropped some of their money on the streets as they departed; coins rested on the ground and some paper money fluttered in the soft morning breeze. Graebe recognized the man as Fritz Germ. A day earlier, Graebe had watched as Germ led an SS officer and several militiamen through the streets outside of, and adjacent to, the ghetto. Germ would point to a certain house, always one occupied by Polish citizens, and the guards would crash through the door or a window, emerging with a family and the Jews whom they had hidden. The fate was the same for the rescuers as it was for the Jews. This occurred at four or five different homes.

Fritz saw an opportunity for revenge. Walking back one or two blocks, he found a German patrol and told them that a man was collecting and hiding money. He was going to sneak it out of the ghetto, exchange it, and reap a profit. When they arrested Germ, his pockets were stuffed with Ukrainian currency and Reichmarks. Fritz says, "I could not have Germ arrested for what he had done to the Jews and the Polish people so I managed to have him taken away for something else—the effect was the same."

Later that day, Graebe and Zimmerer met at the Jung office. The experience had devastated Zimmerer. The two men tried to console each other, but it was in vain. Graebe could not tell Zimmerer about his rescue efforts so there was little more the two men could do; the delaying tactics had failed, time had run out. They were powerless and the control had been shifted. While they talked, Graebe's switchboard lighted up. He could see that the call was coming from an office that was vacant—its Jewish occupants were all dead. He ran to the phone and listened to a woman's voice.

"Herr Graebe, this is Frau Glueckson. You must help me!"

"Wait there for me. I'll come and give you a hand shortly."

Fritz excused himself for the interruption, saying that one of his German workers needed some help moving an instrument. Zimmerer left for his office. With the cunning elusiveness of a cat on a night hunt, Fritz moved through the ghetto, taking the longest, least direct route to the dormitory, hoping to elude any pursuers or observers. It was possible that the SS had left behind sentries to watch for escaping Jews, or perhaps there were informers around. If he were caught, he would have no excuse for being in the ghetto or in the allegedly empty dormitory. When Graebe finally arrived at the dormitory, he found a terribly frightened, famished, and dehydrated woman, one of his workers. Frau Glueckson had gone into hiding two days before the Action began. She was now like a caged lion: every sound thundered in her ears; she was in a state of shock from her fear. Rats had wandered around her at night, but she could not light the single candle she had taken with her for fear that she would give away her position to the police or to a curious German staff member. Near the end of the Action, a patrol had come within five feet of her hiding place. Hysterical, she was too terrified to scream, but to her it seemed that her heart was a tympanist drumming, threatening to reveal her hiding place. Fritz tried to comfort this pitiful soul whom he did not even know. Her plight aroused his compassion, and his caring ways quieted her enough so that he could fetch water for her.

Because there were still troops and police working in and around the ghetto confines, Fritz could not remove the woman from the dormitory for several days. Each night, he would travel a different, roundabout route, avoiding detection as he delivered food and drink. Eventually, it was safe enough to transfer Frau Glueckson by truck to the offices in Rovno and later to Poltava.

These Actions contributed to Graebe's exhaustion. He became fatigued and withdrawn, but would rally his energy once more to continue
the rescue work. *I cannot go on seeing these things—it is too much for me,* he
thought. His resilience was fast disappearing.

It was only a matter of hours before word reached Graebe that nearly
one thousand of his workers had been executed during still another Action on October 14 in Mizocz. He was surprised, however, to learn
that many of them were hiding or had escaped the terrors of the mass
graves. Sdolbonov had inadvertently served as an early warning for many,
but not early enough for most.

Gebietskommissar Marschall was very displeased about the small body
count in the Mizocz Action and had special signs posted offering rewards to those who disclosed the hiding places of "Jewish renegades"
and threatening the severest punishment for anyone who aided the Jews.
Many in the citizenry complied, denouncing the Jews and often their
neighbors.

One night, about two weeks after the Sdolbonov Action, Graebe listened as the senior police official from Sdolbonov, Herr Butenhoff, described how Marschall had been alerted to two groups of Jews hiding in
cellars of private homes in Mizocz.

"Marschall chose his most effective killers. He sent Attinger and Wacker
to investigate and resolve the problem of the hidden Jews."

They found two cellars connected by a tunnel. As Attinger fired an
automatic weapon into the cellar, Wacker filled the area with straw,
leather straps, and gasoline-soaked rags. A flaming rag set a smoky fire
in the cellar that forced five young Jews to flee. Six older men died of
suffocation. Attinger made the survivors retrieve the bodies and then
executed them. Meanwhile, SS units followed their routine practice of
brutal searches and rounded up those who had escaped the initial phase
of the Action. In spite of the modest body count, Marschall declared
the area to be *Judenrein*—although it did take two weeks for the official
announcement to be made.

Graebe sensed that a quick trip to Mizocz would have been futile, if
not dangerous. After the Sdolbonov Action, he was certain that Puetz,
Koeller, and Marschall had conspired to strip him of power and effectiveness. Also, any Jews who might have survived the Sdolbonov Action
would have been deprived of rescue if Graebe had departed. But late in
the afternoon of October 14, after learning about the atrocities in Mizocz, Graebe decided to go to Ostrog. What compelled him is unclear,
because he was emotionally drained from the worry and the terrors.
Fritz took Bronka with him, the secretary who had replaced Maria and

who was becoming a close colleague in the rescue efforts. Because she was multilingual, she could be very helpful to him if he were able to locate Jews in hiding anywhere in Ostrog. Bronka already thought of herself as Graebe's confidante and co-conspirator; she had earned his trust very quickly. Like Maria, Bronka would soon both witness and facilitate many acts of kindness and bravery. On the afternoon of October 14, Bronka remembers, Fritz returned to his office:

> He was pale as chalk. His eyes were red from sleeplessness. As always, when he was filled with tension, he was totally silent. I could not tell from his face what he was thinking or feeling. Then, late in the day, as if he had a vision, he came to life.

"We must go to the office in Ostrog. I must see what is happening there," he said with great urgency. Graebe had approximately thirteen hundred Jewish workers in Ostrog and was using two Jews, Rosenberg and Chunison, to coordinate building demolition and the storing of bricks. While Bronka and Fritz waited for his car, Bronka tried to change his mind.

"It is a very dangerous place to go. They may have set a trap for you. The militia will be shooting and the whole thing will be chaos."

Her reasoning failed to dissuade him. In complete silence, they drove directly to the Jung office, which was in a Jewish house on Tatarska Street, at the edge of the Jewish section. In the soft glow of dusk, Fritz could see the remains of an ancient iron gate, all that remained of an old wall that had marked some earlier division of the community. Beyond the house and the gate lay the yellowing fields that sloped gently down to the Horyn River.

At the same moment they both glanced toward the sandy banks of the Horyn and saw what appeared to be a seething ant hill.

"There are the Jews who have been rounded up to be killed!" she cried.

At Graebe's matter-of-fact response, Bronka gasped and felt a cold chill rush through her back. "It will start in the morning," Graebe said. He had witnessed this horror before. His voice was flat, emotionless, reflecting the powerlessness of a beaten man. To sit in the car was to invite arrest, so Graebe parked and they began their walk to the perimeter of the ghetto.

As a prelude to the Ostrog Action, the SS commander played a bizarre cat-and-mouse game with the victims. He called in the leader of the Judenrat, Abraham Komendant, and ordered him to furnish a pair of boots within twenty-four hours. The boots had to be made from the

finest leather. In spite of the nearly insurmountable problems, a cobbler
was found to make the boots. The SS commander received the boots,
but was infuriated by the sight of a small nail that protruded at the edge
of the heel. The sadistic officer detained ten hostages and the cobbler.
The Judenrat was summoned and ordered to provide proper new boots
and other treasures in order to ransom the hostages. The militia had
cleaned the town of valuables long before, but several rugs were offered
with the new boots. Still, the hostages were killed, and the Jewish population of nearly thirty-five hundred were rounded up at the order of
the Nazi inquisitor.

When Graebe and Bronka arrived, they saw the Jews who had been
herded into groups and guarded in preparation for the mass killings.
However, many of the Jews in Ostrog had been able to hide in time
because they had heeded the warnings that had come from Sdolbonov
and Mizocz. Graebe remembers the fear and desperation:

> In some cases it was obvious where people were hiding. In one
> building next to our office the panicked Jews had nailed the
> doors and windows from the inside, but the nails protruded.
> Even a blind Gestapo would see the ruse and capture all those
> in hiding. I tapped on the side doors and windows while Bronka
> spoke to the people in their own language. They were all so
> frightened and most were weeping because of the pressure. Bronka
> finally quieted them so that I could direct them to pull in the
> nails and bend them. I do not know if these people survived.
> Others, though very few in number, either hid or fled success-
> fully.

Most were not so fortunate. Jung employee Joel Rubenstein hid his
wife, his two children, and his mother. For nearly eleven days they
stayed in a hastily dug pit under their house in the ghetto. Desperate to
find food, Rubenstein crept out of the pit under the cover of night, but
he was observed by an informer and his location was reported, for a
nice reward, to the police. The police surrounded the entrance, fired
shots into the hideout, and finally forced the family out. They were
taken to a mass grave site and forced to undress. Rubenstein bolted
suddenly. He ran under a hail of bullets through the Christian cemetery,
finally collapsing, naked but alive, in the forest. The others in the family, Firma, Ethel, Feigel, and Rivel, were executed. Joel Rubenstein was
hidden by a farmer and later by a peasant until he could continue his
flight through the countryside. He had hidden in trees, pits, graveyards,
haystacks, and stables for thirteen months when the Soviet Army finally

liberated the region. His survival was a pitifully rare occurrence.

Graebe and Bronka went to the Jung office, entering through the rear courtyard to avoid the patrols, hoping to find an unlocked door. Every door and window was either locked or barred. But Fritz's small screwdriver was enough to pry some of the bars from the window. Because the front of the house looked out onto the main street and the Action, they had to move through the house behind a dim, flickering flashlight. A lavatory door was locked, so Fritz used his screwdriver to pry at it. He stopped when he heard a muffled moan from behind the door. The Jews were in imminent danger—the town was sealed, SS patrols were on the roads and roaming the country, and soon this building would be searched.

Graebe and Bronka waited the night in the house because it was too dangerous to enter the streets. Shouts, screams, and rifle fire punctuated the night, making sleep impossible. Barking guard dogs welcomed the dawn and signaled the arrival of inspectors, who rapped on the door. They quickly began a search of the house. One policeman banged on a locked storage room door in the basement, while another poked from corner to corner, looking for Jews. A third man questioned the engineer, who had a solid excuse for being there. Bronka's heart pounded and Graebe, fearful that the Jews would reveal themselves, kept repeating the rescuers' plea: "Silence is life! Don't lose your nerve and scream."

Bronka strained to hear a cry, a moan, a shout. Silence! The policeman came up from the cellar, shouting, "There's nothing down here, let's go."

With the dawn, the concealed pits began filling with victims while Graebe and Bronka made their way to the car. It was no longer safe to be in the house, let alone in the region. In the distance they saw another large group of Jews sitting on the damp, sandy banks of the Horyn. Fritz recalls:

> As we walked toward the car we heard a strange noise—a tapping sound, as if someone or something was trying to attract our attention. The noise appeared to be coming from above. As we got some distance away, we could see the roof. Bronka let out a small laugh as she relaxed and spied a stork roosting on the tartar tower of the house. He was making the strange noise with his beak. Here is life, she cried. We both chuckled over our nervousness because of the raucous noise of the bird. Our eyes must have once again come down simultaneously from the stork to the scene at the banks of the Horyn, because we both

sighed heavily. Bronka broke the sanctity of the silence. "Oh my God, Herr Graebe, there must be two thousand Jews down there." There were easily that number, certainly more, surrounded by the militia, who made them squat in or prostrate themselves on the wet sand. Once again I felt the deep sadness and despair of helplessness. There was nothing that I or anyone else could do for them. Bronka began to sob—I was afraid that she would not be able to stop. Finally, she pointed to the stork, there is life, and looking to the river, there is death. We had to leave or risk being seen. The next day Ostrog was *"Judenrein."*

In four days, the number of Graebe's employees and his rescue network had dropped from six thousand to fewer than three thousand people. It was not his style to allow the executioners the final word, so he went to *Gebietskommissar* Marschall, who previously had not been willing to receive his visitor. With a chill, assured voice and a wave of his forefinger before the brutal Nazi, Graebe said, "You have killed my best craftsmen! You have taken more than three thousand of my workers. Don't blame me when the military command comes complaining that they cannot fight on the North Ukrainian Front. You are the traitor! You and your friends are the ones who sacrificed the innocent." With his piece clearly spoken, he turned in defeat and proudly marched out of Marschall's office.

Bronka's postwar assessment, supported unanimously by the other survivors, was that many Jews had lived for so long or survived at all because Fritz Graebe struggled to win contracts so he could employ them, because he requisitioned them for the work, provided them with documents and food, and relocated them. The Jews of the Ukraine were subjected to extermination and died in massive numbers. Only those Jews under the protection of Fritz Graebe had some hope of surviving. In spite of the fact that the several Actions of 1942 claimed the lives of more than three thousand of his workers, thousands of others escaped or were otherwise protected. After October 1942, however, the numbers to rescue were smaller, the risks greater, and the opportunities for contracts fewer. The *Einsatzgruppen* had decimated the Jewish population.

Fritz Graebe was an accomplished actor on the stages of life. He could shout, confront, ingratiate himself, bluff, storm, lie, and, if necessary, shuffle. He could make his face blank or assume the air of confidence of those with secret authority. But now, after so much effort, after so much killing and frustration, he was physically and mentally exhausted. Everything about him had turned ashen and his back was stooped. He arrived in Poltava, complaining of terrible chest pains. He had pushed past one limit too many, borne one worry, retained one hideous memory, seen one murdered child too many.

This chapter of Fritz Graebe's life did not actually close, though, until 1945. In that year he was able to retrieve the employment rolls from the Jung office in Sdolbonov. Using these rolls, he was able to help construct a list of the names of those working for him who were murdered during the Action. Thus the murdered Jews did not remain nameless, nor was their fate lost to their witness, Fritz Graebe.

Perhaps a chapter never really ends. In 1961, Maria had remarried and was living in the United States. Her work in a medical research facility was interrupted by a summons to testify, with Graebe, at the murder trial of Georg Marschall in Germany. Maria was reluctant to ask her American employer for time off, because she was at a critical point in her work and there was no one else who could easily manage for her. She had not confided in her employer or coworkers that she was a survivor and a principal witness in a much-publicized trial. One day in the lunchroom, she and a coworker on the project were talking. The woman asked Maria why she seemed so distracted and upset. The question caught Maria unsuspecting and at a vulnerable moment. Maria began to tell her friend about the trial and her role in the rescue efforts along with the man who was the chief prosecution witness.

The woman asked Maria for details. Maria told her more, and identified the locations of the operations.

"Maria, did you have an office in Sdolbonov?" the woman asked.

"Yes, of course. It was our main office."

"Did you know, Maria, that I came to Sdolbonov from Ostrog fleeing an Action?"

"No! Oh, my God, no!" Maria exclaimed.

"Was the German engineer Graebe your boss in Sdolbonov?"

"Yes, of course, yes!"

Maria and Rosa Schachter had not met in Sdolbonov because Maria had moved to Poltava by then. For three years the two women had worked daily, side by side in an American research laboratory. Rosa volunteered to take over Maria's project while she went with Graebe to Germany in order to testify against Marschall.

(above left) *Fritz Graebe (circa 1922) as he was completing his engineering studies and as he and Elisabeth announced their engagement.*

(above right) *Fritz Graebe in 1939 while completing his assignments on the West Wall fortifications in the Eifel Mountains.*

Fritz Graebe in a light mood shortly after arriving in Sdolbonov to manage the Jung firm offices in 1941.

(above left) *Fritz Graebe was photographed for U.S. military identification purposes in Wiesbaden, Germany, 1946.*

(above right) *When Fritz Graebe was honored at Yad Vashem on September 20, 1965, he was presented with a photo album that included this formal portrait as well as other commemorative pictures.*

At that same occasion, he planted a carob tree on the Avenue of the Righteous and this name plate identifies him as one of "The Righteous."

Fritz Graebe's workers struggled through the cold winter months to complete a roundhouse in the Ukraine. Graebe had arranged for these workers to wear a warm felt cover to protect their feet.

The workers had to carry bricks and supplies on their backs to the construction site because wheelbarrows were not available.

The brutal, anti-Semitic construction-site manager, Max Schmale, stood with two German officers who visited the Ukraine in order to inspect progress on railroad contracts.

The torn, wrinkled snapshot of the Jewish worker, Diener, who was executed in Sdolbonov. Groups of Jewish workers were forced to look on as a warning against disobedience to the regional government. Fritz Graebe carried this picture as a graphic reminder of the horrors he resisted.

Maria Warchiwker, Fritz Graebe's secretary, with Friedel Graebe on the porch of the Jung firm office in Sdolbonov prior to the Rovno and Dubno massacres.

8. "Snapshots"

Many of us have seen snapshots or scenes from movies taken by Nazis: photos of helpless people being chased and beaten in the streets; scenes of old Jewish men being humiliated; of naked Jewish women being pushed into the streets, forced to sit in gutters under the glaring eyes of the German SS; and photos of the doomed children, their faces incredulous, shocked, terrified. We see these pictures, are outraged and, along with that of the victims, our humanity is violated. But we can close our eyes, look away, and in time forget the haunting photographs. Imagine, though, being unable to wipe the images from your mind because you were there to see and to experience them. Tears will not wash the memories away; you cannot escape them. Sometimes they make you feel your humanity with greater intensity.

Not all of Fritz Graebe's experiences were of the magnitude of the Rovno and Dubno killings, yet all profoundly influenced him. What follows are his remembrances of several encounters with the Nazi killers and their victims during 1942, encounters whose cumulative impact has remained with him all his life.

Two days after the Action in the City of Ostrog on October 15, 1942, a slight Jewish child—she could not have been more than fourteen—came to our work site. She had been terribly frightened by the massacre, the violence, the wounded people crying out and being shot again. Another of my secretaries, Bronka, brought her to me saying, "We must save her. All of her people have died in the Action."

So we hid her, but she became impatient; she wanted to join the partisans. Two young men from the Underground were recruiting her to join with them. They were not the best kind of people; they really did not have anything for her, they only wanted to use her. Bronka and I tried to talk her out of her decision, but she was convinced that she should go with them. She was so young, so innocent, and she did not know what was in store for her. I never saw her again.

The following was a scene replayed thousands of times on railroad sidings and in the forests off the beaten path: Someone would dig a very deep pit under the supervision of the militia guards. Then the people would begin arriving, and the SS guards would force them to undress, placing their clothes in neat piles. They would then line up at the edge of the pit and the guards would shoot them.

In Mizocz, people brought a certain Jewish man to me at the construction site. He had survived one of the Actions that had happened far from us. When they shot him, he had fallen into a mass grave. Then his mother had fallen on top of him and bled to death. His wounded brother lay beside him. Late in the night, this poor man was able to push his way out of the bodies and run for cover. There was no one there to stop him. He ran naked and covered with blood for thirty kilometers to a farm where he was comforted and protected. They brought him to me and he worked for us for a time.

A Jewish physician, Josef Lubicz, and his wife escaped from the Action carried out in Kostopol, the Ukraine, in August 1942. They were able to move quickly through the area past the SS patrols that scoured the area in search of hidden or escaping Jews. Lubicz and his wife found their way to Sdolbonov, where people spoke of the kindness of a certain German engineer with the Josef Jung firm. The couple then approached me, and I immediately registered them on the company books as Polish nationals. After the customary questions about being recognized, I sent the couple to the construction site in Slawuta.

On October 3, 1942, Bronka was working the switchboard when the call arrived from the police in Slawuta. She was informed that the Lubiczs had been arrested on an affidavit charging them with being Jewish and concealing their identities. Bronka was advised to send someone to retrieve business papers and funds belonging to the Jung firm. I went immediately to Slawuta and confronted the police inspector. At length, he handed me a formal copy of the charges. As it happened, the Ukrainian Orthodox priest of Kostopol had been visiting in Slawuta, recognized Lubicz, and had promptly betrayed him to the police as a disguised Jew. Lubicz had not been able to deny his Jewish heritage under the pressure of police questioning. I demanded that I be allowed to speak with my employee, but was informed that the doctor and his wife had already been shot. They went to their deaths without exposing the rescue efforts.

Hanna Prussak was the nineteen-year-old daughter of the late director of the cement works in Sdolbonov. It was a warm, pleasant evening on August 20, 1942. The dew-filled air contained a slight hint of the changing seasons. Hanna and a friend sat on a bench in front of her home in the Jewish ghetto of Sdolbonov, enjoying the momentary peace, the quiet of a late summer's eve. They were ignoring the curfew.

Two slightly intoxicated Ukrainian militiamen happened by the bench. They ordered Hanna and her friend to go home. Hanna resisted, but her friend left. The two Ukrainians began pushing Hanna. The pushing led to a punch and then a brutal assault with rifle butts. Her screams aroused a number of Hungarian militiamen stationed in the area. They rushed to the scene, but by then Hanna was dead. They took the two Ukrainian militiamen and beat them so badly that they had to be hospitalized.

Word of the vicious murder spread quickly and threatened to cause a major confrontation. Symcha Schleifstein, the leader of the Judenrat in Sdolbonov, went to the office of Reich Commissioner for Jewish Affairs, Otto Koeller, to protest the killing and to demand that something be done to punish the offenders. Koeller stopped Schleifstein before he could complete his sentence. "Herr Schleifstein, that charge is just another one of your Jewish lies. You are trying to cause more trouble in my district."

Koeller ordered Schleifstein to summon the Jewish elders immediately, and before he could respond, a soldier roughly pushed the old Jew out the door. When the elders had all been summoned and gathered, Koeller addressed them: "You have twenty-four hours to bring me the Jews who killed this girl, seeking to stir up trouble for me."

Schleifstein protested, "Jews! Herr Koeller, it was the Ukrainian militia who killed her!"

"You are a liar," Koeller snapped. "It was a Jewish plot to discredit the Reich administration. Your people killed one of their own. You give me the killers or you give me ten Jews as hostages."

Schleifstein came directly from the meeting to my office. I had once helped Hanna Prussak, and she had worked for the Jung firm. This seventy-year-old leader was crying on my desk. "What can I do? I know they killed her, but now they have turned the tables on me."

"Be calm, my friend, and we'll find a way."

"It's no use. I cannot bring them the killers, and I cannot bring innocent hostages. Who can I bring? What should I do, Herr Graebe?"

After the war it troubled me that the Judenrat was so severely accused. I was in close contact with the Judenrat in Sdolbonov, Mizocz, and Ostrog. I held the leaders in great esteem. They had to make choices where no real choice existed. They were accused of showing cowardice, whining for mercies, and of seeking special favors and advantages for themselves. Yet as far as I know, virtually all of the Judenrat perished. They were truly tragic characters in all of this. Three or four times each week they were commanded to present themselves to the German authorities, who humiliated and abused them. Some people think of the Judenrat as pawns—and some may have been—but those known to me were more like buffers, standing between the murderer and the victim. Schleifstein, before he was tortured, sent on to Rovno, and killed, was regularly boxed in the ears, but he could not defend himself or complain. He had to quiet the people of the ghetto, but he could never tell them what he was doing to secure food, papers, and warm clothing. People like that were the real heroes of the hour. They did things that were impossible, that no one else knew about or appreciated.

I decided to intercede with Koeller. I assumed a quiet, concerned, almost humble demeanor for our meeting. I suggested to Koeller that it would be in his professional interest to secure the peace and stability of the area by bringing the militiamen to trial and punishment.

Koeller exploded at me. "You are a liar, too, and a dupe! Are you crazy? The Ukrainian militia! Get out of here, now!"

Nothing could be done; it was hopeless. Schleifstein brought the ten hostages, including his mother-in-law because the peo-

ple accused him of selecting only from their people and not
from his own family. On August 24, Otto Koeller had all ten
of the hostages executed in public.

Two weeks later, a grief-stricken woman appeared at the Jung
switchboard. She explained to Maria that she wanted to see the
German engineer and thank him for his help and kindness on
behalf of her daughter, Hanna Prussak. When I came out of my
office, our eyes met. It was the same feeling I had when my
eyes met those of Rosenzwieg after that first Action in Rovno in
November 1941. Frau Prussak fell crying into my arms. All the
work in the office stopped at the sound of her sobs and at the
sight of me, a German, comforting the Jewish mother. I felt
very ashamed. I had not been able to do anything for Hanna
Prussak, and now her mother was crying in my arms, thanking
me. I did not deserve it. I wished her God's blessings and she
left. I doubt that she survived the war. Why should she have
wanted to live after all that? She disappeared October 13, 1942.

During the Action in Ostrog on October 15, 1942, there was
a certain Jewish medical doctor who did not have a German
name. When the Action started, he was able to get away and
hide. Some of the farmers found him and hid him. Many of
them were cruel, as cruel as the Nazis. They made him hide
with the pigs. He slept with pigs. They made him eat what the
pigs were eating. Can you imagine that? He was a Jew, and they
made him be with the pigs and eat like the pigs. When I saw
him much later, he had gone insane. It was so sad. He must
have been a brilliant man, but now . . .

In an Action near Sdolbonov in 1942, a Jewish woman who
was obviously pregnant came swimming across the river toward
me. She was screaming and struggling. I went into the water
and helped her to the shore. I had to place my hand over her
mouth because her screams were sure to attract the militia. It
was too much for me. She was so traumatized and so desperate.
They had killed her husband, and she had no one and no place
to go. I tried to quiet her because I knew the guards had to be
nearby. Finally, after a very short time, I pushed her into a
haystack at the side of the road. I told her, "Be very quiet. Don't
make a single sound or they will come and kill you and your
little one. Be very quiet."

I do not know what became of her. She disappeared just like that. Because of the many soldiers nearby, I had to leave her.

In Rovno, after the July 1942 Action started, people were forced into the trains. One tiny Jewish girl, wearing only a small skirt and otherwise completely naked, was running back into the ghetto, crying "Mama, Mama." A husky SS guard, about forty, caught the little girl, swatted her behind, and told her, "Go this way, here, go this way—poor child."

He pointed her back to the train. As the child ran to the train, the SS man came over to me and said, "Sometimes you need a heart of stone to do this."

I didn't answer that. I watched the little girl run to the train. I do not know if she found her mother.

It was not unusual for me to receive orders that I was personally opposed to and that I therefore ignored. On one occasion, I went with Stabsleiter Erich Habenicht to visit SS Major Dr. Puetz. I needed once again to plead for a delay in an Action. The SS Major was predictably irritated.

"Graebe, I am tired of your requests for delays. This is the last one. You will learn that every Jew that dies brings Germany one day closer to peace." The postponement he offered me was conditional. "You will treat those Jews with the brutality that they deserve. They are lazy, so you will beat out of them the greatest amount of labor. If any one of them slacks or performs badly, you will shoot three of them and let them rot, publicly, for three days."

Dr. Puetz began to snicker as he realized the connection between a dead Jew and three days—an accidental allusion to Easter. "Let them rot," he shouted at me. "It will serve as a warning to all who want to challenge my authority."

I was able to delay the execution of the order for a lengthy period. The Action was not postponed indefinitely.

There was another aspect to Fritz Graebe's memory. If his mind's eye captured the overwhelming scenes of death and suffering he saw around him, his mental camera rescued the two endangered sources of meaning and joy in his life: his relationships and his work as an engineer. His portraits of colleagues, friends, and family represent moments of peace and renewal in the midst of turmoil and dislocation. Graebe seemed to have known instinctively that the scenes of death were fixed permanently in his mind. But what he feared most was the loss of perspective, the loss of the memory of things humane, caring, and precious. The Holocaust had a way of fixing the former and eradicating the latter.

The mental photographs Fritz took were evidence that death and despair were not the final verdicts of the chaos he lived through. The courts and history are filled with many photographs but need the eyewitness accounts, the mental snapshots of those who opposed the violence and covenanted with the dying to "never forget."

9. The Conspiracies: Health and Enemies

In the early phase of the war with Russia, Hitler's primary military strategy had been to secure the Ukraine, defeat the Soviet Army at the Dnieper River, and destroy Stalingrad, one of the two "Holy cities of Communism." Field Marshal von Rundstedt's offensive in the autumn of 1941 had buoyed Hitler's hopes for a renewed sense of purpose for the military.

The Germans were ill-prepared, however, for the onset of the severe winter of 1941, the season of rains and mud. A combination of critical factors virtually halted the German efforts and led to major military setbacks. Retreats, resistance, and forced changes in the command structure decimated the strength and morale of the German armies.

While the Eastern Front war raged on during 1942, the *Einsatzgruppen* continued their merciless work. Then, on November 19, 1942, barely a month after the German and Ukrainian forces had completed the mass murders of the Jewish population in the Sdolbonov District, the Soviet Army launched its major counteroffensive at Stalingrad. Fritz Graebe's Poltava operation was situated only about one hundred kilometers from Kharkov, which would be one of the first cities to be captured if the Soviet counteroffensive were successful. The soldiers and equipment of the German Sixth Army began flooding into the region. Field hospitals serviced the hundreds of German casualties. Railroad services falteringly struggled to maintain the flow of fuel, supplies, and soldiers headed east, while evacuating the wounded and dead on the return trips. Every phase of this conflict threatened the Poltava group.

The Poltava Jung office still existed without the knowledge or approval of the Jung headquarters in Solingen. The office was staffed and directed by twenty-five Jewish men and women whom Graebe had supplied with false papers and work permits. They supervised the few negotiations and contracts they could secure. The majority of the work was limited to cutting firewood, salvaging materials from sites, and doing odd jobs in order to make ends meet. Alex Dutkowski supervised nearly all this piecework being done around Poltava. Additional funds came from Fritz Graebe's personal accounts, but as the work force grew, more funds were needed to secure food and supplies, which were being commandeered by the army and not shared with the labor contractors.

It was his compassionate nature that led Fritz Graebe to board a train and travel east to visit his Poltava staff. He had to assure himself that they were not endangered by the Soviet counteroffensive or exposed to the suspicions and ravages of the Sixth Army soldiers. In spite of his own extreme exhaustion and the trauma of the Actions, Graebe wanted to personally bring the tragic news that the *Einsatzgruppen* had murdered the friends and relatives of the Poltava group.

In mid-December 1942, Graebe removed five thousand marks from a private box in his safe at the Jung office in Sdolbonov. The marks were converted to the currency of the Ukraine, *Karbowaniec*. (Ten *Karbowaniec* were equivalent to one mark.) Fritz placed the currency in a briefcase and set out for Poltava by way of Kiev, where he transferred to another train.

The train trip provided brief periods of restless sleep. Fritz would begin to relax and then his sleep would be interrupted by nightmares of the horrible Actions. This sensitive German's conscience could not quickly exorcise the demonic visions of destruction. Nor could his body, exhausted by long days and nights of work, relax and revivify itself.

Finally, the bouncing, soft rocking motions of the train quieted Graebe, sending his weary mind into the dreamy twilight of sleep's first moments. After the Actions, he had continued his heavy work schedule, with one eighteen-hour day flowing into another. There were still people to be rescued, though nowhere near the number seeking sanctuary before October.

Graebe dozed and recalled the faces of the Polish peasants who regularly camped in the forests outside of Sdolbonov. Graebe or one of his secretaries often aided the elders and children, who always needed food or shelter or clothing. He would requisition temporary space or give them food; and sometimes he could even locate medicines to help the sick. Once the people were attended to, some of the healthier ones worked in the columns before continuing their trek to some anonymous, distant place where there was no war.

The screaming whistle of a westbound train awakened Fritz with a terrible jolt. Sweat poured from his forehead and a shortness of breath sent pains crushing down across his chest. The presence of war and suffering were never far away. Collecting himself after the rude awakening, Fritz glanced out the window only to be confronted by the blurred, bandaged faces of wounded soldiers in the passing train. Glazed stares, bloodied bandages, draped corpses rushed past in a surreal blur. Image merged with memory, and both mass graves and youthful warriors proclaimed the victory of death in war.

Graebe used the remainder of the journey to Poltava to develop plans and alternatives in the event that the Soviet counteroffensive succeeded. His labor column had been incapacitated by the loss of more than three thousand workers. Contracts and schedules could not be honored. Soon Dr. Dorpmueller, director of the Reich Railroad Administration, and then officials from the army would be complaining, pushing, demanding. The Solingen office would be suspicious and send its own investigators. The presence of the Poltava group might be uncovered by the investigation and all the people endangered. A cruel irony confronted the engineer: The many contracts that he had successfully sought in order to support the rescue efforts now threatened the survivors.

Graebe thought of Maria and Bronka. These two loyal workers covered for him and handled as much of the detail as they could wrest from him. It was they who saw the ruinous effects of his ceaseless pace and the tensions that afflicted him. It was they who endured his preoccupied silences and his quick temper. It was they who knew the danger signals expressed by his emotions and who sought to relieve him by easing some of his burden or planning a celebration. The pleasing memory of a birthday party lingered in his mind: it was June 1942, and the staff had remembered him with a song and an ornate, handcarved wooden case that was engraved, TO THE CHIEF.

> As I reflect back on this birthday celebration I realize that through all of my life I have been privileged, no, blest, to be surrounded by wonderful people. They cared for me and helped me and in that awful time they even found it within themselves to have a happy time—even if it was a brief moment.

The rough and noisy rail line kept Fritz awake for the rest of the trip. The pensive rescuer began to look forward to the reunion with his beloved staff in Poltava. They were not just a group of persecuted refugees, not a mass of nameless faces. On the contrary, this group of men and women had become Fritz's friends, confidants, and co-conspirators in the struggle to preserve humanity in spite of the Nazi atrocities. They had shared his danger just as he had offered himself in the face of their peril. A sense of melancholy swept the rescuer; the faces of his friends replaced his own reflection in the darkened glass of the coach window.

Poltava faces mixed with the faces of the young boy and the father, with the twenty-three-year-old woman, the gray-haired grandmother, and the thousands whom he had helped but never known, only seen face-to-face for a second. Fritz did not indulge himself with self-recriminations. He had done all that was humanly possible to save these people. And yet their deaths weighed heavily on him. One does not easily accept a loss of this magnitude—not after such commitment, not after such strenuous efforts.

As the train neared the Poltava station, Fritz began to understand why he had traveled this distance. The isolation and loneliness had taken their toll; he needed the support, the embraces, the affirming dialogues and presence of the ones who had become his extended family. Their presence and touch would release the haunting memories, the agony of defeat, the loss of so many. With the Poltava group he would be safe. He could ease up, sleep, and renew himself for the struggles that lay ahead.

The severe cold of the winter winds whistling around the train station at Poltava was diminished by the warm reunion of the German engineer and his Jewish friends. The first night sped effortlessly into early morning as Fritz shared news from Sdolbonov. Somehow the word of the Actions had reached Poltava ahead of Graebe, and all that remained was to share the details and to mourn together for lost friends. News and tears eventually turned to progress reports and shared concerns for the Soviet counteroffensive.

In Poltava Fritz found a well-ordered operation and good spirits among the people. Maria's presence had significantly influenced both order and morale. Immediately upon her arrival she had thrown herself into the work of monitoring, organizing, and supervising the diverse group of Jung workers with ten Poles, a dozen Ukrainians, forty or so Jews in addition to the core leaders, three German staff, Soviet prisoners of war, and refugees drawn from the labor columns.

After a few hours of rest, Fritz met privately with his trusted friend and co-conspirator Tadeuz Glass. Together they reviewed the few active contracts that Glass had managed to secure. Glass was caught in a precarious dilemma. On the one hand, he had to have enough income-producing work to feed and house his workers, and the work had to have some strategic significance in order to justify the continued presence of a civilian work project so near a combat zone. On the other hand, Glass had difficulty ordering and receiving materials because the Jung home office did not know that the Poltava project existed. All orders were necessarily routed through Graebe. If and when the materials were procured, there would then inevitably be delays in delivery. But delays of any sort were guaranteed to lead to angry visits by irate officials, which in turn could mean investigations and possible exposure of the project.

The Soviet counteroffensive was causing other problems for Glass and his people. More German troops were moving through the area. The increased military presence meant more interactions between Jung workers and officers and hence even greater risk of detection. Fritz and Tadeuz discussed the competition for the dwindling food and supplies. Since the military had all the power, Graebe counseled his friend to maintain a cordial relationship with the middle-level officers of the command and to provide useful, low-risk services for the military. The two men also began considering plans in the event that the Soviet Army started to advance. It would be necessary to dismantle the operation quickly, put it on the Jung train, and move it back to Sdolbonov before the military commandeered the train.

The remaining hours of the morning were spent touring the work sites and visiting with the Jung German staff. Graebe questioned them about their work and their contacts with family at home. It was clear from their remarks that they had no idea of the secret nature of the project or that Solingen was unaware of their activities or location.

Late in the morning, the cold and fatigue took their toll on Fritz. Uncharacteristically, he excused himself and returned to his room to compose himself. He was restless and sleep eluded him, so he called for Maria to take dictation. When she entered the room, he was slumped on his bed and breathing unevenly. While he was dictating the first letter, he clutched his chest and grimaced. He quietly brushed aside Maria's questions and concerns, but in minutes the pains returned. Maria watched as Fritz's face became ashen; his eyes rolled back and closed.

"Heart attack! Herr Graebe's had a heart attack!" Maria's screams brought the women from the next room.

As frightened staff quickly gathered at the door, Tadeuz Glass pushed his way into the room, took one look at his friend, and raced away to find help. In this region, there were few trained doctors and probably none who spoke German. Suddenly Tadeuz remembered that there were German physicians at the nearby army field hospital and evacuation center. Terror gripped him as he ran, but it was not enough to stop him. As he came to the enemy encampment, he wondered if they would detect his slight Jewish accent. Would someone notice his "Jewish features"? Would he be stopped by a guard and questioned? But now nothing mattered to Glass except the well-being of his friend and rescuer.

A young German doctor was Glass's first contact. Glass hastily explained the situation to the doctor and described Graebe's importance to the war effort, as if that might further speed the physician's decision to respond. The doctor accompanied Tadeuz back to Fritz's room and quickly confirmed that Fritz had had a heart attack. But it was too late, too cold, and too dangerous to move the stricken engineer. Throughout that night the loyal staff took turns watching Graebe, administering the medicine, and stoking the warming fire in the stove.

The next morning, the doctor and several corpsmen arrived to take Graebe to the military field hospital, where he could be observed and tested. Without protest, he allowed them to take him to the hospital in an army ambulance. The scene at the hospital upon their arrival was unbelievable. Rows of beds were crowded together. The horror of the Soviet attack was etched onto the faces of the wounded and dying men. Doctors and corpsmen rushed about the hospital while the wounded stared glassy-eyed at private, distant scenes.

Fritz was placed on a cot and propped up with pillows while the young doctor gently tried to reassure his patient. "In three or four weeks you'll be rested enough to return home. I don't believe there will be any lasting damage to your heart."

But instead of comforting the weary engineer, the doctor succeeded only in making him fearful.

"I cannot wait three or four weeks. The killing will eventually come here and I must protect my workers."

"What are you thinking about so seriously, Herr Graebe? You look very troubled!"

"I am troubled! I cannot just sit here for weeks on end. I have a project, and administration—"

The doctor interrupted this typically logical train of thought flowing from a stricken managerial-type man. "It's better that you rest here where we can watch you. You won't be any good to the war effort if you go out from here and die."

"Don't scold me, Doctor, just get me well enough to go back to my office."

"For now you are too weak and you are my patient. Rest—don't fight me, and I will do everything I can for you."

After two days, Maria managed to extricate herself from the office and get to the hospital to visit Graebe. She had not succeeded in getting a message about his heart attack through to Sdolbonov because of strict military rules of secrecy. When she arrived at Fritz's cot, she was appalled by the sight. He was obviously still weak, ashen, and losing weight. The ward was cold and chaotic. The wounded were moaning, and the doctors were preoccupied with ministering to the incoming patients from the front. Graebe's spirits were low because of his weakness and because of his brooding on the prospect of a two-week enforced rest and on the dangers that were closing in on his operations throughout the Ukraine.

Maria wasted no time in finding the young doctor.

"I want to take Herr Graebe back to the Jung office."

"I don't think you under—"

The doctor could not complete his objection—Maria was convinced and presented her argument, the final word.

"Wait a minute, sir. We can watch him there better than you and your staff can here. I can keep him warm, quiet, and fed. If he has a problem we will come and fetch you immediately. Besides, you need all the beds and doctors for the wounded."

Her confident arguments were sound, and there was no point in disagreeing with Maria. In short order, Graebe was at the office in a comfortable bed, next to a warm stove, and attended to by six or eight willing Jung workers. The attention he received was more like that given the rich at a luxurious spa than an officer in a railroad construction company. Maria carefully monitored visitors, moved the office work to another area in order not to tempt the hardworking German, and personally assumed responsibility for Graebe's recovery.

The relocation to familiar surroundings did speed Graebe's recovery. He started eating, his sleep was less fitful, and his spirit began to renew itself. Soon he was asking for work, trying to direct the staff, and anxiously wanting to return to Sdolbonov. One day after the doctor had visited, Alex came in. It was time for Fritz to walk—too much bed rest was weakening him, the doctor had said. Alex was strong and willing, attentive almost to a fault. He helped his friend dress and, taking him by the arm, practically carried him around the room.

"Don't worry, Herr Graebe, I am right here. . . . Do you feel any pain, anywhere? Don't walk so fast. . . . Let me hold your arm so you don't fall. . . . How do you feel now? . . . Do you want to rest now?"

It was too much! "Alex! Alex! Alex!" Fritz waved his finger. "Don't treat me like an invalid."

Soon the solicitous entourage of Jung workers who had gathered to offer their encouragement were sent packing back to work by the protests and chiding of their irascible boss.

Each day brought new strength and resolve to the German engineer. He was spending more time reading reports, receiving his German staff, reviewing plans to transfer funds to Glass, and joking with Maria. Maria confessed to him that she had only sought his transfer from the hospital after she had seen an obese, short-tempered Polish nurse give him a shot.

As days turned into weeks, Graebe grew increasingly anxious to return to Sdolbonov. He worried about the length of his absence and his inability to communicate the reason for his absence to his staff. He could not call Sdolbonov because the army continued to preempt the phone lines. If he wrote, there would be a Poltava postmark on the envelope, and that certainly would cause questions—in fact, the letter might never leave Poltava because of the censors. He wanted to write Elisabeth and Friedel in Solingen to inform them about his condition and reassure them, but the postmark and censorship were deterrents. His anxiety was beginning to wear on the staff.

Then one day Fritz suddenly hit on a plan. Within minutes, Maria was at his side taking dictation. Between letters he would chortle to himself, "There! I've cheated them again!"

All day and into the evening words flowed from Graebe through Maria and onto the paper. On each envelope he wrote the date and the initials *O.U.* That designation, short for *Orts Unterkunft*, was part of a military procedure that provided secrecy for those laboring or fighting in hostile territory. The initials warned the postal clerk and recipient that the letter came from a secret zone. It would not be censored; those who received such a letter would not know its place of origin, and yet no one would become suspicious.

So a flurry of such letters were dispatched in the intervening days. In the meantime the doctor was running tests that would indicate whether or not Graebe would be allowed to return to Sdolbonov. The day finally arrived when he was declared well enough to travel. The doctor warned him that he had to slow his pace when he got home, that he would have to carry his burdens less personally, and that he had to take his medications regularly.

Graebe did not argue with the doctor. He listened, asked a few questions, and thanked the young physician for his care and concern. Maria and Tadeuz interrupted almost simultaneously that something was not as it should be.

"You cannot go back to the same routine—you'll die."

Tadeuz had reasoned everything out in anticipation of Graebe's stubbornness. "You've saved so many people already—now you must save yourself. Elisabeth and Friedel need you; anyway, the war will soon be over."

As Graebe started to protest, Maria asserted herself and spoke her lines. "We have a plan of which everyone approves. You will go back to Solingen and continue to provide a cover for us. Tadeuz and I will take over your duties and responsibilities here and in Sdolbonov. You must let us do this—it is too dangerous for you to continue. The Gestapo are looking for a scapegoat."

Fritz listened patiently, quietly, pondering the suggestions and the implications. Here he was being given the opportunity to look out for himself: he was off the hook, no more risks; he had done everything he could.

"No. I am sorry, I cannot accept your plan. We will never split up. Together we must continue our work. We have come this far together, we can do the rest."

The three argued back and forth, but it was clear that Graebe would prevail. He was stubbornly resolved, as he recalls:

> I was not going to be convinced by any arguments. Saving Jewish lives and protecting innocent peasants were my sole priorities. We had to win at this level or there would be no postwar Jewish population. I felt that the German war effort was flagging. The military could not win the war under the direction of a deranged man like Hitler. After all, look at what was happening to the Sixth Army just a few kilometers from my office. No! It was an obsession with me. I had saved so many lives only to watch them die when the next *Einsatzgruppe* came through. I would not allow the rest to suffer and die. Maria, Tadeuz, and I would continue together.

The next morning Fritz and Tadeuz were walking together. Glass was trying diplomatically to convince Graebe to go home to his family.

"Don't worry, my friend. We all know that you did everything you could and more. One day, when it is all over, we'll meet again in Warsaw. It will be a grand reunion of compatriots."

Maria came running out of the office and down the street toward the two men. A letter had arrived from Bronka in Sdolbonov.

"There is trouble in Sdolbonov," she shouted. "Bronka wants you to return immediately."

The urgency of the letter, which contained no details, was unmistakable, and it put an end to the argument.

Speculation and innuendo about Graebe had been spreading among the German workers in Sdolbonov. Before his departure, Graebe had been seen at the safe in the Jung office counting out thousands of marks and placing them in his personal suitcase. Herr Spicharts, the deputy manager, presumed it was embezzlement and carefully spread his suspicion to other workers. In a conversation with Herbert Moennikes, formerly the site foreman at Dubno, he confided, "I don't think Graebe will be back. Maria disappeared earlier, and now Graebe. I think they have run off together—what do you think?"

Spichart's concerns were not in fact for the firm's funds but were rather for assuring his own position in the firm.

"We cannot go on like this without a manager," he told Bronka. "I have notified Solingen and told them that I would serve as manager . . . unless they wanted to send someone all the way from Germany."

Moennikes asked, "Do you really feel that it was necessary to write Solingen?"

"Damn it! Take off your blinders—Graebe has run off with Maria and the firm's money. Of course it was necessary."

In Solingen, Spichart's communiqué unleashed a flood of activity. Accountants and executives began reviewing contracts, accounts, and requisition forms, looking for any discrepancies that would give evidence of embezzlement. Graebe had never been a popular man with Frau Emmy Jung. After her husband Max's unexpected death, she and her brother-in-law, Fritz Mandler, had taken charge of Jung. The independent, tough-minded engineer was too much of a maverick for the new officers of the firm. Frau Jung needed only a slight pretext to change the leadership and revamp the Ukrainian operation. While her staff reviewed the records in order to find evidence to file criminal charges against Graebe, she set in motion her plan to send in a group of loyalist workers to take over the Sdolbonov office.

While the Solingen office was abuzz, Graebe was finally leaving Poltava. His departure was filled with emotion. No one knew about the dangers that he would face in Sdolbonov. Everyone feared for the stress on his weakened heart, and all his Jewish workers appreciated his unwillingness to retire and be reunited with his family. A last-minute briefing with Alex convinced Fritz that the German Sixth Army would not be able to resist the Soviet assault. This information had come from a highly respected partisan group that worked around the fringes of the battle and in the German encampment.

"Alex, be careful of your contacts with the partisans," Graebe advised. "It is dangerous for you and for the others who are here."

Tadeuz and Maria reviewed with Graebe the plans to evacuate the Poltava workers in case of an advance by the Soviets. Because no one knew what had happened in Sdolbonov, contingency plans were established in case Graebe was unable to continue or to coordinate an evacuation from Poltava.

As bad as things had been over the previous two years, no moment portended more ominously than the one that now clouded the spirits of the conspirators. No one could avoid the possibility that this was a final farewell. Tears spawned by appreciation, love, and fear mingled together.

At the last possible minute, since the train trip back to Sdolbonov would be long and arduous, Maria, Tadeuz, and Alex decided to accompany Graebe as far as Kiev, where the doctor had said they should stop and rest for Fritz's sake. There, if necessary, they could rent a house for two or three weeks so that he could rest and exercise. The confinement to bed had weakened him and caused a painful backache. The trio convinced Fritz that they would not force him to stay in Kiev and that if he went on from there to Sdolbonov, they would simply return to Poltava.

The trip to Kiev took five harrowing days. Every lurching stop, every unevenness in the track sent spasms of pain through Graebe. Sleep completely eluded him on this train trip. The journey took longer than usual because of the security checks at various crossings and because the train had to yield to troop and supply trains, which commanded priority over the rails. Once they arrived at the snowbound capital of the Ukraine, Graebe agreed to stay and rest. His body had been weakened by the stress of the trip. Maria argued convincingly that it would go better for him if he arrived in Sdolbonov rested and strong. So he rested and exercised with the help of Alex and Tadeuz.

After nearly three weeks of travel and rest, Graebe resumed his rail journey alone. The conspirators had an emotional departure, each recommitting to the others the covenant to continue working and agreeing to meet again after the war.

Graebe arrived in Sdolbonov late in the evening and went straight to his house. Early the next morning Bronka left Mass and went directly to Graebe's house to check to see if he had returned. Bronka was ill-prepared for her first sight of him. He was pale, drawn, and thin. As she em-

braced him she exclaimed, "Oh, my God! I had no idea that you were
so sick. Look at you!"

"Don't you start treating me like an invalid, too!" Graebe responded.
"Bronka, tell me precisely what has happened. Why the secretive, urgent letter?"

"Herr Graebe, there are big problems. . . . I'm very worried."

"Good! I have not had a single challenge for six weeks—I am ready
to do something."

"This is no light matter, Herr Graebe," Bronka chastened. "I have
been replaced as secretary, a new worker now operates the switchboard,
and Frau Jung and her brother-in-law sent three people from the offices
in Hamburg and Solingen to take over the management of the contracts."

The brother-in-law had brought two of his cronies, something that
Fritz found amusing.

"Look at that! They need three men to do the work that I could do
alone."

"Herr Graebe, this is no joke—these people are saying that you took
money from the firm and that you ran off with Maria. One of them has
a warrant for your arrest, and the militia has been instructed to take you
away."

Because he would never risk walking into the Jung office unprepared,
Fritz carefully planned his entrance to yet another stage and role. Meanwhile, Bronka was to go back to the office and start her work day as if
nothing out of the ordinary had occurred.

Later, with his usual carefully rehearsed theatrics, Fritz entered the
office. The engineers were leaning over their boards, while one of the
new staff members, Sam Obendorf, and an unidentified Solingen staff
member were at a desk going over books and records. Before a word
was spoken, Graebe's commanding presence had turned the heads of
several employees.

"Herbert, it looks like everyone is hard at work. Good for you!"

"Herr Graebe! Herr Graebe!"

Herbert Moennikes, surprised by the unexpected appearance of his
superior and by his startlingly sick countenance, could only repeat his
name. It was as if a ghost had entered the room.

"How are you, Herbert?"

"Fine, I am fine, sir, and you—how are you?"

"I am feeling much better and ready to work. Obendorf! What are
you and these men doing so far from your comfortable offices in Solingen?"

Obendorf, a former insurance agent, was the ultimate company man, a loyalist through and through. Ignoring Graebe's taunting comment, Obendorf officiously responded, "You have been fired as manager, and I have here an order for your arrest and immediate return to Germany, where you will stand trial."

"What have I done to deserve this honor?"

"You know very well that you absconded with company funds and ran off with your secretary, Maria."

"May I see the official charges?"

Obendorf handed the document to Graebe, who was laughing in his face. In an instant, a look of anger raced across Graebe's own face as he placed the offensive document in his coat pocket.

"I am going to keep this for now."

"You can't do that!"

"It has my name on it, so I'll do with it as I please."

The bewildered Obendorf was about to counter when two Ukrainian militiamen walked through the door to arrest Graebe. Apparently, they had been alerted by the ambitious Spicharts, who had slipped unseen out a side door when Graebe arrived.

Graebe swung around to face the two militiamen. Their premature arrival had caught him off guard but not unprepared.

"If you gentlemen will follow me."

With a regal, sweeping motion he pointed to each of the new Jung staff members and then to the militiamen. With the studied deliberation of an actor who had no more lines to speak and only one critical moment left on stage, Graebe ostentatiously removed a key from his vest-pocket and walked to the safe.

Every person in the office watched in silence as Graebe opened the safe, withdrew a small, locked cashbox, and handed it and the key to Obendorf.

"Open it!"

His sharp words hung in the air.

"Come on now, in front of these witnesses, open it!"

Now more bewildered than ever, Obendorf emptied the contents of the box onto a small drafting table. It contained ten thousand *Karbow-aniec* and an officially stamped, signed receipt, which Graebe ordered Obendorf to read. Humiliation replaced puzzlement as Obendorf nervously cleared his throat.

"Quit stalling! Read it for us!"

"Fifty thousand *Karbowaniec* in payment of five thousand Reichmarks, received from Engineer Herman F. Graebe in the form of a bank draft drawn against his private account. Cologne, this 20th day of September 1942."

"Herr Obendorf, is that all that you find written on the sheet of paper?"

Obendorf hesitated, adjusted his glasses, studied the remainder of the paper, shifted his weight from foot to foot, and then read it all again.

"Read it!"

"Signed by Karl Rodolph, Senior Bookkeeper, Jung, A. G., Solingen and Cologne."

"Herr Obendorf, is that his true signature? Tell me. Now! Is it Rodolph's signature? Yes or no, Herr Obendorf."

Fritz Graebe was relentless when he wished to drive home a point or subdue a foe. His words ripped through the air. Finally, without looking up from the paper, Obendorf muttered, "Yes."

"Count my money—every single piece of paper. Do it now, in front of these militiamen."

With the skill of a trained actor, Graebe spun toward the two startled militiamen, demanding, in his most officious and commanding voice, "Arrest this man and that one over there."

The two officers, who knew Graebe, hesitated for a split second, but when Obendorf began to speak, he was unable to finish his first word before the two officers grabbed him by the arms. Over his vociferous complaint, Fritz's voice rang out: "They have committed treason against the Fatherland by impeding my work, which is the work of the Reich and the official work of the Reich Railroad Administration."

Bronka restrained herself with difficulty from laughing and crying. Somehow Graebe had extricated himself from yet another impossible dilemma. If anyone had told her that morning that the roles would be reversed so quickly and that she would be returned to her position as secretary, she would have laughed in their face. Fritz, in the meantime, removed the warrant from his pocket, ripped it into small pieces, and poured them into the wood stove.

"My friends and colleagues," he said in a soft voice, addressing the workers, "it is good to be back with you. Let us now return to our labors."

Fritz recalls:

> I remember all of this as if it were a fairy tale. It does not seem real to me. Those men from Solingen arrived with an order to fire me and with a court order for my arrest. What a joke! They did not know how to conduct themselves. In one hour the ta-

bles were turned. I was again the manager. I knew that I had to plan and prepare for the future. I was certain that Obendorf would go right back to Solingen and plan something to get back at me. I was right about that.

About an hour later, Moennikes knocked at Graebe's door. Bronka, who had been briefing Graebe and reveling in this dramatic transformation of the office, excused herself.

"Herbert, it is good to see you again. I was not so sure my heart would cooperate and permit me to return."

"Thank you, Herr Graebe. It is good to see you after hearing that you were so sick."

"I had a very serious heart attack, but I am fully recovered and ready to work again."

"Sir, what will happen to those men who were taken to jail?"

"Herbert, I am sick of this whole thing. I work very hard and loyally for the company. What do I get? A stab in the back, an arrest warrant, and it takes three of them to do my work."

"Of course you are right, but what will happen to them? It can only make matters worse for you—and for us."

"They'll be out in a few days. A little jail time will serve them well. They are soft—it is too easy to sit in Solingen making plans and hatching conspiracies. The jail will toughen them for their trip home."

Three days later, Graebe went to the jail, signed the release papers for the workers, and, flaunting the status of his position, drove them to the train station in his Mercedes—the same car in which he had chauffeured his beloved and endangered Jews. The train station was predictably chaotic. Wounded soldiers rested on the platform and in special hospital cars. There seemed to be many more of them. Fritz thought to himself that the Stalingrad counteroffensive had been successful for the Soviets, and that soon everything would change.

> I remember thinking, it is all such a waste—these young men torn apart by the bullets and bombs; the innocent Jews killed in forests, streets, and camps; the poor peasants, robbed of even their meager belongings. . . . They were not even interested in politics. . . . Damn Hitler.

Graebe was roused from his musing by Obendorf. They had reached the civilian passenger car, and Obendorf was resolved to have the final word. The screaming whistle and the noisy arrival of a materials train nearly drowned him out.

"Graebe—we are going to finish you! Wait and see."

In typical form, Fritz smiled defiantly and, shaking his finger, whispered to Obendorf, "Be careful my friend. Be careful. Otherwise . . ."

No purpose would be served by completing the threat. The three days in the Ukrainian jail were all it took to back it up.

As the train pulled slowly out of the Sdolbonov yard, Graebe wondered whether it was too late to rescue any more Jews. *The Underground needs my skills—perhaps they can protect the Jews more adequately than I*, he thought. Late in the afternoon, Graebe told Bronka that he was interested in aiding the Underground.

With a burst of joy she hugged him and said, "I knew you would help us!"

"How could you know such a thing?"

He smiled and picked up a fresh batch of forged identity cards that awaited his signature.

Early on a cold February morning in 1943, agents of the Criminal Police and the Reich's internal revenue service conducted a raid on the Graebe home in Grafrath. The raid was prompted by secret charges that the engineer had evaded paying upward of fifteen thousand marks in taxes and that he had hidden another thirty to fifty thousand marks in his house. The agent in charge of the raid directed Elisabeth Graebe to have her husband return home at once to face the charges.

Two letters arrived in Sdolbonov on February 24, 1943. In the first, Elisabeth wrote her husband describing the frightening raid and reporting the stern warning from the authorities. The second letter was from Ernst Schade in Wuppertal-Barmen. Schade was the certified public accountant who prepared Graebe's taxes and who did much of the bookkeeping for Jung because Fritz had directed contracts to him. The letter informed Fritz that his taxes for 1939 and 1940 were under question, that there was nothing that he, Schade, could do, and that Graebe should immediately release power of attorney to him.

Schade was an ambitious man who had risen to a position of great power in the National Socialist Party. He wanted also to have a significant future with Jung. On several occasions he had expressed his desire to become the administrative manager of the Sdolbonov office.

Immediately, Graebe made arrangements to leave. After four days on the train, he arrived in Solingen, where Elisabeth met him at the train station. Through her tears she admonished her husband, "Why didn't you pay the taxes? It could only cause us trouble."

"Don't be silly, Elisabeth. I have paid everything I owed the government. It is dangerous not to pay taxes, especially under Adolf Hitler. Do you take me for a fool?"

Fritz had decided in Poltava not to write Elisabeth and Friedel about his heart attack. The worry that it would create in Grafrath would not be justified, given his increasing strength and improving health. When he told Elisabeth now, she received the news very calmly. She had expected the workload, rescues, and tension to catch up with her husband and was relieved to hear about the reductions in work and what appeared to be a lessening of the tension. After the brief reunion and the reports on the heart attack and on the fate of the Jewish people, they agreed not to discuss the rescues or the heart attack anymore.

Graebe next went directly to his bookcase and found his hidden account ledger. He had carefully placed it in the midst of other books so that it would not be conspicuous. The ledger contained all his account records beginning in 1930. It was a custom every other year to have a police tax inspector review and sign each page of an account ledger that was accurate. Once signed, the pages could not be added to or subtracted from. All Graebe's documents from 1930 to 1940 were duly signed by the police inspector. From 1940 to 1942, all his accounts had been kept by the Jung accountant and the taxes had been paid through the company. He withdrew fifteen hundred to two thousand marks each month, and that too was recorded by the company staff.

The morning after he returned to Grafrath, Graebe met with Inspector Hennenberg from the Criminal Police division assigned to handle tax evasion charges. Graebe wasted no time in coming to the point.

"I want to know who brought these charges against me."

"I am sorry, Herr Graebe, but I am not permitted to divulge that information."

Hennenberg reviewed all of the documents in the ledger and the receipts of the Jung firm. There were no irregularities.

"Herr Hennenberg, do you know what I do for the war effort? Do you know that my work is of the highest importance to the war effort?"

"No sir, I was unaware of your work."

"Several months ago the strain of this crucial work caused me to suffer a heart attack less than a hundred kilometers from the Stalingrad front. As weak as I am and as far behind as I am in my work, I came here, voluntarily, to face these absurd charges against my loyalty to Germany. I must know the name of the traitors who brought all this about. Was it my accountant, Schade?"

"Herr Graebe, you are a very brave and loyal man for all that you have done and suffered, but I cannot tell you the names of any who put these wheels into motion. However, I think you would be well advised not to allow Herr Schade to do any more of your work."

"Will you give me a written statement that I can use to clear my name at the company now and in case further charges are brought?"

Hennenberg sat down at Graebe's typewriter and prepared an official exoneration, which read:

> I testify that after an investigation of Fritz Graebe, Jr., in Solingen-Grafrath, Schulstr. 53, he is not guilty of the charge of tax evasion.
>
> /S/
> STEUERINSPEKTOR HENNENBERG, DÜSSELDORF,
> 9 March 1943

Graebe took the letter and went directly to the Jung office. There he presented the paper and ordered one of the staff to go immediately to Schade's office in Wuppertal and reclaim all the firm's account records and all of Graebe's personal account records. Graebe told him, "If Ernst Schade gives you any trouble, phone me from his office. Tell him that if he does not cooperate, I will employ certain measures that will cause him to regret his actions for the rest of his life."

Within two hours the courier returned with all of the documents.

> I believe much of this happened at the urging of Frau Jung's brother-in-law, Mandler, and his colleague Obendorf. They hated me and I believe they suspected or maybe even knew something about my work on behalf of the Jews and peasants. I suspected that one of their Ukrainian messengers, Kryloff, was telling them about me and my work. He asked too many questions about too many sensitive things for someone who was only a simple messenger.

Within a week, Fritz released Kryloff and another employee, Max Schmale. Schmale had worked on the staff at Sdolbonov and had regularly associated with Kryloff. His anti-Jewish sentiments were well known in the office, where he, like Kryloff, had asked questions that were quite inappropriate, given his assignments. Bronka had been concerned about them and had related her fears to Graebe. Because both Kryloff and Schmale happened to be in Germany at the time of the tax investigation, Graebe decided to dismiss them then. Kryloff was no problem, but Schmale would have to be handled discreetly. Fritz went to the office of the military draft and informed them that Schmale's services were no longer needed; he was available for conscription into the army.

By the end of the week, Schmale was protesting at the front door of the Graebes' home in Grafrath.

"How could you do this to me? Don't you have something I can do?"

"Max, what are you talking about?" was Graebe's indifferent response.

"I have been called into the army."

"You don't have to cry over that, Max. You can be proud—you'll wear the uniform of Hitler, something that should make you proud."

The next day Graebe returned to Sdolbonov to continue his work and his rescue efforts.

While Fritz Graebe was attending to the fraudulent tax evasion charges in Solingen, the Soviet Army had made a short-term breakthrough in the Stalingrad counteroffensive, moving nearer to the city of Kharkov. The German regional command immediately issued orders for the speedy evacuation of the inhabitants in Poltava. The Germans had plans to burn the city after it was evacuated; therefore even the local Ukrainian residents were forced to pack and leave.

The total evacuation took several days to orchestrate. The scene was one of complete chaos. The army was furiously rounding up the people, carting goods to the train station, and arguing over who had priority interest in the few trains that could get through.

The army had no authority over the Jung staff because they were Reich Railroad Administration and therefore not under civilian or military authority. Tadeuz Glass demanded and finally succeeded in securing space for the staff on a military train. He also was able to take important Jung documents with him. However, he was not allowed to move the office, the machines, or the engineering equipment. It all had to be abandoned.

At the railway station was an incredible mob scene. Huge numbers of civilians and refugees mingled with retreating soldiers, the wounded, and the general staff. Children were separated from their parents, the sick were trampled underfoot, and all the trains were either delayed or rerouted. People had tried to put their lifetimes' belongings into boxes and suitcases, which now littered the platforms, further contributing to the confusion. The cold winter months were not good for the mass movement of entire populations, but there was now no alternative. The lack of sanitary facilities, health care, and food led to rebellions among the evacuees.

When a train finally arrived, the Jung staff pushed through the swarming people, boarded their cars, and headed for Kiev, where Tadeuz Glass

maintained an apartment. They stayed in Kiev for months, waiting for
the Eastern Front to stabilize so that they could return to Poltava. While
in Kiev, officials regularly questioned the papers and purpose of the Jung
staff. Because Tadeuz had brought the checkbooks, documentation, and
records for the company, he was able to convince the officials that they
were temporarily assigned to Kiev while awaiting the successful advance
of the German Army into Poltava and beyond. Had they identified
themselves as evacuees they would have been forced to move completely out of the region and this would have greatly diminished the
likelihood that they could return to Poltava. "Once we return to Poltava," Glass argued, "we will continue our vital work for the Reich Railroad Administration." The argument worked and eventually they were
allowed to return.

The German Army did not liquidate the city of Poltava; the Russians
were pushed back from Kharkov to Stalingrad, and the majority of the
residents and the Jung staff were permitted to return home.

> I was jubilant! Now that the Russians were out of Kharkov, and
> the German troops were avoiding the region, Maria and the
> others could safely go back to Poltava to re-establish the net-
> work. I could stop worrying about their safety and that of the
> Jews in the region.

Though the Germans had not burned Poltava itself, by spring the
central city was ruined by bombs that made housing and workplaces
unsafe. For this reason, when the Jung staff arrived in Poltava they were
not allowed to go back to the safe houses where they had lived. Instead,
they were required to rent cottages and rooms on the outskirts of the
city. Coal and wood for heating stoves and cooking were virtually non-
existent. Fortunately, it was a very mild spring season. People could
easily protect themselves from the chill of the night, and by day the
sun offered enough warmth.

The Jung staff continued to work during the intervening months before the second and final evacuation of the city. Fritz Graebe, working
from both the Solingen and Sdolbonov offices, stayed in close contact
with his staff during this time, but there was little he could do for them.
Tadeuz Glass kept the workers busy dismantling some of the equipment
in preparation for another emergency evacuation.

Graebe's confrontation with the owners of the Jung firm through their
administrative staff had bought him some time, but he knew that matters
were far from resolved. Clearly, a file was being maintained and fed by
anti-Jewish and disgruntled employees. His vindication on the tax charges

and the transfer of the new employees served at best only to slow down his pursuers. Fritz warned Bronka that she should listen carefully to the Sdolbonov grapevine, and that her partisan colleagues must watch for signs of impending betrayal.

The Jung owners and the Gestapo were momentarily restrained, but Graebe had been warned. Yet there was little that could slow his pace. On his return to Sdolbonov from Solingen, he and Bronka held a hasty consultation. They shared news and predictions about the progress of the war, considered staff needs, and discussed the ever-increasing difficulty of securing the delivery of supplies. And there was another crisis even more urgent than these bureaucratic inconveniences. People were sick, medical staff and medicines were again scarce, and there were no reliable hospitals in the vicinity.

Graebe had befriended a sympathetic army physician, Captain Voigt, who was assigned to the Reich Railroad Administration. Graebe pleaded with the doctor for help:

"My friend, I must have a regular clinic in Sdolbonov. My people are not recovering properly. We cannot continue sending them all the way to Rovno for treatments. Their lingering illnesses slow our work. There are refugees who come to us and we can do nothing for them."

This report did not catch Dr. Voigt unawares. He had been concerned about these matters since the small storefront medical office had closed months earlier. Because he divided his time among the five or six cities in his region as well as a dozen or more railroad projects, he could not devote his attention to the specific needs of Sdolbonov. The request of the German engineer was an often-heard one, but for a friend he would see what he could do.

"If you could requisition a site for a clinic, I think I could put my hands on some supplies and perhaps train a nurse to do some of the work in my absence," the doctor promised.

Within two weeks, three houses had been commandeered by the Railroad Administration. Dr. Voigt brought in two nurses; they were paid out of Fritz Graebe's personal accounts because the Jung auditors would have quickly discovered such unauthorized costs. Graebe also purchased uniforms so that the medical staff would be spared endless questions from the militia and the Gestapo.

Dr. Voigt, realizing that he would not be in Sdolbonov more than a few hours each week, trained a nurse to act as a paramedic. Soon there were four houses serving as makeshift clinics and hospitals. All were filled to capacity as word of their existence reached outposts in Ostrog and Mizocz. A small, precious cache of medicines was maintained for the most serious cases. Virtually all medical supplies in the area were being directed to the front or held in reserve in case the Soviet Army prevailed in its counteroffensive; requisitioning too many medical supplies would have eventually caught the eye of the army supply officer and the attention of the investigators.

In times like these, there were no typical days, and yet there was a sort of rhythm to the fast-fleeting hours of each day. Most evenings, until eleven or twelve o'clock, Graebe would organize for the next day and look ahead to the succeeding weeks. His great strength was his ability to organize and plan. With this sort of planning he was free to participate with the underground, to meet refugees, build clinics, and arrange for forged papers.

Each evening, sitting in the private office he kept in his small home, he carefully prepared his lists. So many board-feet of timber had to be located and delivered to the roundhouse project; so many pallets of bricks had to be prepared and delivered to the signal building project; so many linear feet of cable and steel had to be requisitioned for the radio tower construction; pay vouchers had to be reviewed and signed so that contractors and workers were appeased. These were the business routines of nearly every evening in the Ukraine.

But there was still more to do. The workers needed food, shelter, shoes, warm clothing, adequate tools, and protection from both the hounding military and the impatient site supervisors. Morale was a problem. Wages were very low, but people had to work for the Reich projects or they likely would not work at all. The Jews were permitted to receive only eighty percent of the wages earned by the Polish civilians. But wages really did not matter that much; what the people needed was food. Food meant more paperwork, more delays, shuffling of funds and bartering with local farmers and suppliers.

Graebe finally had to build an infrastructure of food procurers. He appointed one man as the commander of the food gatherers. This man in turn had five or six underlings who regularly traveled to the little villages and outlying farms in order to buy the food products.

A typical day began for Fritz at sunrise or earlier at the firm office. The plans of the preceding evening were set in motion. Fritz reviewed his arrangements, and when staff arrived he carefully and quickly gave orders and briefed them. Soon the office was teeming with draftsmen, secretaries, suppliers, subcontractors, and a stream of railroad officials. Refugees moved around the perimeter, seeking whatever aid they could wrest from the people. Bronka tried to monitor and field the comings and goings of these people, but it was a difficult chore because they could arrive at any moment, unannounced and in great need.

While Bronka worked with the refugees, Fritz visited project sites, reviewed plans, and attempted to sign new contracts. He also watched for needed supplies, met with the underground, and settled disputes between the staff and the workers. Whenever he met with resistance from workers, staff, suppliers, contractors, or military, he would revert to his carefully rehearsed, officious personality. The lines always seemed to bring him through.

"What do you mean, this cannot be done? Listen, my friend, don't fool around with me. My work has the highest priority."

The response was always the same: "Where do you get this highest priority?"

"I can only tell you, Berlin, no more. It is secret." If pressed for additional information, he would simply shake his finger, cock his head to the side, and tell the inquisitor, "Better for you that you do not know. Now that's all I will tell you. You do understand? My secret is that we want to win the war, isn't that right? So you don't want to interfere with me. It could be very serious for you."

This strategy worked literally hundreds of times. Almost no one in the hierarchy wanted to challenge this approach.

During this period (from late winter into mid-fall 1943), Fritz traveled to Rovno and Ostrog twice each week. Once a week he went to Mizocz and Dubno, and once or twice each month he went to Kiev, Lvov, or one of the more distant cities. This schedule enabled him to maintain close touch with his workers.

While Graebe and his colleagues were struggling to rescue Jews, the Allies convened the Bermuda Conference on Refugees. Noble resolutions were being enacted by various governments, including the United States, while ignoring warnings like this cryptic one sent by Myron Taylor (a well-placed American diplomatic observer) to Assistant Secretary of State Breckinridge Long, on March 26, 1943:

> Gravest possible news reaching London last week shows massacres now reaching catastrophic climax particularly in Poland also deportations Bulgarian, Rumanian Jews already begun. . . . convoke immediately . . . conference for action not exploration, otherwise too late rescue single Jew.[4]

On April 19 the Bermuda Conference on Refugees opened with very pessimistic reports on the likelihood of timely, effective rescues and relocations. The defeatism of the delegates assured the failure of the conference while assuaging the consciences of the world leaders who had convened it. No effective actions on behalf of Nazi victims resulted from the conference.

While the delegates at the conference sought ways to avoid implementing the politically difficult and unpleasant solutions needed to rescue the Jews, Nazi troops, accompanied by Ukrainian, Latvian, and Polish militia, moved against the Jews remaining in the Warsaw ghetto in Poland. On May 16, 1943, nine days after the formal conclusion of the Bermuda Conference, the Warsaw ghetto was liquidated and declared free of Jews.

At about the same time, Bronka discovered the plight of nearly four hundred Polish peasant refugees and a few Jewish refugees. She entered Graebe's office crying.

"They are staying in the forest about twenty-five kilometers from here. They have no food, and the babies are dying."

Graebe sent for a car and drove with Bronka to the forest to see the problem firsthand. He was appalled by the scene.

> I decided that I could best help these people by integrating them into my work details. There was no other way that I could bring that many refugees into Sdolbonov without raising great suspicions. I determined that I would justify their presence on the grounds that so many of my other workers had been killed. It was a cruel irony. By allowing me a justification, the dead were life to these other people.

It took four days and three trucks to transfer all the refugees and their goods. Only a third of them were strong enough to work for Jung. The rest needed medical attention and nourishment. Again using his own funds, Graebe was able to purchase, for very inflated sums, two weeks' worth of provisions for the refugees, and he had his medical staff minister to the sickest of them. In those two weeks, twelve children and infants and several adults died from the effects of starvation and disease. Jung carpenters were diverted from their assignments to build coffins and prepare burial plots. A priest was brought in to conduct funeral services for the Christian dead—an act that restored a measure of dignity to the survivors.

Many of the people continued to live and work in Sdolbonov, while many others left the region to wander in search of a new, less threatening existence. Graebe turned his attention back to the routines of his engineering and to his plans for a withdrawal of his people when the army went into retreat or was defeated.

10. The Ending of a Time in History

Throughout the summer of 1943 the partisans attacked more and more German supply and troop trains. Fritz and his crews were being called out to repair rail lines and to remove the remnants of trains shattered by guerrillas' bombs. German soldiers patrolled the lines in the country, but to be effective there would have had to be one soldier stationed at every hundred yards. When a squad of soldiers appeared in an area, the partisans simply went farther down the line, demolished those tracks, and disappeared; or else there was a sudden, bloody assault that left dead soldiers by the track side.

One cold, autumn morning, SS Lieutenant Beck sent a messenger to the Jung office in Sdolbonov. Beck needed to have tracks cleared after a partisan attack, and he wanted Graebe on the assignment at once. When Graebe arrived at the scene, it was immediately clear that the partisans had simply removed two pieces of track. This had caused an engine and the first five cars to derail.

As Fritz stepped out of his car, he saw the bodies of two soldiers, stripped naked, being placed in a truck. Nearby, Beck was talking to a contingent of SS and Ukrainian militiamen and gesturing vigorously into the air. Beck turned as he heard the door on Graebe's car slam shut.

"Over here, Graebe! Look what these bastards have done—in broad daylight, no less!"

Fritz's response was aloof and confused: "Why do you call me? I have no knowledge of military operations."

Beck pushed, as if he knew or suspected something about Graebe's involvement with the Underground. "Herr Graebe, there's nothing you can tell me about all this?"

The sullen, condescending tone disarmed Graebe for a moment. "*Herr Leutnant,* sometimes you startle me. What do you think I am, a traitor?

Do you think for one minute that these partisans are making my life easy? Every time they blow up one of your trains I get pulled off my contract work and waste two or three precious days cleaning things up." Fritz was furious because of Beck's veiled allegations. "Damn it! These bastards are making *my* life hell, too! By the time they finish with you, and I complete the cleanup, they are off blowing up my installations!"

The tables turned again, and Beck became defensive, speaking without even the slightest hint of a conspiracy.

"Herr Graebe, I don't know what to do—the partisans are everywhere."

"Then put your soldiers to work and stop blaming me for your problems. I have only refugees and poor, tired, starving peasants working for me—no guns, no bombs. Do you understand that?"

The SS and militiamen had drifted away from the heated conversation. Beck too turned away and began giving directions without answering Graebe's question. His silence did not really matter any longer. Within weeks the Soviet Army would break through the German lines outside of Stalingrad. The total Nazi war effort in the Ukraine would dissolve, the suspicions and charges would be packed in crates along with the German command files, and the Reich would begin its orderly retreat from the region.

The sounds of artillery bombardment were a constant but distant reminder to the Germans that their days left in Sdolbonov were limited. The dull pounding of the guns soon became like background music: everyone was aware of the noise, but took it for granted. Occasionally, a loud thud would shatter the night and awaken a few light sleepers or turn a few heads toward the windows, but the guns were still too distant to be taken seriously.

Meanwhile, in Poltava, the severe cold spell that had hit closed the few remaining work details supervised by Tadeuz and Maria. One hundred kilometers east, the war situation was obviously turning sharply against Germany. Tadeuz and Maria began carefully packing the critical records and documents of their work. Alex supervised the careful packing of the engineering hardware. All that was missing were an order to depart and the crating of the larger machinery. There would be no time for further packing when the order to evacuate finally came.

The order did come in September 1943, and the final evacuation from Poltava began without delay. The ill-tempered, harried German soldiers brutally beat and pushed their way through the civilian population. This time the command decided that the people could remain behind and fend for themselves. The retreating army had no interest in the fate of the city nor any plans to level it. However, anyone or anything that got in the way was killed or destroyed by the retreating troops.

Initially, Tadeuz had prepared to take his staff by train back to Kiev, regroup, and then move west to meet up with Graebe and the Sdolbonov contingent. The German command scuttled that plan when they closed the Kiev rail line to all but essential military personnel and equipment. Moreover, there was no way to fight that decision.

After several telephone consultations with Graebe, Tadeuz decided to take a southern rail route, toward Rumania. Going into Rumania would be safe because the people would not be easily recognized as Jewish there. Polish spoken in a Jewish dialect would not be understood by the Rumanians. The Glass group would remain in constant contact with the Sdolbonov group and would eventually try to move north to be reunited with them, so the plan went. On the day of the departure, the German soldiers refused to allow Tadeuz and Maria to take the machines and the sensitive engineering equipment that belonged to Jung. It was only because of his persistence that Tadeuz was even able to take several cartons of documents and records.

During the journey, which lasted for nearly four months, it was impossible to settle and establish a base of operations. The three-hundred-member Poltava group stayed in six different cities; each city eventually was threatened by the advancing Soviet Army. The Reich Regional Command would then force the Poltava group to pack and depart. Whenever the group would disembark at a new city, Tadeuz would report to the authorities, explaining that his group was assigned to the Reich Railroad Administration and was waiting reassignment orders for a neighboring region.

This excuse was usually enough to guarantee a stay of at least two weeks. Whenever a meddlesome or officious member of the command staff questioned or challenged Tadeuz, he simply started pulling official documents and work orders from the few boxes he had managed to take with him. On several occasions Graebe had been able to forward permits and travel papers from Sdolbonov to the Poltava group as they arrived in a new city. But if papers were not available from Graebe, Tadeuz carefully forged the necessary transit or residence forms.

Living conditions for the Poltava group were very Spartan. They had little money and only what authority they could assert by bluffing. Quite often they had to stay in crowded peasant quarters and share their limited rations as barter. No one save the German command lived in comfort or had sufficient supplies.

In the first hours of the new year, 1944, the German retreat was officially called in Sdolbonov. That morning when Fritz arrived in the office, Bronka was at her desk writing, a draftsman was setting up his table, and several others were chatting in a small group. In a subdued, matter-of-fact way, Fritz spoke.

"We are leaving."

The orders were given, people began to dismantle the office, and Fritz retired to plot a strategy. He decided that he would take all his staff and his workers. Since winter had set in and rail lines were being bombed, there were no assurances about the time required to travel to wherever they would be reassigned. With this in mind, Graebe directed his workers to stock the train with enough provisions to last six months.

All the German officials were scrambling to locate and commandeer every available freight car. The retreating army too was taking whatever rail equipment it could find. But Graebe was able to claim two engines and, amazingly, forty-two cars. Many of the cars had been scattered at work sites and on sidings. By acting quickly, Graebe was able to assemble the cars and begin loading them before the military realized what was happening. The Jung staff worked tirelessly and with great speed, filling portions of each train car with engineering equipment, desks, supplies, tools, files, construction machinery, and finally with the few personal belongings of the staff and workers. Next came the provisions for the trip, along with chickens, cows, goats, a horse, and two mules. All the houses, clinics, offices, and storage areas were stripped of anything that might prove useful to the travelers. Three cars were set aside for special use. An office was set up in one car. Another car was Graebe's private room and study, and the final car was reserved for the new secretary, Elizabeth, and her mother. Elizabeth Radziejewsha, a Polish Jew, had replaced Bronka as the primary secretary after Bronka had left the train in Lvov to join her colleagues in the Underground; it was the last time that she and Fritz Graebe would see one another. The remaining workers and staff would share sleeping spaces on cots in the freight cars.

In another part of Sdolbonov, the German staff were boxing the offices of the Reich Regional Command. Fine paintings were boxed and stored, priceless oriental rugs were rolled and wrapped, records were carefully labeled in boxes and sealed files, and the safe, which contained the valuables of murdered Jews and refugees, had been carefully locked and sealed under the watchful eye of Lieutenant Beck.

On January 9, 1944, Graebe entered the offices of the Regional Command to pay his respects. It was a decent gesture considering that he had rarely agreed with the staff on any issue, that they had argued constantly, and that they suspected Graebe of espionage and treason.

His was indeed a decent gesture, but then no action taken by Graebe had only a single purpose: this visit was a safeguard in case any of them met again en route to the end of the war.

Graebe's presence was announced by a military orderly who stood guard at the door. Lieutenant Beck, who was staring out a window, spoke without turning to acknowledge his guest.

"They are just fifty or so kilometers from Rovno, Herr Graebe. They have taken Kiev and now they are in Zhitomir. The Russians are everywhere."

He slowly turned and walked over to a large map on the wall. Locating Sdolbonov, he tapped the spot, again and again.

"There—there—there, and there! Within a few days they will be here."

Fritz broke the melancholy musings of the frustrated official with a bouncy, "Well! It is good-bye, then. We part having done our best."

"Have we?" The young officer's thoughts trailed off. "I don't know where I'll be going. Marschall is to be posted in Kostopol. The Underground there is too strong, and the high command wants him to use whatever tactics he wishes in order to clean it up. It will be very unpleasant."

The sentence was spoken as the officer stared directly at Graebe. The two men stood silently, staring at one another. There was no rancor in Beck's voice; he was speaking about torture and summary executions as if he were ordering a glass of vodka. Fritz broke the silence.

"I have a great deal to do before I leave, Lieutenant. I came to bid you farewell."

"That's a warrior's life, isn't it, Herr Graebe? And where are they assigning you?"

"I will go first to Warsaw and there await my next assignment. Now I must go. Good-bye."

The soldier extended his hand, but did not release the handshake. He began speaking again.

"It will not go well from here. Germany is finished. I haven't lost faith, don't think that! But we cannot win the war. It has been hard here, but at least we were not like some of the others in the Reich. I hope that you will remember that."

Fritz freed his hand and somehow restrained his anger and revulsion at this whimpering failure of a human being who, "like some of the others," had killed anyone he pleased—especially Jews.

"You and your superior, Marschall, must forgive me, but I will not allow myself the luxury of an easy resolution and a defeatist attitude. Again, good-bye."

On January 10, with the Wehrmacht in full retreat from the Soviet Union, Graebe boarded his train and looked out over the city that had been his home and base of operations for more than two years:

> As I stood on the platform of my train I looked out over a city that tested my soul. I do not know that I have ever experienced such emotions in my entire life. Maria's husband and hundreds of other Jewish men died behind the cement factory; I had learned of the Rovno murders here; I made up my mind to begin saving Jews here; my faith in myself and in humanity was on trial here; everything I valued in life was endangered here. Too many people died, but many others lived. I stepped onto the train that day knowing that the killings would soon stop, but it was too late, in spite of our best efforts. I regret that I could not have done more.

The Jews to whom Graebe referred as "my people" reluctantly began to board the train. They carried all their worldly possessions, their history, memory, faith, and destiny packed in knapsacks on their backs as they boarded a train that would take them into an unknown, uncertain future.

It was a clear, cold winter day in Sdolbonov. On the horizon, the roof lines of the houses and the church looked as if they had been painted onto the deep blue sky. In spite of everything, life in Sdolbonov had been relatively secure for Graebe. Now he did not know what lay ahead for him, for Elisabeth and Friedel, or for his precious human cargo. His pensive, troubled face drew the attention and concern of his people. An old, stooped Jewish woman left her place in the line before the freight car door to speak with Fritz.

"Are you worried, Herr Graebe?"

He was worried, but with a reflex response he said, "No. Don't you worry either; everything will be all right for us."

Soon the train whistle moaned balefully. People scurried about, hugging those in other cars as if they were parting company forever. Nearly all the workers and staff leaned against the doorways of their cars scanning the scene, forging a memory of a hostile land in which there had existed an island of compassion and hospitality. After another series of mournful flutings from the steam whistle, followed by the sharp report of steel couplings slamming together, the train began to move slowly out of the Sdolbonov yard.

Graebe stayed at the door of his car until Sdolbonov was completely out of sight. His mind turned from Sdolbonov to his friends Maria,

Tadeuz, Alex, and the others of the Poltava group. Where were they at that moment? Were they safe? Were their papers enough to protect them? Would their provisions sustain them? Would someone accidentally betray them, or would some functionary in the Party or the army discover their true identities? It was a time of powerlessness for a man who was accustomed to directing and controlling. There was little he could do now, even for himself. There was no point in worrying; it would place unnecessary stress on his weakened heart.

Graebe's train headed southeast to the Ukrainian city of Lvov. A forty-two-car train was an impressive sight in Central Europe during wartime. It advertised that important personages were aboard and deserved certain courtesies not afforded to civilian or military trains. When the train pulled into Lvov, it was too long for the yard. The stationmaster inquired hopefully if the train was moving directly on to Warsaw. Fritz's affirmative response brought an audible sigh of relief from the man.

It took several hours to fuel the train and gain clearance onto the track to Warsaw. The train finally pulled out of the yard on a trip that would take nearly three days to complete. The trip was further complicated because the train could make lengthy stops only at the larger stations. Mainline and spur tracks had to be cleared or prepared for the train. At each stop, Graebe would go to a phone or radio to contact the railroad yards in Warsaw, alerting them to his arrival and requesting that they arrange a work schedule for him and his staff.

Their arrival in Warsaw was a local spectacular. No one could remember when a train of this size had entered the city. Warsaw was not able to take the full train, and the stationmaster insisted that it be divided. One portion could stay in the Warsaw yard, but the other had to be moved about two miles down line, where it would not interfere with the functioning of the station. Fritz appreciated the plight of the stationmaster and chose not to argue about the placement of his cars.

Unfortunately, the railroad staff in Warsaw had no work for the Graebe crews. It was a cold winter, and there was little opportunity to make progress on any of the work assignments. But there was no reason to move on, so Fritz decided to wait in Warsaw and try to contact the Poltava group moving southwest. It took nearly a month to locate them; then he discovered that they were having difficulties with papers, food, and petty bureaucrats. Fritz took one of his engines and twelve cars and headed for Kirovograd, several hundred kilometers away, where the Poltava group had been laying over en route to Chernovitz, on the Rumanian border.

Meanwhile, the Reich Labor Service was in desperate need of workers back in Germany. A plan had been devised in which a special Gestapo battalion would move through the occupied territories detaining and then transporting refugees and local civilian professionals to Germany. The Germans grabbed men and women who were walking on the streets or standing on the corners. They moved into the market areas and surrounded the train station. Everyplace where people had normally gathered suddenly became a collection point. As word spread, people ventured out of their homes only if it was essential and with great fear. Special trucks rolled up to the various locations, and heavily armed soldiers forced people at bayonet point or with wildly swinging rifle butts onto the trucks and took them to specially designated train stations from which they were sent directly to the factories in Germany. It was a very tense and dangerous situation. The soldiers were impatient and would not accept excuses from the people. Families were brutally separated without warning; abandoned children could be seen crying on some streets.

One of the special Gestapo groups had moved into Kirovograd. Graebe arrived in the city on the second day of the labor roundup. While he was standing on a street corner with a group of his employees discussing work assignments, two truckloads of Gestapo pulled up. A palpable wave of fear surged through the frightened workers as they started to scatter in every direction. Fritz walked directly over to the ranking officer. He addressed the man in German, explaining that he was preparing his railroad workers for a special assignment that would start in several days. In a calm and commanding voice, Graebe made it very clear to the officer that under no circumstances were the Jung people to be deported to Germany to work in the factories. The officer, to Graebe's astonishment, responded very positively and respectfully. All the Gestapo reboarded the trucks and departed without even asking for papers.

During his brief stay in Kirovograd, Fritz worked feverishly to find a way to stay in contact with the Poltava group while he would be in Warsaw. A supply of new papers and documents to forge was passed to Tadeuz. There would be less danger now that the updated documents were in hand. Once satisfied that his friends were secure and could more easily proceed to Chernovitz, Graebe returned to Warsaw to rejoin his divided train. He thought to himself, *If only there was a way that I could get the permits to move Maria and Tadeuz onto the Warsaw track.* Strictly enforced military law made such a detour impossible. Graebe could only return to the main task at hand, keeping the people in Warsaw fed, healthy, and on board the trains, and intercepting inquisitive officials who might challenge the presence of the group.

After several weeks in Warsaw, Graebe contacted the Poltava group. He decided to leave the workers in Warsaw again and join the others en route to Chernovitz. The Poltava group had been delayed because tracks had been bombed and were just being cleared. Graebe feared that they would not be able to find work in Chernovitz and that they would be in need of more forgeable papers.

Shortly after Graebe met the group, a freak late-winter storm dropped a large amount of snow onto their area. The train stopped near a small army outpost at the edge of a village. Everyone huddled together for five or six hours trying to keep warm. Impetuously, Alex Dutkowski decided to venture over to the army base in search of coffee. Late in the evening, Fritz discovered Alex's departure and his long absence. Fearing that Alex might have become lost in the snow, Graebe set out and followed Alex's footprints in the powdery waste. The trail led directly to the outpost.

Upon entering what appeared to be the office of the outpost, Graebe found an older sergeant in charge. A guard entered from another room. As Graebe glanced in the direction of the guard, he spotted Alex sitting forlornly in a small jail cell. Fritz informed the sergeant that he had come to retrieve his worker and wanted to know why he had been detained.

"They suspect this man of being a partisan spy and a collaborator. He was found wandering around in the snow. His clothing made the guards suspicious and he speaks only Polish. I am holding him for interrogation. Under no circumstances will we let him free."

Like many Polish civilians, Alex wore a heavy winter overcoat made of sheepskin. The wool was worn on the outside, a Polish custom not practiced by either the Rumanians or the Germans. Aside from his attire, there was no reason to hold him.

"I want to speak with your commanding officer at once!" Graebe ordered.

"I cannot disturb him. It is late and he is sleeping."

"You wake him now or when I make my report to Berlin it will not go lightly for you or him."

Once again the actor's bravado worked, and in ten minutes a captain entered the room, rubbing his eyes and fumbling with the buttons on his shirt. He tried to size Fritz up by his attire: Graebe wore civilian clothing with high-top black boots that made him look like Gestapo.

"Who are you and what is your rank, sir?" The inquiry was accompanied by a clicking of heels and a sloppy salute.

"I am Fritz Graebe and, my friend, it is better for you that you not know my rank. You have one of my men in your jail and it is a problem for me. I want you to release him. He's not a spy or saboteur. I personally vouch for him. The poor man simply went for coffee and warmth."

At this hour of the night and with the intimidating man standing in his office, the captain was in no mood to argue. The fact that a ranking German took responsibility for the prisoner was sufficient for the captain. Papers were signed and the guard brought Alex out of the cell. The captain, who was now waking up, started a line of questions about the group, where they came from, what they did, where they were going, who handled their assignments. As Alex entered the room, Graebe seized the opportunity to divert the questions. He winked at Alex, who caught the signal and joined the act. Fritz shouted at Alex in Polish and translated into German for the captain.

"Alex, damn you! Why the hell were you out wandering around in the snow? You fool! You could have gotten lost or shot and endangered us and these brave soldiers. What if they had been forced to spend the night in the cold, wet snow looking for you?"

The captain solicitously interrupted the heated outpouring. "Don't be so hard on him. It was a mistake on our part, too. We should have looked for you and the others. We were waiting until morning."

"It's all right, captain, this man should know better." Turning to Alex, Graebe began to shout, "Get out of here! Now! Get the hell out of here, go back to the train!"

As Alex closed the door, the captain, who was by now fully awake, invited Fritz to sit down and join him in a cup of coffee. In the course of their conversation, Fritz complained about the plight of his people. "We've been standing in the snow for eight or nine hours—women and children, too. It is so cold and we have neither food or coffee."

"I have not space for you in our barracks, but have your people come in. I'll send someone for them."

A guard was sent to the train while the sergeant ordered a group of soldiers to clear the tables and go outside in order to make room for the guests. The grumbling soldiers reluctantly complied. The guard returned ahead of the Jung workers and excitedly whispered to Fritz, "Are you entertainers? I saw your accordions."

For some inexplicable reason Fritz played into this story—it seemed a logical, safe reason for their presence. The guard had seen several of the office typewriters that were stored in containers that resembled accordion cases. He also had seen special engineering instruments wrapped in cloth and wooden containers. Having discovered what he thought were accordions, he naturally assumed that the other items were related to performance.

When the Jung workers began entering the room, Graebe started identifying them to the guard. "Keep this our secret, but she is a dancer, as is she. That one there plays the accordion, and that one the piano. She sings and they also dance."

Several of the staff who had gathered around Graebe were initially confused, but they then picked it up and joined in the charade, pretending to be exhausted, sick entertainers who had narrowly escaped from the advancing Russians. Word spread quickly and quietly through the ranks of the Jung workers. But there was a problem that Graebe had not reckoned on when he first affirmed the guard's inquiry. The soldiers now wanted a performance.

"Please play for us—entertain us," pleaded the soldier.

Fritz responded quickly. "I am so sorry, but we cannot. I know you need this, but my people are totally exhausted and their nerves are shot after our harrowing experience."

"We need your acts to cheer us—we are just poor devils."

It was true. They were just poor, ignored soldiers stuck in a lonely outpost, probably even forgotten by the Reich High Command.

"They cannot," Fritz insisted. "Believe me. If the sick ones sing, they will hurt their vocal cords. Soon everyone will be demanding a performance. No. Let us get warm and rest."

The next morning Fritz quickly gathered his people onto the train and resumed the journey to Chernovitz. The beginning of the trip was complicated by the accumulation of snow on the train cars, but the soldiers and the Jung workers shoveled it off. Had they stayed longer, the persistent soldiers and their captain might have tried to force them to entertain and their safety would have been jeopardized.

When the train finally arrived in Chernovitz, Graebe made several attempts to find work for his people. After several days of futile effort, he made arrangements to return by train to Warsaw. He wanted to get back to check on his group there and to work on contracts that might enable them to remain in Poland and be reunited with the Poltava group.

In the very early spring of 1944, without any prospects for work in Poland, Fritz decided to take his Warsaw train across the country, through Germany, and on to Junkerath in the Eifel Mountain region. There he expected to find work for his people, even if the risks were higher. When he shared this decision with his workers, the Jews became terrified and enraged by the prospect of a trip into the enemy homeland. It was the equivalent of holding an executioner's gun to one's own head. Finally, after much discussion and weeping, the Jews consented to go to Germany with the man who thus far had protected them. On the appointed day, the train moved out slowly from the snow-filled Warsaw yard, coupled with the other cars two miles further on, and began the journey westward.

During this time, there was an intense internal power struggle going on at the Jung headquarters in Solingen. It was a critical year for the firm. Josef Jung, founder of the company, and his son Max, were both dead. This left most of the management to Graebe, who was fully engaged in work in the Ukraine. In Graebe's absence, one of the sons-in-law, Fritz Mandler, vied for power and control of the company. Had Graebe relinquished his rescue work and returned to Solingen, he most certainly would have become the principal in the business. But he did not return, and the power vacuum enabled Mandler to instigate a series of actions against Graebe.

The other executives in the firm were antagonistic toward Graebe and the power he was able to maintain even at a distance. Secretly, decisions were reached and plans developed to oust Graebe from Jung by any means that might be effective. Rumors of the plot reached Graebe, but they were too vague and insubstantial to be considered seriously. In spite of the rumors, Graebe was more concerned about securing work in Germany for his Sdolbonov group and about ultimately reuniting with his other group, now somewhere in Rumania.

The three-week cross-country trek from Warsaw to Junkerath was miraculously uneventful. Border crossings were easy to manage; there were no surly officials to complicate either entry to or departure from the stations. No one challenged the size of the train, and fuel was available at every stop. The worst, slowest parts of the trip were across large sections of track that had been bombed. Crews were working feverishly at most of those points and made every effort to get this official-looking train past their particular points.

When the forty-two-car train pulled into the tiny village station at Junkerath, Graebe faced the same problem that he had encountered in Warsaw. Once again, the train was too large and had to be separated. Half the train was to be taken to Cologne while the other half could remain in Junkerath. The section of the train that was headed for Cologne held most of the materials and supplies for the work that would be sought. Fritz decided to keep the nerve-center cars—those with the offices, the bookkeeping functions, and the records—in Junkerath where he could control them. He dared not risk compromising or endangering any of the documents and records.

> It was very important for me to find work for these people. If I did not find work, it would draw suspicions, which could have led to real trouble. I found a few easy things for the people to do and instructed Elizabeth [the secretary] to start seeing what she could do to line up some contracts. I was feeling very insecure at this time. Word reached me about problems developing for me in the Jung office. I would have to pay attention to it soon. Also, I was not convinced that my Jewish workers were safe in Germany. For their security and because I was having a difficult time finding useful work in my own region, I decided to return to Warsaw. I contacted Maria in Chernovitz, where they had been stalled by weather conditions and other factors beyond their control. I instructed her to go ahead of me and start looking for work in Warsaw. I told her that I would try to get there within two weeks. In hindsight this set of decisions was very unwise and clearly reflected my fears and the uncertainty of the times.

During these months, plans were being formulated to deport Hungarian Jews to Auschwitz. A radio transmission informed Graebe that Sdolbonov had fallen into the hands of the Soviet Army and that the Soviet forces had captured Chernovitz. Maria had reached Warsaw after putting the remainder of the Poltava group on Bulgarian trains headed for frontiers beyond Rumania. Fritz could only pray and hope that his friends would not be caught in the vise that was clamping them between the advancing Russians and the defeated Wehrmacht.

When he departed from Junkerath for Warsaw, Graebe left Elizabeth in charge of the office and bookkeeping operations. The other staff were told to complete the record-keeping and documentation on the work that had been done in the Ukraine. Because of their unpredictable, hasty retreats and evacuations, the staff had fallen behind in its recording procedures. Fritz took one other step before leaving. He wrote a letter for Elizabeth that placed her in command of the train, staff, and all records. It forbade her to permit anyone, under any circumstances, to have access to the records in the office. She was directed to notify Graebe in Warsaw if anyone even inquired about the group's activities.

When Graebe arrived in Warsaw after two weeks' traveling, he found Maria waiting for him at the prearranged time and location. She had

been completely unsuccessful in securing work. Her underground con-
tacts had informed her that the Germans were secretly evacuating Warsaw and that there was no hope of finding work. After several days'
searching together for contracts and meeting with underground leaders,
Fritz and Maria grudgingly accepted the fact that there was no work,
and that they had to solve the dilemma of the unemployed workers in
Junkerath and the plight of the Poltava remnant escaping through Rumania by other means.

A member of the Underground contacted Maria as she and Fritz were
seeking some solution to these quandaries and preparing to leave. The
Underground had a serious problem with which they hoped she could
help. In December 1943, a Polish underground intelligence man, Lieutenant Colonel Marion Drobik, had been arrested and taken to jail.
Later, his sister, his brother-in-law, and their daughter were also arrested and taken to jail near Warsaw. Drobik, whose code name was
Szieciol ("woodpecker"), had been tansferred to the infamous Gestapo
prison Pawiak, in Warsaw. He had very sensitive information that could
endanger many people. He had to be liberated or assassinated before he
was tortured into divulging the identities of other key people. It also
had been learned that the women had been transferred to the Gross-
Rosen concentration camp. There was nothing that could be done for
them.

The question put to Maria was, "Would you convince the German
engineer to help the Underground free Drobik before he talks?" The
Underground would provide assistance and cover, but could not pene-
trate the prison. Fritz was selected because his reputation with the Underground was very solid and because only a German could get inside
the prison. Graebe agreed to help, and he set about developing a plan.
He would enter the prison disguised as a German army dentist assigned
to conduct routine examinations of the prisoners. However, as the plans
and props were being arranged by the Underground, something went
wrong, though Graebe never learned what, and the entire effort was
scrapped.

In the meantime, Graebe received an urgent telegram from Elizabeth.
The message urged him to return to Junkerath immediately. During his
absence, uniformed members of the Party, the local police, and the
Gestapo had come to the train demanding to know what assignment
kept them in the region. They also demanded an audience with Graebe,
and they were prepared to board the train in order to examine the records of the firm. Elizabeth, faithful to her charge, informed them that

her boss was in Warsaw, that she was in command, and that they would necessarily have to wait until Herr Graebe was present before they could look at anything. The leader of the eight-man group threatened to arrest Elizabeth and the others on the spot for interfering with the work of the Reich. In spite of her terror, Elizabeth held firm and produced the letter of instructions from Graebe. The men studied it quietly and carefully. For reasons that have never been clear, the authorities did not pursue the matter any further than to direct Elizabeth to wire Graebe, and they advised her that they would return to meet him.

This was the third action instigated against Graebe. His careful record-keeping had protected him against the embezzlement and the tax fraud charges. This time, the authorities had more nebulous charges to bring—it was a case of pure harassment. The charges were of protecting Jews and providing Jews with special considerations (food, shelter, employment, papers, money), and the unauthorized transporting of Jews from a region under the jurisdiction of the Reich Regional Command. A warrant had been issued for Graebe's arrest, but it could not be served until he returned from Warsaw. In his own land, he was to be accorded the right of due process, whereas if he had been in Poland or the Ukraine he might well have been summarily executed.

During the weeks before Fritz returned to Junkerath, Elizabeth took it upon herself to visit the chief of the military police to discuss the case. As it turned out, the man had a Polish name and spoke fluent Polish. Because of Elizabeth's concern, he became sympathetic. He told her to follow her instructions and that because the case was under his jurisdiction, he would handle any problems until Graebe returned. Elizabeth represented herself to this man as yet another Polish citizen who was not tolerated or accepted by the Germans. Of course, she never let on that she was Jewish.

Several days later, six of the original group of officials returned to the train. Elizabeth could honestly say that she had wired Graebe (which she was certain they knew since the Party monitored all phone and Telex communications) and that she had no idea when he would return. She boldly advised them that the matter was at rest until the return of the German engineer, and that everything was under the jurisdiction of the chief of the Military Police. They did not return again.

As soon as Fritz arrived back in Junkerath, he went straight to Elizabeth. When she saw him, the emotional dam burst. She was terrified and could hardly stop crying long enough to share the details of the encounter. After hearing the story and identifying the cast of characters, Graebe began plotting his strategy.

"First thing in the morning I will contact my lawyer in Solingen to see if he knows anything. He can advise me. Then I shall go directly to Gestapo headquarters in Cologne and try to get the file they are building on me."

"Herr Graebe!" Elizabeth protested. "Are you absolutely out of your mind? They will take you to a camp and kill you."

"I don't think they have enough on me to even detain me. They have been fishing for evidence, but I think I can turn the tables on them— even if they know some of the things I have been doing."

The next morning, after a nearly sleepless night spent carefully planning his script for the encounter, Graebe called his lawyer. Fritz was stunned by what the lawyer related. The lawyer revealed that he himself had been a faithful member of the Party for many years. Without notifying Graebe, the lawyer had sat with Gestapo and Jung officers while they discussed the plan to indict and remove Graebe from the firm. The lawyer represented the interests of the Party at the meeting, but had not revealed that he was also Graebe's attorney.

"My old friend," said the lawyer, "let me give you some important advice. It is you or them—just like in war. One of you will be the victim. This time they are being perfectly scrupulous in their charges against you. Their intention is to charge you—a warrant has been issued—and place everyone in your family into a concentration camp."

This revelation had a deadening effect on the ill-prepared rescuer. After the phone call he had second thoughts about his plan to confront the Gestapo in their own offices at Cologne. *Perhaps,* he thought, *I should return to Warsaw and hide there until the war is over. But what will become of Elisabeth and Friedel?* Time was short. By now the lawyer might have warned the others that Graebe had returned.

If he tried to escape, he would look guilty. This might further endanger his family, and he could not protect them if he was hiding in Warsaw or traveling with a group from the Underground. The alternatives were dangerously limited. He decided to take a regular civilian train to Cologne in case he changed his mind; he also feared that the authorities would be watching for his private train.

I decided that I would continue my plan. I truly believed I could use a bluff to get out—just as I had done so many times in the Ukraine. The authorities in Cologne were unlikely to be aware of my style. My lawyer was willing to take my defense, but it seemed too much a conflict of interest and his final words hung heavily in my mind: "You can no longer stand out against the Party and you must leave the Jung firm."

Fritz Graebe was ready to terminate his association with Jung, but all his assets were tied up in the firm. So one more stop was necessary before boarding the train for Cologne. Fritz went to visit a trusted confidant, Rudolf Wasserlos. Wasserlos had advised Graebe's father and Fritz on financial matters and once, in 1942, had visited Graebe while he was on leave from Sdolbonov. At that time Fritz had shared with Wasserlos the news of the massacre in Rovno. Wasserlos felt that Hitler was unaware of such things and that this practice reflected the attitude of middle-level functionaries whose behavior was sabotaging the decency of Adolf Hitler's rise to power.

This current visit with Wasserlos in 1944 was an opportunity for Fritz to explain how and why the Jung firm wanted to dismiss him.

"Why, Fritz? Why would they wish to harm someone with a record as distinguished as yours?"

"Because, Herr Wasserlos, I have employed Polish civilians, refugees, and others who—"

Wasserlos's face flushed as he interrupted. "Enough! Enough. I don't want to hear anything more."

To hear something in those days was to be complicit in the very act itself. However, Wasserlos agreed to help Graebe if he was indeed fired from the firm. Graebe left Wasserlos's office for the Junkerath train station and the short trip to Cologne.

When he arrived in Cologne, Fritz carefully worked himself into a theatrical rage in preparation for the confrontation; it was much like the times in the Ukraine. He walked up and down the street until he was certain of his strategy and that he was prepared to be assertive. He burst through the door of Gestapo headquarters, walked past the guards at the desk, entered the office of the chief, and presented himself, saying, "I am Fritz Graebe." He then carefully spelled out his name.

The Gestapo chief stared at Fritz, but failed to offer him a chair, so Graebe pulled up his own chair and made himself comfortable. Dramatic silence punctuated this ritualistic entrance.

Graebe had carefully chosen his clothing for the occasion; he knew that most German officials made certain immediate assessments based on appearance. They would make assumptions about Graebe's position in the command hierarchy based on his clean, sharp attire and his high-topped black boots.

Graebe initiated the confrontation. "So! What do you have for me that keeps me from my important work?"

"Herr Graebe, you will let me do the talking and you will answer my questions."

"No! Now you wait. I have my own questions and first we will deal with mine, not yours."

An argument ensued over the priority of questions. The chief was raising his voice, demanding that his questions be treated first. Fritz saw the opportunity to shift the flow of the event. Leaning across the table, he banged his fist on the desk and, half-enraged, half-pensive, he spoke.

"It's crazy—beyond belief. We need to win the war. You want that, I want that. I go to the Ukraine and work my damned ass off and people sit in the comfort of their fancy offices far from the fronts and innocently sabotage the war effort. Isn't that crazy?"

"What do you mean by that charge, Herr Graebe?"

Graebe relaxed. He had triggered the defensive response that he wanted. The chief continued.

"Here in Gestapo headquarters we have our own suspicions about you."

"Oh, really? And what is it that you suspect about me?"

"Herr Graebe, don't pretend that you are unaware of the Jewish matters against you."

"Yes! I have heard vague rumors that are being spread by others. But are you aware of directives originating in Berlin, commanding us at the front to use all available forms of labor? I hire every worker I can find. How else can I advance the cause of the war effort? I had four thousand men and women working all winter out there in the Ukraine. I don't give a damn if my workers are Poles, peasants, or Jews! All I want is hard work, progress, and no troubles. Do you understand what it takes to win a war using railroad lines?" Fritz spat the words out of his mouth without pausing to take a breath.

"Herr Graebe, wait a minute. You don't need to get mad. What it takes to win a war is a military matter—"

Graebe could now spring the trap. Almost as if he were alone and speaking to himself he said, "I knew it. You've sat in a comfortable office for so long that you have forgotten the unity of this effort. Every day I see wounded soldiers who give up their precious German blood on the front, and I rededicate myself to win the war. Refugees, Jews—damn it, all that is irrelevant to the war effort."

During this outpouring, the Gestapo chief had reached nervously into a drawer, removed a thick file, and placed in on his desk. He opened it carelessly and was thumbing through it as Graebe continued. Never once did Graebe look down at the file.

"I must report all of this to Berlin—the traitors who—"

"To whom do you report in Berlin, Herr Graebe?"

"I cannot tell you."

"You mean you don't know."

"On the contrary, sir. It is better for you that you do not know to whom I report." Leaning over the desk again, Fritz waved his finger at the Gestapo chief. "I cannot answer your question because the answer is a secret."

With that, Graebe stood up and looked directly at the file. It was nearly an inch thick with official letters, even a few pictures, and several letters on Jung stationery.

"Sit down, Herr Graebe."

"Tell me something, Herr Gestapo Chief. Do you have the other file on me, too?"

Absolutely confused, the chief again stumbled. "What other file?"

"You know the one. My file with the positive answers to all the treasonous charges contained in your petty files. The file that documents all that I and my workers have done for this war effort. You are wasting my time. Twice before, people from the Jung firm tried to sabotage my part in the war effort—now this, and from the military! Certainly you know better than to believe people who are consumed by a struggle to take charge of a big, prosperous company."

Graebe slowly, carefully pushed his chair back, stood up, adjusted his coat, and walked out of the office. It was obvious that his dramatic presentation had upset and confounded the Gestapo chief. The chief, who at one moment had thought he had a solid case, was now beset with doubts and confusion. The Gestapo did not call Fritz again.

If one confrontation was such a success, two might be good security, or so Fritz thought. He next headed for his lawyer's office. With the Gestapo disarmed, it was now time to slow the pursuit by the Party leadership. His visit to the lawyer was brief. After he recounted the incident with the Gestapo chief, Fritz concluded, "What did I do—am I having my head cut off because I am a patriot? Because I built railroad lines and laid track in the Ukraine?"

The lawyer, who was by now not unsympathetic, responded, "Be cautious, Herr Graebe. They will continue collecting things."

"Who are they?"

"The Jung people, of course. You'll have to use your imagination to protect yourself. Now, good day, my friend—be careful."

The train trip back to Junkerath, via Grafrath, was a relief. The plotting had been slowed, and the officials at each level had had to regroup and begin again. It had been a success. A brief two-day stopover at home with Elisabeth and Friedel offered the rest and love that Fritz needed to release the tensions of the past month. It also gave him an opportunity to terminate his responsibilities with the Jung firm. Their decision to force Graebe out had been reached some time earlier. When Graebe now arrived at the office, there was a nasty encounter with the widows of Josef and Max Jung and with Fritz Mandler. In his usual unrelenting style, Graebe held out. He threatened, and finally settled for a cash buy-out by the firm. Mandler raged during the entire three-hour meeting, protesting that the concessions were too large. The firm's lawyer finally spoke, warning Mandler, "Don't push Graebe too far, because we don't know how much Herr Graebe has in his files."

Graebe took their bank draft and left the office. It was a depressing moment for him; he had hoped to make a career of engineering in his own community.

Now, having some funds, he returned to Junkerath where he had determined that he would seek contracts for himself, keep the supply train, and all the materials and equipment. Arriving in Junkerath, he found Elizabeth in hysterics. While he had been away, a group of uniformed soldiers had raided the train. They had taken one hundred of the Jewish workers to Cologne. This action was more than harassment. The Jews had been without a contract and were therefore technically unemployed. A labor recruitment unit had previously spotted the idle workers, checked with the military authorities in Cologne, and taken the people to work in some factory.

Graebe went directly to his colleague and adviser, Rudolf Wasserlos, and complained bitterly. "These people in Cologne are crazy. All they do is harass me. First they call me from my work, then they arrest my workers."

The next morning, Fritz and Wasserlos took the train to Cologne. It rained the entire day. For an hour they stood in the rain arguing with the Jung supervisor who was now in command of the workers, and with the Gestapo officer in charge of labor recruitment. It was no use. Soaking wet, the two men returned to Junkerath on the afternoon train. The worst fears of the Jews now in custody in Cologne had come true.

That night Fritz reviewed the railroad and military maps for the area, trying to anticipate where he could find work for the remaining people. Suddenly, it occurred to him: The Gestapo had crossed over their boundary to arrest his people. The train and its workers were under the jurisdiction of the army office in Westphalia. It was a small technicality, but it might work. The next morning found Graebe in the army headquarters for his region.

"I am on a secret mission and I have lost my workers to the officials in Cologne. They cannot know the secret details of my mission, and they refuse to return my workers. You must accompany me to Cologne and help me retrieve my workers."

"I must know what your mission is and to whom you report."

"Forgive me," Graebe shot back, "I cannot divulge that information to you for the same reasons that I cannot tell them. Later, when I file my reports in Berlin, perhaps they will tell you. My report will, of course, note whether or not you were able to help me in this difficult matter."

Another trip to Cologne, another confrontation—it was becoming a habit. This time Fritz and his new army ally went directly to the district superintendent of railroads for the Cologne-Düsseldorf region. Graebe let the army officer do the talking. After patiently listening to the banter between the two men, Graebe interrupted.

"Gentlemen, this is all well and good, but I have a time schedule to keep. Can you not settle your territorial disputes and make up your minds to return my workers?"

"Patience, Herr Graebe."

"Patience! When I file my report in Berlin they will not be interested in my patience. They want results. My report will indicate responsibility and consequences—nothing about patience."

The district superintendent was a very territorial man. He was quite possessive of his limited authority and of any staff or workers in his area or command. His reply was terse.

"Don't threaten me with your talk about consequences, Herr Graebe."

"Do I take my workers or not?"

"You do not take them."

"Then my report will talk about consequences—for both of you."

"Herr Graebe," the army officer interrupted, "would you let us speak privately for fifteen minutes?"

Graebe agreed and waited outside. When he was called back into the office, the district superintendent asked him to submit a list of the people who were to be returned. He returned to Junkerath, prepared the list, and shortly the workers were all returned. Graebe's Jews were again safe.

The petty harassments continued. The SS made regular raids on the train and on a warehouse used by Graebe. They carefully studied every detail of his current reports and requisitions, hoping to find that Graebe was issuing too many rations or hiding supplies. The SS occasionally followed Graebe, trying to trap him. They tried to trick him into some complicitous acts so that they could arrest him. Building inspectors and city engineers seemed to take extraordinary interest in every detail of a plan, a drawing, or a project.

One day when Fritz was in Solingen on business, a city engineer stopped him on the street.

"Herr Graebe, we need to talk to you."

"Yes."

"You know that the Americans are close, very close. We must build a series of residential bunkers for the sentries and civilians. We want you to design and build them."

"Isn't this a little late if the American Army is indeed that close? And why do you ask me when there are so many other companies in Solingen—all of them bigger than me?"

"Herr Graebe, we know all about your work in the Ukraine. All the other companies have no guts. You do. We'll give you all the materials and supplies that you'll need. Will you do it for us?"

"Of course—I have built many bunkers. Call me in Junkerath and we can begin working on the details of your concern."

They shook hands and parted. It was a confusing situation: Was it a conspiracy to trap Fritz? Were they setting him up for another Action?

> I knew that my work was good and that I was a respected engineer, but I was suspicious of this offer, coming so soon after the confrontations with the Gestapo and with the continuing harassment of the SS.

Even if the offer to build the bunkers had been legitimate, it was too late. Allied troops were moving from the west, and some of the divisions were reported to be within one hundred fifty kilometers of the region. The bunkers were never discussed again, nor were they ever built.

The summer of 1944 was fateful for the Third Reich. The Soviet Army was nearing the eastern borders of the Reich, while the American and British Armies were preparing to move against the western borders. In Berlin, conspirators among the top generals on Hitler's command staff were secretly planning an assassination, using the code name "Valkyrie." On June 6, 1944, the Allies launched their surprise invasion through Normandy. By July 4, the Russians had opened the Polish border region and were moving through Poland toward East Prussia. On July 20, Colonel Klaus von Stauffenberg detonated the bomb intended to kill Adolf Hitler. The barbarism that followed the unsuccessful plot was virtually without parallel in the annals of war. Trials and killings continued into 1945. And the war was finally converging on Germany. For the first time in years, German soldiers were to be required to fight on German soil to protect their country.

In Junkerath as Fritz Graebe pondered the fate of his country, he decided that he had to reunite his family. Elisabeth had placed Friedel in a small, private residential boys' school in Pruem, near the Belgian frontier. Fritz called Elisabeth, shared his plan, and drove to the school, which sat behind a massive, eight-to-ten-foot rock and concrete wall.

When he arrived in his Mercedes, he found many frustrated and enraged parents standing in front of the locked steel gates of the school. He asked as to the problem. One man reported that the school's headmaster was refusing to release the students to the custody of their parents. Apparently the headmaster had been directed by the military authorities to have the young boys clear antitank trenches in the area near the two-thousand-year-old Roman city of Trier. Hitler's Panzer units were on the move, and the military was anticipating the arrival of the Allied tanks. The trenches were an essential line of defense. To make the trenches operative, hundreds of boys between the ages of twelve and sixteen were being forced into the labor columns.

Graebe rang the bell at the front gate. Shortly, a man came to the gate, opened it, and asked, "What do you want here?"

"I am from the Reich Railroad Administration, and I must speak to the headmaster."

"What is it about?"

"It is a very private matter which I dare not discuss publicly."

Fritz was escorted to the office of the headmaster, an unctuous hunchback named Dr. Nieman. The two men exchanged pleasantries for a few minutes. Nieman asked Graebe who he was and what he did. Graebe described his work, embellishing its importance to the war effort, and concluded, "My son Friedel is one of your students."

"Ah, yes. I know him. He is a very good student."

"I have come to remove him from the school. I have been transferred several hundred kilometers away and I want him to be near me."

"You cannot take him."

Fritz laughed and played along. "You don't understand, Dr. Nieman. I have a car and it will not be a problem."

"You don't understand, Herr Graebe. It is not that you cannot take him; you are not allowed to take him. I am under orders from the military command to place all the boys at the antitank trenches."

Fritz insisted that he at least be allowed to see and to speak with Friedel. One of the monitors went upstairs and brought Friedel down.

"Friedel, I have been transferred. Go pack your suitcase and prepare to leave at once."

Friedel knew about the work assignments in the trenches, and his eyes shifted from his father to Dr. Nieman.

"You cannot do that, sir. These boys are needed for the total mobilization of the Fatherland."

Graebe looked directly at his son and ordered him, "Go! Pack! Now! Don't make me angry."

As Friedel raced up the stairs, the headmaster continued to protest, but to no avail. Friedel came downstairs within twenty minutes. Together the two walked quickly to the front gate. The monitor opened the door, which had a handle only on the inside, and slammed it shut as soon as they crossed the threshold. The waiting parents were astonished.

"How did you get your son out?"

"I am transferred and I told the headmaster that I was taking my son with me to another school."

Graebe drove away as the parents banged on the gate and shouted their protests to those inside in the school.

> I had heard that the military command might use children to
> build the antitank barriers. This was particularly dangerous work.
> As it was, nearly sixty boys from the Pruem school died building
> those barriers. Most were crushed by tanks or walls caving in. I
> thank God that I had the strength to rescue my son.

Fritz drove back to Junkerath, called Elisabeth in Grafrath and, later the same day, put his son on a train to Solingen. With his wife and son safely reunited and away from the war zone, Graebe reviewed the plans he had been making to get his people out of the area.

In the early days of September 1944, the Reich Security Police issued orders to evacuate the Junkerath region. All German nationals and all assigned workers or refugees were immediately moved east, into the interior part of the country.

Graebe refused to obey the order from the police. Soon a small contingent of indignant Security Police were knocking at the train station office in Junkerath. They demanded his departure; Graebe refused. When they challenged his authority to disobey an official order, Graebe reverted to what had become a ritual excuse.

"Gentlemen, I appreciate your concern, but I have received different instructions from higher authorities. These I must obey, not yours."

The Security Police insisted, but Graebe continued the litany. "If you try to force me I will include that fact in my report to Berlin and you will be held responsible. The consequences will be quite unpleasant."

It sounds unbelievable, but it worked again. One might imagine that the frequent repetition of this excuse would eventually devalue it as the authorities became accustomed to it, but Graebe knew the German mind. He knew that a lower level of officialdom would rarely question a higher level for fear of bureaucratic reprisals. The secret was not to overplay one's hand. Fritz was careful about being sincerely officious rather than bullish and frothing. It worked!

Graebe and his crew, which included Maria (she had been unable to meet up with the Poltava group after they had left from Chernovitz, so she had traveled by train from Warsaw carrying official Jung transit papers and a visa) languished for two weeks more in the no-man's-land of Junkerath, between the Siegfried Line and the Belgian border. In those first weeks of August 1944, the U.S. First Army had moved through Belgium, capturing Namur and Liége, and then east, taking the city of Aachen. The U.S. Third Army moved from the south through Verdun and on to the French city of Metz near the border of Luxembourg and Germany. Fritz Graebe knew what the Allied forces would soon discover for themselves. The highly acclaimed Siegfried Line was nearly abandoned and unarmed.

11. Bearing Witness to the Unspeakable

The few remaining days on German soil were frighteningly quiet for Graebe's group. A stillness settled over the area as the Allies and the Germans moved into and secured their respective positions. Fritz and Maria discussed the limited number of options available to them, and they decided that a westward movement would be the safest possibility for the group. Because Graebe had no way of predicting what fate he and his colleagues would meet, he decided to leave Elisabeth and Friedel in Grafath, not even telling them that he was moving his workers. It would be safer for them, and he could eventually find them after the war ended. In the meantime, Maria met with the Jews and other Polish workers to present the alternatives and to invite their participation in the decision. The prospects were not good for any who remained in that region because the Security Police and local citizens could turn against the unemployed Jews at any moment. There was no guarantee that the U.S. Army would liberate the area in time to save them should such an Action begin. To follow the general evacuation into the interior of Germany would be even more dangerous. Jewish refugees were still being pursued and summarily dispatched either to labor camps or to extermination sites, or were killed on the spot.

The majority of the group elected to remain with Graebe, and only about seventy ventured off alone. Preparations were begun for an evacuation late that very night. The route of escape would be to the southwest, through the Eifel Mountains, to Belgium and a hoped-for linkup with the Allied forces. Several people were posted as sentries around the train in the event that the SS decided to stage another raid. Others packed their few goods and possessions and loaded them onto horses or one of the several wagons that had been commandeered. Some of the engineering equipment was loaded, but most was left behind in order to make more room for the passengers. All the essential papers were placed in six or seven crates and loaded on a wagon.

The Jews were about to set out on yet another phase of this twentieth-century exodus. Like Moses on Mount Nebo they felt as if they were halfway between the Promised Land and the pursuing armies of Pharaoh. The Moses of Rovno was again their leader, but even he did not know what awaited them beyond the mountain range.

When they began the journey late in the night, the group included a pregnant woman and her husband. Many of the younger children were on the wagons; most of the one hundred thirty walked in small clusters behind the wagons. Fritz and Maria rode on the wagon that contained the engineering equipment and the vital records of their work.

Graebe had directed his office staff to identify every Jewish worker on large payroll ledger forms, including the victims of the tragic Actions in the various towns and work sites. If this wandering group of refugees did manage to find safety and sympathetic soldiers, the records would be very important. Graebe would have a record of their existence. The chronicles of names would be testimony to the tragedy that befell the Jews in the Ukraine. Fritz was determined that the record of their existence not be lost, not to history or to prosecutors. The crates also contained Fritz's personal diaries, written in a complicated script known as "shorthand-shorthand." (It is said that Adolf Hitler too had used this script because so few people knew how to decode the words.) Graebe's mother had taught him this style of notation in his early years, as a means of improving the accuracy of his classwork and to give him a competitive edge over his classmates.

The group walked until early the next evening, pausing only to rest briefly. They entered a German village from which the civilians had been evacuated. As people were getting settled, Maria and several others scouted the area and went through the empty houses. They discovered some food in a few of the houses, but hardly enough to help feed the group. What little they did find was of great value, however, because they had been unable to secure many provisions in Junkerath.

One of the fears of the group was that German patrols would circle back into the area to check on foreign troop movements. Fritz recalls that first night in vivid detail:

> I remember the fear on that night in the abandoned village. We knew we could not set cooking or warming fires because the smoke might attract soldiers, who would assume that we were part of an advancing army group. If the Allied forces were nearby,

they might believe that we were part of the German Army. In either case we might draw fire. If the Gestapo happened to be in the area searching for stragglers or refugees and observed the smoke, they would arrest us all. We did set up several sentry posts, but the people were so exhausted that they could not really serve as guards against the many dangers that were lurking about.

The group decided to remain at the village for two days. There was a stillness about this isolated mountain region. It was a restful counterpoint to the chaos and fury that had encircled and followed Graebe, Maria, and the others throughout the years in Sdolbonov and Poltava.

Early in the morning on the second day, Maria remembered that she had left some tomatoes in a wagon that had been carefully hidden on higher ground. The crisp smells of the autumn morning and the stillness of the sparsely wooded hillside filled Maria with serenity as she walked to the wagon. Only as she started back to the village did she notice the strange silence of the birds. At the same moment she spotted six soldiers with fixed bayonets and rifles at the ready, moving cautiously through the trees. The men appeared to be wearing SS uniforms and were walking down the trail that led to the village.

Carefully, quietly, Maria lowered herself and the two baskets of tomatoes to the ground. It was too late; one of the scouts had seen Maria, and suddenly six rifles and a pistol were aimed at her. Because of the distance separating them, it would have been futile for the soldiers to shoot. Maria ignored the shouts and signals of the patrol leader, who was obviously an officer, and walked quickly back to the village. She even bent down to pick up the baskets of tomatoes. Though she could not bring herself to turn around to look, Maria knew that the soldiers were following.

Graebe had fallen very sick, with flulike symptoms, shortly after he had arrived in the village. Severe stomach cramps kept him confined to a bed. Elizabeth, who had been looking after him in an upstairs room, met Maria at the door of the house. Everyone could hear the panic in their voices.

"Oh God, Elizabeth. The worst has happened. An SS patrol spotted me and followed me here. They'll be here any minute!"

Without warning, rifle butts banged against the hastily barricaded door.

"What shall we do?" Elizabeth screamed. "They'll throw grenades and kill us all."

"Quick, quick! Open the door before they start shooting!"

Maria pushed away several chairs as Elizabeth turned the handle. Suddenly the door burst open and all six riflemen crashed simultaneously through the tiny door jamb. The several men in the room were hastily pushed, face first, against the walls, while the women were moved at bayonet point to the opposite wall. The soldiers were talking rapidly while their commanding officer shouted over the din. It was obvious that everyone was terribly frightened, especially the soldiers themselves.

Elizabeth, who spoke six languages fluently, started explaining in German that the entire group was composed of unarmed German civilians. Elizabeth's elderly mother, who was facing one of the finely sharpened bayonets, whispered, "Elizabeth, you fool. Those are American soldiers. Not one of them is a German."

To Maria and Elizabeth, all soldiers looked alike with their helmets, green-brown uniforms, and rifles. The insignia meant little to the uninitiated civilians. The group turned out to be composed of an American major and scouts who were checking the area before a full column of American troops advanced into the area.

The major had many questions for this group. Because Elizabeth spoke reasonably good English, she was able to answer most of the questions. The major wanted to know about Germans in the area, but no one knew about the troops. Elizabeth explained that they were on the Siegfried Line, but that it was mostly abandoned by the soldiers and civilians, who had moved farther into the central areas of Germany. She told them about the German who had helped them and who was ill and resting in the upstairs room.

While two of the soldiers searched the house and another went up to check on Fritz, Elizabeth began relating the experiences of the refugees from the Ukraine. The major must have known something of the horror, but he had no real understanding. One report after another shocked him into a realistic awareness of the Nazi regime and its persecutions. Elizabeth also was quick to point out the kindness and bravery of the German engineer.

It was clear that the immediate vicinity was part of a targeted war zone. It was not safe to sit there and talk any longer. The major could not leave the people in the area because he could not verify their stories and because it would soon be under attack by fighter planes and ground troops.

"There is a tunnel nearby. I must take all of you with me to this place. Please prepare yourselves quickly and travel with a minimum of luggage."

No one in the group was aware of a tunnel in the area, but that did not slow their excited preparations to move toward safety and away from the Nazi dangers. Within the hour, everyone was ready to travel, the phone lines were cut, and Fritz was carried downstairs and placed into a waiting wagon. He was still too sick to walk or even to be questioned at that point. As they approached the abandoned train tunnel, the contingent of refugees and soldiers had to cross a wide-open expanse of ground.

Suddenly shots rang out. Bullets struck all around the group, while the American soldiers returned the fire. Elizabeth was with the man who had the horses. The gunfire frightened the horses so much that they had to be cut free. Mercifully no one in the group was wounded, but several soldiers were hit. All the people, soldiers and civilians, made it into the protection of the tunnel.

American troops were massing on the other side of the tunnel. They had been alerted by radio phone to the impending arrival of the refugees. They heard the shooting and sent a group of sharpshooters to assist the others and to return the fire. A medic immediately began to treat the wounded and then turned his attention to the ailing engineer, whose face and body were now covered with blisters and seeping sores. For the next two weeks the refugees lived in the dark, damp tunnel.

By day, German patrols ranged through the area, firing on anything that moved. The American soldiers who stood guard entertained themselves with card games. By night, the Americans made small reconnaissance sorties into the hills and forests. To the refugees, the war seemed now to be at a standoff. The First and Third American Armies, which had made rapid, significant advances from the Normandy coast into the interior of Central Europe, were strangely calm. The supplies they needed to continue the fighting were unavailable unless they were dropped by parachute or trucked four hundred miles across the country from the beachheads. In the meantime, the demoralized Reich High Command began to obey Hitler's admonitions to protect the Fatherland and, in turn, the beleaguered troops and newly recruited soldiers rallied behind the generals. For three months, the military efforts were stalemated on all sides.

During the two weeks that the refugees lived in the tunnel, Fritz slowly recovered and both Elizabeth and Maria told the American officers about the exploits of Graebe's groups. Knowledge of Graebe's activities influenced the Americans to treat him with respect and as an ally rather than as a prisoner of war. Because supplies for the Front were limited, the Americans decided to evacuate the Graebe group through the tunnel and relocate them in the Belgian city of St. Vith. In evacuating the refugees, the Americans admitted that their war efforts were not going well in the region. Once through the tunnel, the entire group was loaded onto trucks and driven to St. Vith.

Graebe's health fully returned during the two months that the group was in St. Vith. Maria spent most of her time befriending American soldiers of Polish descent. Surprisingly, the days were not spent in debriefings or interrogations. The military attention was directed at breaking the stalemate. The cold weather of the early winter had set in, keeping the people and the armies fairly immobile. Early in December, one of the young Polish-American soldiers presented Maria with a goose that he had shot. The goose was left hanging outside in the cold to be cooked for a holiday dinner.

This period, though relatively inactive, was hard on everyone. The soldiers were preparing for what would become a protracted battle. Other armies were having no success in challenging the defense of the Fatherland. The presence of so many strange, foreign-speaking refugees, with their gruesome tales of life under the Nazis, made the soldiers even more nervous.

On December 16, 1944, the worst fears of the Allies became reality as the German counteroffensive, known as the Battle of the Bulge, began. Prior to this counteroffensive, members of the U.S. Army Intelligence Corps in Verdun, France, had received and reviewed reports on Graebe's unusual group of Germans and Poles. They made an initial contact with Elizabeth, but the St. Vith area was too dangerous. The Americans prepared to take Fritz, Maria, and Elizabeth to the city of Verdun and there interview them. The other refugees were to be moved southwest out of the battle zone.

The evacuation of the three leaders proved to be a complicated task. They had carefully shepherded their records and documents in order to have some proof of the Nazi atrocities. Maria would not go anywhere without the documents. But the crates became a logistical problem. The soldiers wanted to leave them in St. Vith. But Maria prevailed, and the crates were finally loaded onto trucks amid the chaos created by the British Air Corps bombing runs.

Fritz, Maria, and Elizabeth were placed into the custody of an American counterintelligence unit that would move them to the noncombat zone for the continuation of the interrogations. For reasons that are unclear, the three got as far as the Belgian city of Liége, where they were placed in a large detention camp with civilians and soldiers from Poland, Yugoslavia, Czechoslovakia, Russia, Italy, and various other countries.

Their entrance into the camp was very unpleasant. The surly guards, fearful of spies and infiltrators, nervously handled their charges with an abrupt, pushy kind of behavior that alienated the detainees. As part of the reception and processing, men and women were separated and all personal effects were searched. Maria's suitcase contained an expensive, small-caliber pistol that Graebe had given her for protection. Maria feared that the discovery of the pistol would certainly make matters worse for everyone and lead to a special jail cell for all of them.

Before she would submit her luggage to a search, Maria demanded to speak with a Polish liaison officer. The guards refused, stating flatly that she could meet the officer only after she had been processed, but Maria argued on. Finally, in order to speed the process along, Major Kempinski, who was a member of the Polish government-in-exile, arrived to meet with Maria. Obviously inconvenienced by her vociferous protests, Kempinski was very unpleasant and short-tempered.

"Lady," he said in Polish, "I don't know what you are doing, but you are bringing shame to Poland by your attitude and behavior. Now just what do you want?"

Maria exploded, "Now you listen to me! I went through hell in the Ukraine while you sat in London. I am a Jewish woman who somehow got away from the Nazis. Either you help me, as one Pole to another, or get away from me, now!"

Kempinski quickly softened his position and, in a conciliatory spirit, offered to help. Maria explained that she had a weapon in her luggage. Kempinski offered to get rid of it and directed the guards not to search that one suitcase. He then did a cursory search, located the gun, and placed it in his pocket without anyone noticing. Later, Maria let him have the gun as a gift from her and Graebe.

Kempinski reviewed the relocation files on Maria and Elizabeth as the two women repacked their suitcases.

"Could we please talk over here for a while?" he asked them. The Polish officer took them to a separate room and began asking questions.

"Why isn't Herr Graebe kept with the other Germans, and why are you traveling with him?"

Maria informed him that for now, it was not his business and that he was asking the wrong questions. Instead of dealing with his agenda, Elizabeth and Maria spent the next six or seven hours relating to him the outline of their experiences and their eyewitness accounts of the fate that befell Polish Jews at the hands of the *Einsatzgruppen,* the labor columns, the Gestapo and SS units, and the antagonistic civilians. The major was dumbfounded by what he heard.

"Are you trying to tell me that the Jews are all dead?"

The women were silent.

"Are you trying to tell me that the Germans did all of these things?"

The women stayed silent.

Maria finally spoke, her voice breaking at each word. "Major Kempinski, I am not *trying* to tell you anything. I *am* telling you exactly what I saw with my own eyes."

"What about your friend, the German engineer? How does he fit into all of this?"

Maria retold the incidents from a different point of view. She described Graebe's compassion and bravery in detail.

Kempinski stood up at the end of the presentation. He started for the door and spoke numbly.

"You must tell these things to military intelligence. They still do not believe that these things have happened in the east."

"We have tried to tell them," explained Maria, "but they are preoccupied with other things. We thought we were going to Verdun to offer this testimony, but what happens? We are locked away in a detention camp."

Kempinski excused himself from the room and asked a guard to take the women to more comfortable quarters.

Soon several American intelligence officers presented themselves, asking to meet Graebe, Maria, and Elizabeth. They spoke English and German but not Polish. Nevertheless, the leader brought each of them into the room separately and began the questioning. The Polish major elected to be present for the questioning in case the women needed help with translation or support in describing their harrowing experiences.

"Did you see dead bodies?"

"Of course, I saw many dead bodies—almost all Jews."

"Did you ever witness an Action?"

"I have direct knowledge of one Action in which my husband was murdered and Herr Graebe knows of many other Actions."

Each of the three poured forth their testimony, memories, and nightmarish visions from those days in the Ukraine. At one point, when Graebe recounted the Rovno Action, an interrogator became physically ill and had to leave the room. Graebe volunteered to use his extensive archives to document the horrors, but the officers did not want to hear or read any more. Maria was called back to be asked more questions about Fritz Graebe's role in the rescues. They wanted to know about his evidence. Was it accurate? Who maintained the files? Maria's response closed the questioning.

"We Jews worked for him, and at his direction we kept lists, records, letters, diaries, and census reports on the workers." The testimony of the two Jewish women corroborated Graebe's account exactly.

Maria listened as Major Kempinski spoke in English to the intelligence officers. "This is a story for Severin Kavin—can you locate him?"

Maria, who did not know the meaning of the word *story*, grabbed at Kempinski's coat. "What did you say?"

Annoyed at this interruption, Kempinski pulled his jacket back into place and continued with the officer.

Maria pulled at him again. "What did you say?" she demanded.

"Please, you are interrupting me. We can talk more later."

Once more Maria demanded to know what he had said to his American counterpart. Realizing that he would not be allowed to continue until he explained, he gave Maria her information in Polish.

"I want you to tell your experiences to an American officer, Severin Kavin. He is a reporter assigned to the intelligence service and a specialist in psychological warfare. He is gathering stories like yours."

Maria's eyes filled with tears. "Oh, my God! I think I know him. He is my cousin."

Maria's response changed the nature and tone of the interview. The American quickly left the room and Kempinski questioned Maria about Kavin.

"What does he look like?"

"I don't know because we have been separated for many years."

"Where does he live in the United States?"

"I don't know that either, but my uncle could tell you because he kept in touch with them."

"Where did he live when he resided in Poland?"

Maria named the small village outside of Warsaw. Things began to check. By a bizarre twist of fate, Maria's first cousin, Severin Kavin, was assigned to this very camp. They had been raised together and had played together until early childhood, when Maria's uncle had taken Kavin's family to live in America.

Kempinski excused himself and came back in about twenty minutes with a photograph of two Germans and an American. All wore helmets and uniforms. Maria, who had no eye for the subtleties of military attire, was uncertain about the identity of her cousin.

"Listen, Maria, Kavin is my friend and if he is your cousin he can help you. I'll try to locate him."

"I am sorry. I have not seen him since 1928—nearly seventeen years since our childhood days."

Soon word reached the interrogation room that Kavin had departed for Paris to complete an assignment for the army. For the next five days, the intelligence staff continued their interrogation of the trio of rescuers. These sessions were halted when German V-2 rockets began falling in the countryside near the Belgian border. For security reasons, Graebe, Maria, and Elizabeth, and their interrogators were moved to Paris. Maria was certain that she would be reunited with her cousin.

Once in Paris, she began asking everyone about Kavin. Finally, she was told that he had left for the Belgian border—the area from which she and the others had just been evacuated. For two more weeks the group was questioned, and reports were developed. Once it was safe, they were taken from the army dormitories in Paris and were moved back to Verdun, where the intelligence forces were establishing their temporary headquarters.

Graebe, Maria, and Elizabeth were given rooms in a commandeered hotel that was bombed on the second day of their residency. As it turned out, the hotel also served as a residence for an important American general, who was the target of the bomb. One day while they were eating, an American officer at another table took exception to the presence of a German, Graebe, in the American officers' mess. He came to the table where the three were sitting and began to accuse Fritz of being a spy, suggesting that he ought to be arrested and detained in a special prison. This unnecessary and humiliating encounter led to an informal house arrest or detention for the three rescuers.

Undeterred by the harassment, Elizabeth tried to use the hotel phones to locate Severin Kavin in Paris. Civilian use of a phone was strictly forbidden, but after a time Elizabeth somehow convinced a soldier of her sincerity. For several days, she would go to the room of the general when he was out and use his private phone. Her persistence was rewarded when an operator in Paris who knew Kavin informed her that he had just arrived. Elizabeth immediately told Graebe, who ran to Maria's room while Elizabeth stayed on the phone awaiting the completion of the connection. When the two cousins were reunited over the phone lines, Maria soon knew that she was speaking with family. At his urging Maria briefly gave Kavin details of their experiences and a report on the fate of Jews in the Ukraine.

Two days later, Captain Severin Kavin and his first cousin Maria were tearfully reunited in Verdun. Kavin listened and recorded every detail of every incident reported by the trio. The combination of Kavin's reputation and the thorough documentation provided by the Graebe group freed the group from further suspicion and detention. It also legitimized the early accounts of the fate of Jews in Reich-occupied territories.

After the long, idle days of waiting in St. Vith, Liége, and Paris, Fritz again felt that he had a mission. The meetings with Kavin were very friendly, affirming, and energizing for the German engineer. Now no one thought of him as a spy or a self-serving turncoat. He was a witness. He could now meaningfully fulfill the covenants he had taken in the town square at Rovno and before the mass graves containing the countless bodies of Jews whom he had tried to help. He no longer had to think in terms of Actions, but instead in the legal category "war crimes."

> Most of the Jews I had saved were dead. I found it very hard to accept the limitations imposed on me by fate. My cunning should have been more effective than all the rifles of the Reich. My only consolation—and it took me a long time before I could accept it—was the knowledge that I gave some people a reprieve, an opportunity, a moment of life in a sea of death. Sometimes, now years later, I think of more things I could have done to save more people. I am not sure that anything would have worked better. I only wish that the people I had rescued could have been saved to see life on the other side of the war.

While Graebe, Maria, and Elizabeth had been living in the tunnel, British bombers had invaded the German airspace. A single squadron dropped nearly one thousand bombs on Solingen that December. Fritz did not learn of this raid until he reached Verdun. Because of the battles that were raging, it was impossible to determine the fate of his family.

Elisabeth Graebe had been told that her husband was a war casualty. This assumption had been made by those who knew of Graebe's refusal to move his people from the Junkerath region before the Allied troops reached it. In spite of her husband's silence, Elisabeth was not convinced by the rumors of her husband's death. She was certainly fearful, but she also knew that he was a resourceful man who could protect himself and his workers. During those days in Sdolbonov and through the days of the Rovno Action, she had released her husband. She knew that he had a mission which might cost him his life, so she had created a life for herself and their son.

After the devastating raids in December, she had many things to do to help her neighbors and family. The bombs had damaged or destroyed some of the buildings. Elisabeth Graebe quartered exhausted young soldiers and gave them the comfort of her home. She spent hours cleaning up, preparing food, making clothing and bandages, and comforting her neighbors. This important activity kept Elisabeth from brooding over the fate of her husband.

Graebe was not an easy man to categorize, particularly because his bold actions were so contradictory in a nation that had willingly followed its leaders into war and acts of atrocity. In Verdun, his interrogators had a very hard time convincing themselves that he was not a spy. The scene was repeated in St. Vith, Liége, Paris, and Verdun. In a chilly room without decoration, sitting on hard, stiff-backed chairs, two officers questioned Graebe. One officer sat opposite him, staring across an empty table. The other man paced nervously around the room, occasionally releasing a volley of questions and then retreating to the dusty window, where he could stare vacantly at the passing soldiers as Fritz repeated his answers.

Once Graebe lightheartedly challenged the men, because he sensed that they were not career soldiers. In fact, they were not. Both men were lawyers who had been drafted and were assigned the task of interrogating prisoners of war for the Twelfth Army Group—the unit assigned to prepare the war crimes cases. Their harshness with Graebe was a mask for their fear and ignorance. They simply did not know how to do their assigned tasks, and so they affected the roles that they believed were appropriate.

This routine of questioning continued as the officers repeated their questions, and Fritz answered them again and again.

"Once more, all right? Who are you—really?"

"I am Fritz Graebe. Herman Friedrich Graebe."

"Herr Graebe, you must appreciate the fact that your story is almost unbelievable. We don't understand how a construction engineer could do everything you claim to have done. What were your duties, again?"

"I've told you what I built and I'll tell you only one more time. I built any installations necessary for the railroads."

"Please give us more specific details."

"I built roundhouses, car barns, maintenance stations, storage bins, radio towers, and switching houses."

"In the Ukraine?"

"Of course, yes."

"During what period?"

"From October 1941, when I arrived in Sdolbonov, until I evacuated my people from Sdolbonov and Poltava on January 10, 1944."

"How were you connected to the Reich government?"

"Gentlemen, we have been over this repeatedly. I am becoming very impatient with you and your questions. I tell you again, for the final time, I was not a part of the government. I was the regional manager for the Jung firm of Solingen. We contracted with the government solely through the Railroad Administration."

The two inquisitors had a final critical question, one that was central to establishing the credibility of the German engineer:

"Herr Graebe, you had your own train. The only people who have their own trains are people who have great power. Your whole damned country is crumbling and you travel across the Ukraine, Poland, and Germany in your own train. Only a spy or a powerful agent of the state has his own train and can travel with such liberty. Which one are you, Herr Graebe?"

"I have had enough of this. I am neither. Either you accept that fact and get on with what is important, or you arrest me and charge me."

Graebe's remark came out of his weariness more than his anger and frustration, though there was a sufficient amount of both. The long weeks of waiting, the endless repetition of the same questions, followed by the same answers, were taking a toll on Fritz. He felt their distrust. He was impatient, knowing that the most important questions were going unasked and therefore unanswered. Fritz Graebe wanted them to ask about the *Einsatzgruppen,* about the mass graves near the airport in Dubno or behind the cement factory in Sdolbonov; he wanted them to ask for his lists of names of those who plotted, tortured, murdered, signed orders, and laughed. He had no more tolerance for mundane questions and routine procedures.

Adolf Hitler's suicide on April 30, 1945, and the German surrender eight days later enabled the Twelfth Army Group to dismantle their temporary headquarters in Verdun and open Operational Headquarters in Wiesbaden. The army units moved quickly into the German heartland. In early June, the Twelfth Army Group reached the Rhine River. They had to cross the swollen, fast-moving river on rubber rafts because all the bridges had been destroyed by bombings and last-ditch counter-offensives. Command jeeps and trucks bobbed on rafts in the river waiting for the orders to begin the crossing. Army sharpshooters with machine guns crouched on each raft, nervously fingering their triggers while scanning the river and the east bank for any signs of movement or hostile activity. Fritz, Maria, Elizabeth, and their intelligence service colleagues were in vehicles near the front of the line. When the signal came to begin the crossing, the soldiers became tense. As the third raft was launched into the river, gunners on the second raft began firing. On the bank, people dived for cover. A partially submerged log drifting by with the current had been mistaken for an enemy saboteur. For the next three hours the soldiers sniped nervously at anything moving in their direction.

On the fourth day, the intelligence officers and six soldiers accompanied Graebe, Maria, and Elizabeth in a search for a cache of documents that they had hidden shortly before their departure from Junkerath. Graebe and Maria had gone into the forested hillside late on a dark, misty night. They had carefully buried the crate and marked the spot so that they could return to reclaim their goods. The crate contained Jung contracts, payroll information, and documents issued in Rovno by Lieutenant Beck. These papers were not as critical as the ones that the trio had carried throughout their trip across Central Europe, but they would help establish the identities of the murdered Jews and offer even more concrete evidence for the prosecution of war criminals.

Months later and in daylight, the terrain was completely different in appearance. After three fruitless days of searching, the decision was made to abandon the effort and rejoin the group in Wiesbaden. The box of files was never recovered. One of the officers and Fritz were resting under a tree when Graebe mentioned that his home was located just over the next range of hills. The area had not been secured by the American Army so they could not visit, but the officer suggested that they might find a hilltop and look at the city. The small contingent of searchers set out for Haan and a small village on a high plain overlooking the rolling hills about fifteen kilometers from Grafrath. When they arrived, one of the soldiers removed a high-powered periscope from its case, scanned the area, and handed the instrument to Graebe. Although it would be six more months before the Graebe family would be reunited, Fritz had a brief, distant glimpse of his home and city. The devastation choked the German engineer. As he sighted his home, the periscope lens clouded with tears. His house had been spared the destruction of British bombers. From one window on each side of the building hung large white flags formed from bed linens. The knowledge that his family was safe and that soon they could be reunited gave Fritz the energy to continue his work with the Americans.

Once settled back in Wiesbaden, Graebe began a written reconstruction of every event and interaction that he had seen and every recollection that he had that related to the years of the Holocaust in the Ukraine. With Maria and Elizabeth, he compiled statistics on the Nazi genocide in the Ukraine. He carefully drew maps identifying the locations of massacres and tracing the movements of the *Einsatzgruppen*. One of the most awesome tasks was to transfer the names of his workers and their families onto lists that supplemented the description of each killing. This list seemed endless. With each name there was a birthdate, a birthplace, and wherever possible the identities of family members who were killed on the same date. Each list ended with a disclaimer asserting that "family members of the persons listed by name are mentioned only as far as these were known with certainty. Their number is therefore not complete." The lists were then read, translated, and attested to by Maria and Elizabeth before they were sworn in front of a representative of the Judge Advocate General's division.

After each of the lists was compiled, Graebe drew a detailed plot plan of the area in which the massacre had taken place. Roads, buildings, geological features, and other related identification points were marked so that the mass graves could be easily located by investigators who were traveling to the sites to prepare their cases for the Nuremberg trials. Following the map-making, Graebe, Maria, and Elizabeth carefully collated the Jung firm documents related to the particular location—contracts, work orders, design sheets, plans, payroll records, requisitions, photographs, copies of communications with the home office and other construction companies, and other general correspondence.

Drawing on his extensive diaries, written in the obscure "shorthand-shorthand," Graebe then began building lists of names identifying those people who were nationals and held regional powers, those who cooperated with the Nazis, those who led or cooperated in the Actions, and those who witnessed the killings. Maria and Elizabeth helped Graebe profile these people with their physical descriptions and write a brief statement about the activities of each.

After all these records were drawn together, Graebe sequestered himself for the most painful and taxing part of the war crimes process. A narrative account of each individual and group murder had to be written. In quiet quarters, months removed from the turmoil, these memories, visions, and promises flooded back into Graebe's mind. Each night brought an exhausting, tortuous alternation between sleeplessness and wrenching nightmares. By day, Fritz carefully and succinctly crafted the affidavits attesting to the murders of Jews, Polish peasants, and dissidents in the underground movement. His writing style was sparse and matter-of-fact, as witnessed in this report on the killing of young Hanna Prussak by the Ukrainian militiamen:

The Jewish girl, Joanna (Hanna) Prussak, born August 8, 1923, in Ogrodzieniec, daughter of the director of the cement works in Sdolbonov (deceased prior to 1939), was slain on August 20, 1942. The ten Jews taken by Otto Koeller as hostages were executed on August 24, 1942.

It was this seemingly emotionless style that was to make Graebe an ideal witness for the International Military Tribunal. What could not be seen in the handwritten, typed, and witnessed reports were the scars on the soul of this man and the private agony he revealed in his diary. The diary describes the blind rage that engulfed him whenever he thought of those to whom he referred as "my people," the ones he had failed to save.

As each affidavit was sworn and witnessed, it was assigned a case number. It then was necessary to go back through the lists and cross-reference the case numbers with the names of the victims, executioners, witnesses, and bystanders.

Because he had traveled throughout the Ukraine and fraternized with the police, railroad officials, military staff, and regional administrators for the Reich, Graebe had regularly heard tales of Actions and killings that he did not witness. The United Nations War Crimes Commission investigators prevailed upon him to prepare statements about even these rumored events and to identify witnesses whenever possible. From these documents the Commission was able to piece together its cases and locate both executioners and witnesses. In some cases, survivors were found and given the opportunity to testify.

For more than a year, this gruesome task of recollection and writing occupied the days and nights of the trio in Wiesbaden. There were few hours allotted for leisure; Graebe saved those for trips home to be with his family. He regularly worked for six straight weeks and then took a six-day sabbatical to travel by train to Grafrath. These family reunions had an uneven quality. Fritz was emotionally spent and physically exhausted from the daily chore of reliving and inscribing the record of the genocide that he had witnessed. Elisabeth and Friedel, on the other hand, rightly expected the full attention of their husband and father. It was not there. It is a testament to their love and mutual respect that the marriage survived those nightmarish months.

On November 10, 1945, Fritz was approached by one of the military lawyers, Herman Marcuse. Marcuse and Fritz had spent many hours together writing, questioning, and discussing. In spite of this, Marcuse's question today was unsettling.

"I want you to write down what you saw at Dubno in 1942."

Graebe's surprised response came quickly. "Why? You've recorded it yourself and I've already repeated it a dozen times."

"Please, Herr Graebe, I just want to see it from your hand in narrative form."

With that, Marcuse handed Graebe a sheaf of blank lined paper and abruptly left the room.

Fritz paced the room nervously for a long time before he could sit down to again reclaim the horror. When he finally began to write, the words flowed uninterrupted from his pen. As always, the words were carefully chosen and bereft of strong emotion. The starkness of the account was its own drama. Elizabeth was asked to translate the document into English, and later it was witnessed by Major Homer B. Crawford of the International Military Tribunal.

On November 13, the visit was repeated. This time the Americans requested a written statement describing the Action at Rovno. Again, Fritz complied, Elizabeth translated, and Crawford administered the oaths.

On August 8, 1945, the four major Allied powers, England, France, the Soviet Union, and the United States, had signed an agreement that specified the procedures and charges to be used in the war crimes trials. Two of the offenses were specified as follows:

> *War Crimes:* Namely, violations of the laws or customs of war. Such violations shall include, but not be limited to, murder, ill-treatment, or deportation to slave labor or for any other purpose, of civilian population of or in occupied territory, murder or ill-treatment of prisoners of war or persons on the seas, killing of hostages, plunder of public or private property, wanton destruction of cities, towns, or villages, or devastation not justified by military necessity.

> *Crimes Against Humanity:* Namely, murder, extermination, enslavement, deportation, and other inhumane acts committed against any civilian population, before or during the war, or persecution on political, racial, or religious grounds in execution of or in connection with any crime within the jurisdiction of the Tribunal, whether or not in violation of the domestic law of the country where perpetrated.

The Americans who were investigating war crimes filed Fritz Graebe's Dubno and Rovno statements with the International Military Tribunal as evidence of crimes against humanity. The statements were consolidated into one affidavit and submitted as Exhibit 494 for the United States. The statements were presented exactly as Fritz had written them. On November 21, 1945, Robert H. Jackson, chief counsel for the United States at Nuremberg, presented the opening statement, noting that:

> It is my purpose to show a plan and a design, to which all Nazis were fanatically committed, to annihilate all Jewish people. These crimes were organized and promoted by the Party leadership, executed and protected by the Nazi officials, as we shall convince you by written orders of the Secret State Police itself. [5]

Compared with the full scope of the Nazi atrocities suffered by European Jewry, the Dubno and Rovno mass murders were diminutive convulsions. Nevertheless, Graebe's account of the suffering there became a critical element in the prosecution's proof that there was an unrelenting "plan and design, to which all Nazis were fanatically committed, to annihilate all Jewish people." These two famous statements are included in the appendices.

The inclusion of this affidavit in the proceedings of the Tribunal and its worldwide circulation made Graebe a marked man in his home country. Though he was never called to the dock, he became the only unindicted German to so testify in cases of crimes against humanity. His testimony set the tone for the cases that were presented and later used against the highest regional officials of the Reich in the Ukraine. The testimony is a standard reference in Holocaust cases and studies. The great wave of publicity that instantly followed brought threats to the Graebe family.

By June 1946, when Graebe's work for the War Crimes Commission was completed, he was receiving threats against his life. He was socially ostracized, excluded from professional associations, and denied the means to establish or maintain a private engineering business. During the next twenty-six months, the Graebe family lived on their fast-diminishing savings and the money Fritz had received when he was bought out of Jung. Graebe did not spend much time seeking employment, trying to open a firm, or competing for contracts. The word was circulated far and wide that he was to be rebuffed. It did not take long to learn that the message would be honored everywhere.

To fill his time, he perfected his skills as an artist and calligrapher. His one friend was Dr. Bethke, a physician who sympathized with his plight and became his confidant and friend. Graebe spent many hours in Bethke's home, sharing his frustrations, doubt, and despair.

I began to doubt the wisdom of my decision to work with Kavin and the Twelfth Army Group. I never doubted my decision to rescue Jews, but I confess that I was riddled with despair about the effect of the testimony. I was most concerned for my wife and son. Now they were suffering because of decisions I had made. It was soon clear that I could not live in Germany. The final straw was when Friedel was threatened by his schoolmates, and their parents, in turn, began threatening my entire family. After several very long talks with Dr. Bethke, I decided to approach the American Jewish Joint Distribution Committee to see if I could emigrate to the United States. All of my friends, Maria, Elizabeth, Alex, and Tadeuz were gone. I really had no reason to remain in a land and with a people who could not tolerate me or my conscience and who ignored their own consciences.

The Graebe family received the assistance of the American Jewish Joint Distribution Committee and won the coveted visas to the United States. Graebe's disabled brother elected to remain in Germany. Because he could not care for himself or ever be fully employed, Fritz and Elisabeth assumed responsibility for him, locating a guest home for him; they sold their own home and many of their personal goods and used the remaining funds to secure his care.

In August 1948, Fritz, Elisabeth, and Friedel boarded a Liberty ship bound for Canada and New York. Their new life would begin to take shape as they settled in San Francisco in October 1948. Their relocation would not be without incident or reminders of all that had happened between 1933 and 1945.

12. Newspaper Attack: Germany, 1965

Fritz worked at several jobs in San Francisco before starting his own business as a structural engineer. In 1960, twelve years after the Graebes' arrival in the United States, Georg Marschall was brought to trial in Stade, Germany, for his role in the persecution and destruction of Jews in the Ukraine. Graebe was contacted by the prosecutors' office and the U.S. Department of Justice; he agreed to travel to Germany in order to testify against the former *Gebietskommissar*. The trial, after so many years, placed an incredible strain on Graebe and his family: nightmarish memories long dormant, visions of death that had faded enough to permit him to sleep, now all returned to torment him. During the trial itself Fritz developed intestinal flu and was sick for several days. In spite of the strain, Graebe could write to Bronka (now living in Poland) that in retrospect he regretted only the absence of Otto Koeller, who should also have stood in the halls of justice with Marschall for his crimes against Jews and Polish civilians.

If there was any pleasure to be had in the return to Germany, it was in returning to Solingen. But the nostalgic visit offered only a brief respite and a bittersweet relief from the trial. A local newspaper highlighted his return to Solingen-Grafrath with the headline HE TURNED HIS BACK ON GERMANY. The article under the headline was replete with vague insinuations about Graebe's past. The paper did not libel the Graebe name by its remarks, because its investigative reporter had not been able to uncover or reveal any improprieties on the part of Graebe or his family. Instead, the paper seemed to pander to those Germans who could not face their own complicity in the Holocaust and who needed a scapegoat for their emotions. In spite of these attacks, Fritz was happy when he saw the city of his birth and wandered through the nearby forest.

Despite the natural beauty of the area and the warm memories evoked from his childhood, however, the fact remained that fifteen years after the war, people still held harsh feelings for him and could not accept his role as a rescuer or as a witness against those who had committed crimes against humanity. His reaction to the newspaper article and its meanspirited attack was demoralizing. It reminded Fritz of the painful lessons he had learned when he returned home following the Nuremberg trials. There was no place for him in Germany anymore. Why this attitude and its continuation fifteen years later? Because Fritz Graebe was a living reminder to a people who wanted to forget and get on with their lives. The price he paid for his honorable life and for the rescues was exclusion from his native land and abuse by the press.

Following his work with the courts in the Marschall case, Graebe returned to San Francisco and continued his engineering career. During the intervening five years, the Israeli government conducted investigations that would lead to the honoring of Fritz Graebe. Many of those whom he had rescued had written to Yad Vashem—the Holocaust memorial and research center in Jerusalem that is charged with, among other things, the responsibility of verifying the humanitarian work of the rescuers and bestowing appropriate honors for their efforts—describing the heroism of the German engineer. On September 20, 1965, Fritz Graebe entered the Hall of Remembrances at Yad Vashem to receive tributes from scores of women and men whom he had saved and to receive the honored title, Righteous Among the Nations, conferred by the government of Israel. The presence of a man of such great compassion, together with many of the people he had helped, was an international media event. The attendant publicity in Germany sparked the interest of people at the offices of the newsmagazine *Der Spiegel*. In late September, a correspondent, Axel Jaeschke, phoned the Graebe home requesting a photo of Graebe to be used in an article on the impending retrial of Georg Marschall. Graebe was shocked to learn that Marschall had successfully petitioned for a new trial. He did not learn of it, however, until much later because he was in Israel.

Jaeschke was informed that Graebe was in Jerusalem and would not be available for some time. Knowing this, the newsmagazine sent Fritz a lengthy questionnaire. When he finally returned home from Israel, Fritz completed the form (even though it was past the stated deadline), reviewed it with attorneys from the U.S. Department of Justice, and sent it to the New York office of *Der Spiegel*.

The article that appeared in the German newsmagazine on December 29, 1965, was shocking. The story called into question Graebe's hon-

esty by suggesting that "considerable doubts have arisen as to the credibility of the prosecution witness Graebe," because of reasonable confusion
over the date when he believed he was expelled from the Party and the
date on which the Party actually struck his name from its official roster.
Furthermore, the story alleged a romantic postwar correspondence between Graebe and one of Marschall's former secretaries, Frau Kosnick,
a spurious charge, which Graebe denied. Remarks from the questionnaire were printed out of context, if they were included at all. Immediately, letters were sent to the magazine by Graebe, by his family, and
by knowledgeable survivors. Jaeschke wrote to the relatives of one rescued person that the article had been cleared by the correspondent for
Der Spiegel in New York, Herr Baruch-Baker; he in turn denied knowledge
of the article. Representatives of the World Jewish Congress and the
director of the Israeli police unit concerned with war criminals assured
Fritz of their unchanged opinion of him and offered to help him find a
lawyer who could bring suit against the magazine. Unfortunately, Graebe's
personal finances made it impossible for him to retain the necessary legal
representation. He was deterred by the prospect of a lengthy and costly
trial.

In the meantime, Fritz and those whom he had rescued wrote numerous letters to *Der Spiegel* rebutting the article. Not one of the letters or
rebuttals was ever printed. Only one of the writers is known to have
received a reply from the German weekly. Finally, in the October 1966
issue of *The Yad Vashem Bulletin*, the full text of Graebe's questionnaire
response was printed with a vindicating summary of the problems. Many
of the questions that were asked in the initial questionnaire had been
connected to unresolved issues from Marschall's first trial and were certain to be issues in the much-publicized retrial.

One of the major issues raised by *Der Spiegel* was Graebe's unwillingness to return for the trial against Koeller in 1963. An official summons
had been issued for that trial, and another one had been issued for the
Marschall retrial. In both cases, Graebe refused to respond to the summons. Following the Marschall trial in 1960, Graebe was accused of
willful perjury in the matter of his membership in the Party. For reasons
that are completely lost to history, the Party did not officially delete
Fritz Graebe's name from its membership list until 1934 or 1935. The
attorneys for the defense picked up a discrepancy between Graebe's testimony and the membership lists of the Party. On this basis they were
able to call into question the veracity of Graebe's general testimony in
the case. Using this data and other legal maneuvers, these attorneys
were able to secure Marschall's retrial.

Graebe responded to the charge of willful perjury in the questionnaire by pointing out that he had no power over the Party records and that he had no knowledge that his name had not been deleted on the same day he was expelled. The entire matter of the alleged willful perjury was never resolved in the courts of Germany. In summoning Graebe for the Koeller trial in 1963 and for the Marschall retrial in 1965, the courts promised Graebe "free escort for a period of five days," provided he made no attempt to escape or leave the boundaries of Germany. In essence, this "free escort" was not in any way an immunity from the scurrilous charges. Graebe could enter the country, but he could not leave. For this reason and because of his distrust of the court system, Fritz followed the advice of his counsel and refused to travel to Germany to testify or to answer the charges of willful perjury. Instead, Graebe volunteered to appear before German attorneys who would come to the U.S. to take any depositions required in the case against Marschall. In fact, depositions were taken by attorneys while Graebe was being represented by the U.S. Department of Justice.

Graebe's decision to remain in the United States and to ignore the summonses to the German courts was also informed by other issues that were raised in the courts by Marschall's attorneys and later reported by *Der Spiegel*. One such matter related to the false charge that Graebe had reported to the Party leadership an alleged indiscretion by a former employer in 1933. The groundless charge against Fritz was that he had informed the Party that his employer, Josef Jansen, had called the *Heil Hitler* greeting nonsense. In answering that charge, Graebe pointed out that Jansen got into trouble not because of his alleged anti-Hitler perspective but because of business and financial improprieties. Graebe's early indifference to the Party and to Hitler and his later complete opposition to them was well established. It would have been completely out of character for Graebe to have acted as an informant for the Party.

A second issue raised by Marschall's attorneys and by *Der Spiegel* involved an insinuation that Graebe had proposed to marry a woman named Kosnick, Marschall's former secretary. Graebe had received a number of letters from this woman, who said that she was in a mental hospital in Germany; she claimed that Graebe had rescued her. These letters appear to have been written between 1957 and 1962. Graebe had responded to the letters in a matter-of-fact way, informing her that he was involved in the Marschall trial and asking if she knew anything that might be helpful to the prosecution attorneys. At no time did Graebe mention marriage to this woman or any other—he was married to Elisabeth. Graebe did not know how the attorneys happened to locate this correspondence, but it opened the door to spurious accusations that threatened the integrity of Graebe's testimony. The fact that the woman wrote him from her bed in the mental ward of a German hospital was proof enough for Fritz that the woman lacked credibility and that the defense team was grabbing any issue that might cause doubt and lead to the vindication of Marschall.

The remainder of the questionnaire, like the challenges issuing from the defense attorneys, raised vague charges and pointed to alleged inconsistencies in his testimony. Graebe, in his response, requested that the newsmagazine forward any testimony that they felt held inconsistencies. They sent nothing.

In publishing Graebe's response to the questionnaire, the Yad Vashem investigators included a preamble that stated their reasons for printing his full account. Both the preamble and the complete questionnaire may be read as a vindication of an honored man by the very people who had the full power to discredit him if he was indeed dishonest in his testimony or actions. The full text of both is included in the appendices of this book. They are included here because revisionists of questionable repute and insincere motives are seeking to deny every aspect of the Holocaust. Acknowledging the article in *Der Spiegel* and printing the full, correct response will challenge any who will use the article to malign the actions and motives of Graebe or the historical authenticity of the Holocaust. It is also essential for the sake of the record to make public the full responses that were denied to the world in the original article and in the rebuttals to it.

13. Postwar Portraits

Following the war and the work of the International Military Tribunal, the principals in this story scattered throughout the world. Some resumed their normal lives; some went into hiding or were tried and convicted by the Tribunal. The war experiences forever marked and changed the life of each person. Daily life regained some semblance of order, but the victims and their rescuers did not flag in their quest for justice. The killers sought anonymity, hoping that they would not be recognized in the marketplace or on a train or in a crowd. Herewith is an account, as far as the facts are known, of what happened to the most important people in this story of Fritz Graebe's remarkable courage and compassion.[6]

Erich Koch: It was to this man, *Gauleiter* of East Prussia, Reich Defense Commissioner for Wehrkreis, Reich Commissioner for the Ukraine and Bialystock, and SS *Gruppenfuehrer,* that subordinates presented a *Judenrein* Rovno District in 1942. After the war, it is believed that this senior official escaped to Denmark, later returning to live in Hamburg under an assumed name. He was arrested by the British in 1949 and surrendered to the Polish government. He was finally convicted in 1959 and sentenced to death for the murder of 72,000 persons, primarily Jews. A report in 1983 indicated that Koch had not been executed but instead was imprisoned at a security institution at Barczewo, Poland.[7] The Soviet Union reputedly has outstanding charges against Koch for the murders of four million persons and the deportation into forced labor of an additional two million people.

Bronka: After she left the train loaded with Jung workers trying to escape the advancing Russian troops, Bronka was reunited with the Polish Underground. She and Graebe have not seen one another since the hours spent in Sdolbonov immediately prior to the departure of their trains. Following the war, she married a professor of law in Poland. They raised two daughters, who now live outside of Poland. Bronka filed affidavits in the Marschall case. She and Graebe maintain contact through correspondence.

Elizabeth Radziejewsha: Following the war and her work for the International Military Tribunal, Elizabeth married an American army lawyer who was adjutant to General Omar Bradley. After he wrote a major historical account of the role played by the Twelfth Army Group, they settled in the Midwest. After her husband's death in the late 1950s, Elizabeth went to law school, graduated, and had a career as a prominent lawyer. Over the years she maintained her ability to speak, translate, and read in seven languages. She also cared for her mother; she and her husband never had children. Elizabeth did much of the translation work at Wiesbaden and later prepared an affidavit for the 1960 trial. She died in 1983.

Maria Warchiwker: Because of her relationship with Severin Kavin, Maria was able to emigrate to the United States. She arrived well ahead of the Graebe family and lived with her sister and family in the Midwest. Later, she moved east, where she met and married a banker. They did not have children; they spent their professional lives in New Jersey. Maria traveled with Graebe to Stade in 1960 and testified against Marschall. Both she and her husband accompanied Graebe to Yad Vashem in 1965 for the honors accorded him by the Israeli government. Over the years, Maria and her husband remained in constant contact with the Graebes. Maria's husband died in 1984 in Florida, where they had been living in retirement.

Otto Koeller: After the war, Koeller vanished from sight until the trials in 1960. At that time he surfaced and testified for Marschall at the Stade court. Later he was jailed, tried, and imprisoned for his role in the horrors that befell the Jews and peasants in the Ukraine. He died while a prisoner.

Dr. Puetz: According to available news stories following the war, Puetz retreated with the SS in 1945 and settled in Hamburg. He committed suicide in that city before he could be arrested and tried for Crimes Against Humanity.

Georg Marschall: The Criminal Police and courts searched a long time before they were able to locate Marschall. His twin brother was arrested by mistake, and it was not until his father correctly identified and distinguished the two brothers that the war criminal was arrested. Following his arrest, he was incarcerated for two years pending trial. Following the trial in 1960, he was sentenced to life in prison, a sentence that was subsequently reduced to five years after a hotly contested retrial.

Attinger: This homicidal madman dropped out of sight for a considerable period of time. He finally gave himself up to the courts in the early 1960s and committed suicide while imprisoned.

Tadeuz, Irene, and Romak Glass: After the war, this family sought to emigrate to the United States. Because they had no American sponsors, they were unable to fulfill this dream, but with the help of a Jewish resettlement agency they were able to relocate to Australia. Tadeuz Glass died in 1955. Irene and Romak still live in Australia.

Alex Dutkowski: This brave Christian man who loyally stood with his beloved Jewish wife, Lydia, and told the militia that he would go to live in the ghetto if that was where his wife was to live, remained in Poland after the war. As a member of the Communist Party, he became a high official serving the nation as a mining and geological engineer. Eventually his wife emigrated to Israel, where she lived in Tel Aviv and worked as a children's teacher. While traveling in Brazil on an assignment for a government agency, Alex decided once and for all that his dissatisfaction with the form of government under which he lived was too great and that he wanted to be reunited with his family. On Christmas Eve in 1961, while on a layover in Switzerland on his return from Brazil, he shared his plight with a flight attendant from an El Al airline. Somehow, without papers or permission, he was able to convince the crew that he was defecting, and they took him to Israel. On that Christmas Eve, he was able to make his way to the door of his wartime friend and associate, Barbara Faust, who then arranged for him to be united with his family. Alex and Lydia were both injured at Lod Airport when a group of Japanese terrorists attacked the civilian lounge. Both recovered from the attack. Following Lydia's death in 1981, Alex resettled in Germany, but lives part time in Israel. He has a daughter and a grandchild living in the United States.

Erich Habenicht: After he was replaced by Koeller, Habenicht was drafted into the Wehrmacht and sent to the eastern front. According to rumors that came back to Sdolbonov, he was killed in action while fighting in the Russian zone.

Barbara Faust: Many husbands died at the hands of the *Einsatzgruppen.* Maria's and Barbara's husbands died in the same Action. Following the war, Barbara married another Polish survivor, and together they made their way to Israel. They welcomed Alex Dutkowski and sped him on his way to be reunited with his family. They have one daughter living in Israel.

Fritz, Elisabeth, and Friedel Graebe: In addition to his testimony at the trials in Nuremberg, Graebe assisted with the logistics of the trial it-self—arranging the design of the room and the seating assignments. He will be remembered for his testimony against the killers. William Shirer, the distinguished historian, recorded the moment when the British pros-ecutor, Sir Hartley Shawcross, read the sworn affidavit recalling the liq-uidation of the five thousand Jews at Dubno: "An eyewitness report by a German of how a comparatively minor mass execution was carried out in the Ukraine brought a hush of horror over the Nuremberg courtroom when it was read. . . ."[8] Although his actions contributed mightily to human dignity and although his testimony earned him the respect of people around the world, it led to harassment and threats in his own land.

The Graebes continue to live in San Francisco. Fritz Graebe worked first as a draftsman and then as a structural engineer in his own firm. His hard work, reputation, and ability to make lasting, important con-tacts helped establish his professional life in America. Elisabeth Graebe saw to the raising of their son and participated in a variety of church and civic philanthropies. The San Francisco Jewish community gener-ously helped place her in a Jewish retirement center near the family home after her health failed. Following a first career as an engineer, their son Friedel later began a second career as a lawyer with a practice in Sacramento, California.

After the ceremonies at Yad Vashem, which included the rekindling of the eternal flame in the Hall of Remembrance and celebrative re-unions with many whom he had rescued, Graebe returned to San Fran-cisco. Later he retired, but served as the manager of a German cultural hall until his complete retirement in 1982. He has had eight heart attacks since the first one that delayed his mission in Poltava. Honors have continued to come to him from the World Jewish Congress, from synagogues, interfaith groups, Jewish foundations, and from his adoptive city, San Francisco.

Fritz Graebe did not forget his covenants, did not rest in his pursuit of justice at Nuremberg, and did not ignore the scurrilous charges and innuendos hurled by attorneys and the press. He has been marked and changed by the horrors he witnessed at Rovno and many similar places. What has not changed is his compassion; it has remained and has been strengthened by all that he has seen and all that he has done in his extraordinary life.

Epilogue

The Lessons of Fritz Graebe's Life:
The Origins of a Moral Person

The Nazi destruction of European Jewry has given humanity a frightening and distorted self-perception. From the time when the first liberators set foot in the extermination camps of Central and Eastern Europe and unearthed the mass graves in countless forests and listened in stunned horror to the eyewitness accounts of the survivors, sensitive people have been forced to confront the difficult question: What kind of people become genocidal murderers? However, this first question of Holocaust studies has provided but a single dimension, a solitary angle of vision into a complex and multidimensional period of history.

The pervasive focus of Holocaust scholarship has been the brutality, the indifference, and the disregard for even the most basic human values. Scholars, novelists, and students attempt to understand the origins of such evil. They probe every darkened recess of the human heart for some evidence, some quirk or gene or personal characteristic that might explain, justify, or excuse all that has happened. It is essential that they record this history of the Holocaust and inquire into its contemporary implications and lessons, for in one generation, the world has witnessed the transition from the theory and practice of genocide to the potential for nuclear destruction of this globe. Because we sense that the past may be but mere prologue, we struggle with Elie Wiesel's observation that "if we were to know the mystery of Auschwitz, I think we could prevent the destruction of the world."[9]

Justice Moshe Bejski of the Israeli Supreme Court, chairman of the Commission for the Designation of the Righteous at Yad Vashem, asked a question in 1974 that suggested an urgent new direction of inquiry by

Holocaust scholars. "Why was it that in approximately twenty states under Nazi occupation or influence, which had the combined population of hundreds of millions, there were relatively so few persons who were prepared to help those who were in such urgent need of relief during that period?"[10]

When people read or hear a recounting of Fritz Graebe's story they often ask what caused him to take such risks. From where did he derive his beliefs, his strength of character, and his skills to stand in opposition to the rulers and the ravaging forces of his culture? The more haunting question is intensely personal: Would *I* be able or willing to take such risks if I were in Fritz Graebe's place?

Graebe's life is a witness to the fact that there is indeed another side to the tales of murder and brutality of the Nazi era. The few thousand men, women, and children who performed often dangerous rescues without thought for reward restore a measure of balance to the self-image and self-respect of humanity after Auschwitz. The lessons we learn from the rescuers may encourage us to practice daily kindnesses and courtesies. Their example has an urgency in this era when most endangered people are at the mercy of random and unpredictable interventions. As moral role models, they give us a view of life that has clear, humane standards and that treasures the rich diversity of human races, cultures, and religions.

Fritz Graebe and most of the other rescuers disdain the label "hero" and all that is implied by the notion of heroics. Most refer to their acts as simple, often inadequate, gestures of human decency. They will tell you that in the worst of times and circumstances they did what they could to help. They will tell you that they merely did what anyone would have done, or should have done. Yet their behavior, which usually was predicated on specific Christian values, gives humanity a contemporary model of the biblical Good Samaritan.

Are these rescuers larger than life, somehow removed from common people? What enabled them to do what they did? Until recently, only two or three social scientists have inquired into the genesis of moral behavior in the Nazi-era rescuers. Perry London's work was the earliest systematic study of this altruism. London, working in the early 1960s, identified three significant shared characteristics in the rescuers.[11] These characteristics were, first, "a spirit of adventurousness"; second, "identification with a morally strong parent"; and third, they were all "socially marginal."

We have seen the spirit of adventurousness in Fritz Graebe as he spent four years teaching himself to stop stuttering. In the same spirit and because of the effect of the stuttering, he taught himself the skills required to pass the tests to become a state-licensed engineer in Germany. Later, during the Nazi era, this spirit was evidenced in his boldly successful avoidance of military conscription; in his entry to the Rovno town square and the circle of death in order to confront Dr. Puetz and save his Jewish workers; and in his entry into Gestapo headquarters in Cologne to effect the release of his staff.

Graebe participated in carefully planned, arduous, high-risk activities that affirmed and energized his moral beliefs and stimulated his desire to continue his altruistic enterprises. He did not seek these activities for their excitement or take them on willy-nilly. Graebe's spirit of adventurousness was humane, calculated, and purposeful.

One of London's most important findings related to the influence of a moral parental model. Graebe's mother, Louise Kinkel Graebe, was his primary moral model. She held consistent, resolute views on right and wrong. She both articulated and practiced her beliefs and values. She stressed qualities of constructive candor, honesty, empathy, insightfulness, and assertiveness; and she directed Fritz to make difficult decisions that would cause life to be better or easier for someone else.

Louise Graebe was a very religious person, having grown up in the Lutheran tradition. Because of certain incidents in her parish, however, she preferred not to associate with that institutional church. She was not doctrinaire but rather exhibited great interest in things ecumenical and egalitarian. Charitable and open, she taught these qualities to her son and expected him to practice them in his life.

Frau Graebe's articulated faith was related to teachings such as the Golden Rule, "Do unto others as you would have them do unto you" (Matthew 7:13); to parables of compassion such as the Good Samaritan (Luke 10:39) and the Kingdom (Matthew 25:31); and to the teaching that people must "love your neighbor as yourself" (Matthew 22:39). In a very homey manner, she would weave these lessons into her talks with young Fritz and use the teachings to illustrate the basis for some kindness that she had performed. Of his mother, Graebe has said, "She was the strong moral figure for me—she knew right and wrong." In another conversation he noted, "She accepted people for their own worth, not because someone else told her about or spoke against them."

London's third characteristic was social marginality. This difficult-to-measure characteristic includes, but is not limited to, such matters as social class, political affiliation and viewpoint, economic status, religious beliefs and practices, educational status, geographic location, family style, and other personal variables. In the case of Fritz Graebe, his stuttering caused him to be the victim of youthful taunting and thereby made him feel isolated or socially marginal. His family was poor but respected, and his mother spoke a dialect of the German language that was not common in the region where the family resided. These factors contributed to Graebe's marginality. The family's association with Jews clearly made them socially out of step with the basically anti-Semitic culture. Graebe's attitude toward the Nazi Party also made him marginal. Of himself, he has noted, "I marched to my own tune. I was not taught to be political. Therefore, I did not oppose or support National Socialism on ideological grounds. I became opposed to it when I personally witnessed its injustice and inhumanity."

Another quality about Fritz Graebe that distinguished him as socially marginal was his disdain for seeking the approval of others. "My mother always urged me to do what I—I, not others—thought was best and right. I do not regret that I have followed this teaching of hers all of my life, and it has served me very well." Peer approval and the slavish accommodation of social conventions do not cause a person to spend four years risking summary execution to save the lives of thousands of persons publicly branded as "parasites."

I believe that there were other factors that contributed significantly to the makeup of a rescuer. Two grants, one a Faculty Research Grant from the Oregon Committee for the Humanities and the other from the Memorial Foundation for Jewish Culture, enabled me to interview the rescuers and the rescued living in various countries. As a result of the first study, I came to know Fritz Graebe. As I interviewed the rescuers, reviewed their files at Yad Vashem, and recorded the rescues from the perspective of the Jews who were saved, a clear pattern began to emerge. These people did indeed have significant common forces at work in their lives. In addition to the three characteristics discovered by Perry London, I have identified seven traits of the caring person—the rescuer. As they are listed, examples will be given from Graebe's life, but the categories are derived from a much larger sample of interviews. It is important to note that these traits are skills that can be learned by anyone and that can be taught by parents.

The first trait is *an empathic imagination*. The essence of empathic imagination is the ability to place oneself in the actual situation or role of another person and to imagine the effect and the long-term consequences of the situation or the role on that person. There is a specific theatrical quality suggested when exchanging roles and projecting oneself onto the stage of life and into the being of another character.

Graebe had a generally active imagination and grew to have an active, specifically empathic imagination. During the war years he was quite able to imagine himself in the situation of the endangered Jews. Exchanging roles by means of imagining engendered a strong empathy and set his mind to creating alternative means by which he could have a positive effect on their lives.

Graebe remembers a practice of his mother's that led to the development of an empathic imagination early in his life. Regularly and in many different situations, Louise Graebe would ask her son, "And Fritz, what would you do?" This was never an idle, rhetorical question. Frau Graebe intentionally employed it as an instructional device, expecting and receiving an answer. The example of his mother's visits to an imprisoned relative caused the young Graebe to ask his mother why she persisted in the face of such intense family pressure and parental abuse. She briefly explained to him her concerns. Explicit in her soliloquy was the empathy that ruled Louise Graebe's life. She then asked her son, "And Fritz, what would you do?" By stating her values in terms of her concern for her sister, she set the stage for an altruistic response from her son, whose empathic imagination was growing.

The extent to which Graebe's empathic imagination grew and developed is shown most deeply at the edge of the mass grave at Dubno. There he watched his contemporary, an anonymous, naked Jewish man, point to the sky and speak to his son moments before the two descended to a ledge in the mass grave and were murdered by soldiers of the *Einsatzgruppe*. In the empathic imagination of Fritz Graebe, he and his own son *became* the two Jews standing before the pit. As he walked from the scene, heartsick, his mother's question crossed into his consciousness: "And Fritz, what would you do?"

The second trait is *a person's ability to present himself or herself and control a critical situation.* Graebe learned a range of theatrical skills through a minor role in a school play, by observing performances of the light opera company, and by teaching himself to stop stuttering. He was a consummate actor, commanding nearly every scene in the dramas of rescue.

In the second trait, the presentation of the self is a major determinant of the outcome of a particular situation. Graebe was intentional and purposeful in presenting himself even in roles as minor as ingratiatingly befriending a petty official or incredibly confronting Dr. Puetz in the circle of death at Rovno.

As evidenced in his preparations for the scene where he had Maria become a Gentile, Graebe rehearsed and worked toward a specific outcome. His self-presentation for the act included controlling his breathing; managing his posture, dress, and location; locating his positions "onstage"; and generally reading the entire scene on his arrival. Because no person can predict every scene or preview every desired outcome, it is important to note that Graebe used his travel and other nonwork time to anticipate scenes that were likely to develop because of the wartime situation. In this low-keyed way he was always alert for events that would potentially require his intervention, and he was usually not caught unsuspecting.

The third trait is *previewing for a purposeful life*. In order to be altruistic, a person must be both proactive and prosocial.[12] *Proactive* (its opposite is *reactive*) and *prosocial* (its opposite is *antisocial*) behavior is characterized by (1) careful planning to act in a cooperative and responsible way; (2) anticipating opportunities for having a positive and beneficial impact in the lives or circumstances of others; and (3) actively promoting the well-being of self and others.

What is sought in this trait is the integration of a person's desire to be caring and helpful with the skills necessary to fulfill that desire. This conception of proactive, prosocial living is based on the assumption that, given the choice, most people would prefer to be caring and helpful rather than the opposite, and that certain skills must be learned if a person is to be predictably altruistic. The skills to live a caring and helpful life are taught, learned, rehearsed, and practiced.

Graebe's life reflects just such an integration. Upon reaching his decision to initiate a large-scale rescue effort, he began to preview the impact that he desired. A plan had to be designed and executed in order to get from the foundation to the completed structure. He undertook his task with the basic tools of his profession, engineering and design. Of course, allowances for variations, changed perspectives, and unplanned contingencies made a certain amount of flexibility necessary. His opportunity to plan and test a strategy and his cautious assessment of the risks fostered a quality of intentionality that separated Graebe from the more impulsive and hazardous (and often unsuccessful) rescues undertaken by less methodical persons.

The alarming and regrettable conclusion of most studies in "Samaritan behavior" is that victims were and continue to be left at the mercy of random and unpredictable interventions on their behalf. Without radical efforts at preparing people to be proactive and prosocial and to act in caring and helpful ways, would-be altruists may be unable to translate their values into actions.

The fourth trait that the Nazi-era rescuers have in common is that most of them had *significant personal experiences with suffering and death prior to the war*. Two such experiences, which are as vivid to Graebe today as if they had occurred yesterday rather than in 1918, were very formative in his understanding of victimization.

At the end of World War I, the very young Graebe watched soldiers return from the battle zones. He remembers one bandaged young man from Grafrath, much of whose face had been blown away by a bullet. Fritz recalls thinking that this man and others like him were going through such unnecessary and wasteful suffering. The image of the soldier from Grafrath and the lesson of war ineptly hidden by the bandage were engraved forever in his mind.

The other incident involved the mistreatment of Graebe's disabled brother by playmates and Louise Graebe's response. Fritz's sensitivity to and awareness of the suffering of others enhanced a caring attitude and encouraged his decision to be a rescuer. The suffering of another human being did not lead him to feel either revulsion or fear. It neither morbidly attracted him nor did it weaken his resolve to combat it. On the contrary, he saw suffering as unnecessary and inappropriate, and he sought to save others from it.

Among the rescuers the experiences with suffering measurably enhanced their empathic imaginations. Their prior sensitivity to suffering contributed to the reality of their wartime planning and decisions to become rescuers. The ones who became rescuers had not been spared the traumas of death, injury, or separation. Instead, most reported that the traumatic impact of a particular incident was shared within the family and given perspective by parents. Because of the times, death was neither sanitized nor encapsulated in a hygienic hospital room. The experience generally was intensely personal.

The fifth trait common to all the rescuers was *their ability to confront and manage their prejudices.* Firmly held and culturally endorsed stereotypes of specific individuals or groups often determine political, social, and legal conventions that result in dehumanizing attitudes toward, and injury to, the individuals or groups. When these stereotypes are challenged or set aside in favor of a greater consideration of human decency or a more pervasive and egalitarian world view, the acts potentially leading to prejudice and brutality may be avoided. All of the rescuers in the studies had developed a certain world view that enabled them to interpret the persecution of Jews and others as morally repugnant.

The research has established that rescues were facilitated by both short- and long-term friendships or acquaintances with stereotyped individuals before the onset of oppression and by a level of knowledge about Judaism and Jewish life. Graebe and his family had significant personal and business associations with Jews over a considerable span of years before

World War II. Graebe himself did business with Jews and his immediate family was attended to by a Jewish physician. Graebe began his journey to rescue by protesting against the abuse experienced by the Jewish merchant Leon Kirschbaum. His involvement increased geometrically when he witnessed an Action and, in a generalized way, as he met or heard about Jews in similar situations.

Opportunities to examine prejudices, to develop broad egalitarian and humanitarian beliefs, and to instill respect for the pluralism of the world before judgments and stereotypes become ingrained are essential if we are to forestall crises in human behavior. Friendship or familiarity with persons and cultures, with traditions and structures that are not a part of a person's usual set of life experiences, are particularly essential. In 1979, a Louis Harris survey for the National Conference of Christians and Jews concluded that "the most salient idea to emerge from the study is the fact that familiarity does not breed contempt. To the contrary, familiarity breeds acceptance and respect."[13]

Few people were willing to assume the risks associated with any form of rescue. Those who did rarely told anyone else what they were doing for fear that they would be discovered or betrayed. Very few rescuers even informed their spouses or families when they intervened. Fewer still were able to surmount the fear and build a cooperative group of rescuers. The sixth trait common to rescuers was *the development of a community of compassion and support.* Unfortunately, this was not practiced by many rescuers.

The majority of rescues were isolated, secret acts of kindness. The rescuers have related the tremendous, nearly disabling fear that gripped them whenever they intervened. Many of the rescuers reported that it took weeks and months to regain courage for the next rescue. They longed to share the responsibility, to increase the scope of their ministrations, to be in a mutually supportive relationship with a confidant and co-conspirator. To their credit these brave persons persisted in their efforts, managing to overcome their terror if not their aloneness.

In those instances where groups of people or whole communities engaged in rescue work, many more endangered people benefited. The risks of infiltration and detection were enormously high, but the results were equally great. There were pitifully few communal rescues, presumably because there is not a common, unifying ethic in most groups and cultures and associations and because the risks were so great. The most acclaimed communal rescues were orchestrated by religiously based groups with a long-term and carefully organized ethic that united the people.

(The interventions by the Huguenots of LeChambon and the protection given by the religious order in Assisi are worthy examples of effective communal rescues.)

Fritz Graebe's rescue efforts were a middle course between the two extremes: singular serial rescues and large-scale cooperative rescues. Had Graebe worked alone on his rescues, he simply could not have saved hundreds of people or aided several thousand refugees with food, shelter, work, or papers. Graebe was too highly placed, too responsible, and his work was too demanding to engage in personal, yet large-scale and successful efforts. On the other hand, he could not have turned to any of the Ukrainian people in Sdolbonov, Rovno, Kiev, or Poltava for sympathetic understanding or support.

Graebe carefully selected the most courageous, intelligent, and compassionate people to serve with him in his secret and subversive operations. The primary rescue team was comprised of Graebe and six others, five of whom were potential victims of the Nazis. Without the support and strength provided by this community of compassion, Graebe could not have been the visionary leader of a successful rescue network. He would not have been protected from the Nazi leadership, his moral values would not have been affirmed, and his exhausted body and spirit could not have been rejuvenated. Had Graebe been arrested, executed, or become incapacitated because of his heart attack, one or more of the six could have stepped in to continue the rescues until alternate plans could be formulated.

A supportive community of coworkers offers the nurturance of a compassionate vision held in common, affirmation of common values, a broad base of mutual responsibility, a diversity of skills, and a system or structure that may guarantee effectiveness and security. Caring and helpful behavior and interventions leading to rescue will be most successful when there is a community of like-minded persons with an organized ethic that supports compassionate thinking and acting.

The seventh trait common to all rescuers is *the ability to offer hospitality.* The rescuers removed endangered people from intensely hostile environments, offering them a respite from the forces that sought their destruction. The rescuers gave the victims whom they aided food, drink, warmth, rest, protection, and other creature comforts. They welcomed friends and strangers alike and provided whatever was necessary and available to them.

Most of the rescuers who had an active role in a church at some time in their lives were aware of the biblical texts that refer to hospitable acts and life-style. The most frequently quoted or paraphrased passage was that of the Good Samaritan, in which an unlikely passerby aids a man who has fallen victim to a band of robbers. The teaching ends with the instruction, "Go thou and do likewise." The second most common reference was to the parable in Matthew 25 where Jesus is identified as having been treated with care and hospitality while he was imprisoned, without clothing, sick, hungry, thirsty, and a stranger. At the end he issues a clear call to his followers to be hospitable: "Whenever you did these things to one of the least of these brothers [or sisters] of mine, you did it to me."

Fritz Graebe's childhood was filled with lessons and examples of a hospitable life-style based on these and other biblical models. Although they were of moderate means, they always had enough to share with an unfortunate sojourner. Louise Graebe regularly assisted the charitable work of Sister Angelica. People in need were simply not turned away from the Graebe home, which was filled with the spirit of openness and sharing.

The actions of Fritz Graebe while he was in the Ukraine can be understood in terms of hospitality. He managed to maintain a complex and demanding job while saving Jews and providing for their needs. While trying to protect himself from malcontents and informers, he was busy arranging for shoes, warm clothing, medicine, and forged papers.

Hospitality is the specific training ground of altruism. Henri J.M. Nouwen, the Roman Catholic theologian, has written a description of the essential qualities of hospitality.

> In a world full of strangers, estranged from their own past, culture, and country, from their neighbors, friends, and family, from their deepest self and their God, we witness a painful search for a hospitable place where life can be lived without fear. . . .
> That is our vocation, to convert the *hostis* into a *hospes*, the enemy into a guest and to create the free and fearless space where brotherhood and sisterhood can be formed and fully expressed.[14]

The Graebe rescue effort practiced a brand of hospitality that welcomed strangers and outcasts, provided them free and unconditional space, saw to their security and physical well-being, and affirmed them as human beings. In the midst of a murderous hostility, Fritz Graebe reached out to others with his loving hospitality.

These common traits of the rescuers are skills that can be taught and learned. As people learn and practice them, others who are in distress are more likely to be the recipients of direct, meaningful intervention. These skill-related traits do not develop out of nothing or come to a person accidentally. They must be rehearsed and affirmed in a way that insures their continued refining and practice.

Appendix I

The Nuremberg Record I

The following documents are the sworn testimony of Hermann Friedrich Graebe on November 10, 1945, in Wiesbaden, Germany, before Major Homer B. Crawford, Investigator Examiner, War Crimes Branch, U. S. Army.

"I, Hermann Friedrich Graebe, declare under oath: From September 1941 until January 1944 I was manager and engineer-in-charge of a branch office in Sdolbonov, Ukraine, of the Solingen building firm of Josef Jung. In this capacity it was my job to visit the building sites of the firm. Under contract to an Army Construction Office, the firm had orders to erect grain storage buildings on the former airport in Dubno, Ukraine.

"On 5 October 1942, when I visited the building office at Dubno, my foreman, Hubert Moennikes of [address listed here], told me that in the vicinity of the site, Jews from Dubno had been shot in three large pits, each about thirty meters long and three meters deep. About fifteen hundred people had been killed daily. All of the five thousand Jews who had still been living in Dubno before the pogrom were to be liquidated. As the shootings had taken place in his presence he was still much upset.

"Thereupon, I drove to the site, accompanied by Moennikes and saw near it great mounds of earth, about thirty meters long and two meters high. Several trucks stood in front of the mounds. Armed Ukrainian militia drove the people off the trucks and [sic] the supervision of an S.S. man. The militiamen acted as guards on the trucks and drove them to and from the pit. All these people had the regulation yellow patches on the front and back of their clothes, and thus could be recognized as Jews.

"Moennikes and I went directly to the pits. Nobody bothered us. Now I heard rifle shots in quick succession, from behind one of the earth mounds. The people who had got off the trucks—men, women, and children of all ages—had to undress upon the order of an S. S. man, who carried a riding or dog whip. They had to put down their clothes in fixed places, sorted according to shoes, top clothing and underclothing. I saw a heap of shoes of about eight hundred to one thousand pairs, great piles of underlinen and clothing. Without screaming or weeping these people undressed, stood around in family groups, kissed each other, said farewells and waited for a sign from another S.S. man who stood near the pit, also with a whip in his hand. During the fifteen minutes that I stood near the pit I heard no complaint or plea for mercy. I watched a family of about eight persons, a man and woman, both about fifty, with their children of about one, eight, and ten, and two grown-up daughters of about twenty to twenty-four. An old woman with snow-white hair was holding the one year old child in her arms and singing to it and tickling it. The child was cooing with delight. The couple were looking on with tears in their eyes. The father was holding the hand of a boy about ten years old and speaking to him softly; the boy was fighting his tears. The father pointed toward the sky, stroked his head, and seemed to explain something to him. At that moment the S.S. man at the pit shouted something to his comrade. The latter counted off about twenty persons and instructed them to go behind the earth mound. Among them was the family which I have mentioned. I well remember a girl, slim and with black hair, who, as she passed close to me, pointed to herself and said, 'twenty-three.' I walked around the mound, and found myself confronted by a tremendous grave. People were closely wedged together and lying on top of each other so that only their heads were visible. Nearly all had blood running over their shoulders from their heads. Some of the people shot were still moving. Some were lifting their arms and turning their heads to show that they were still alive. The pit was already two-thirds full. I estimated that it already contained about one thousand people. I looked for the man who did the shooting. He was an S.S. man, who sat at the edge of the narrow end of the pit, his feet dangling into the pit. He had a tommy gun on his knees and was smoking a cigarette. The people, completely naked, went down some steps which were cut into the clay wall of the pit and clambered over the heads of the people lying there, to the place which the S.S. man directed them. They lay down in front of the dead or injured people; some caressed those who were still alive and spoke to them in a low voice. Then I heard a series of shots. I looked into the pit and saw that the bodies were twitching or the heads were lying already motionless on top of the bodies that lay before them. Blood was running from their necks. I was surprised that I was not ordered away, but I saw that there were two or three postmen in uniform nearby. The next batch was approaching already. They went down into the pit, lined themselves up against the previous victims and were shot. When I walked back, round the mound I noticed another load of people which had just arrived. This time they included sick and infirm people. An old, very thin woman with terribly thin legs was undressed by others who were already naked, while two other people held her up. The woman appeared to be paralyzed. The naked people carried the woman around the mound. I left with Moennikes and drove my car back to Dubno.

"On the morning of the next day, when I again visited the site, I saw about thirty naked people lying near the pit—about thirty to fifty meters away from it. Some of them were still alive; they looked straight in front of them with a fixed stare and seemed to notice neither the chilliness of the morning nor the workers from my firm who stood around. A girl of about twenty spoke to me and asked me to give her clothes, and help her escape. At that moment we heard a fast moving car approach and I noticed that it was an S.S. detail. I moved away to my site. Ten minutes later we heard shots from the vicinity of the pit. The Jews still alive had been ordered to throw the corpses into the pit—then they had themselves to lie down in this to be shot in the neck [sic]."

/S/
HERMANN FRIEDRICH GRAEBE

The Nuremberg Record II

The following document is the sworn testimony of Hermann Friedrich Graebe on November 10, 1945, in Wiesbaden, Germany, before Major Homer B. Crawford, Investigator Examiner, War Crimes Branch, U. S. Army.

"I, Hermann Friedrich Graebe, declare under oath: From September 1941 until January 1944 I was manager and engineer in charge of a branch office in Sdolbonov, Ukraine, of the Solingen building firm of Josef Jung. In this capacity it was my job to visit the building sites of the firm. The firm had, among others, a site in Rowno [Rovno], Ukraine.

"During the night of 13 July 1942 all inhabitants of the Rowno Ghetto, where there were still about five thousand Jews, were liquidated.

"I would describe the circumstances of my being a witness of the dissolution of the Ghetto, and the carrying out of the pogrom [Action] during the night and the morning, as follows. I employed for the firm, in Rowno, in addition to Poles, Germans, and Ukrainians about one hundred Jews from Sdolbonov, Ostrog, and Mysotch. The men were quartered in a building, 5 Bahnhofstrasse, inside the Ghetto, and the women in a house at the corner of Deutsche Strasse, 98.

"On Saturday, 11 July 1942, my foreman, Fritz Einsporn, told me of a rumor that on Monday all Jews in Rowno were to be liquidated. Although the vast majority of the Jews employed by my firm in Rowno were not natives of this town, I still feared that they might be included in this pogrom which had been reported. I therefore ordered Einsporn at noon of the same day to march all the Jews employed by us—men as well as women—in the direction of Sdolbonov, about twelve kilometers from Rowno. This was done.

"The senior Jew [Judenrat] had learned of the departure of the Jewish workers of my firm. He went to see the Commanding Officer of the Rowno SIPO and SD, Major (S.S. *Sturmbannfuehrer*) Dr. Puetz, as early as the Saturday afternoon to find out whether the rumor of a forthcoming Jewish pogrom—which had gained further credence by reason of the departure of Jews of my firm—was true. Dr. Puetz dismissed the rumor as a clumsy lie, and for the rest had the Polish personnel of my firm in Rowno arrested. Einsporn avoided the arrest by escaping to Sdolbonov. When I learned of this incident I gave orders that all Jews who had left Rowno were to report back to work in Rowno on Monday, 13 July 1942. On Monday morning I myself went to see the Commanding Officer, Dr. Puetz, in order to learn, for one thing, the truth about the rumored Jewish pogrom and secondly to obtain information on the arrest of the Polish office personnel. S.S. Major Dr. Puetz stated to me that no pogrom [Action] whatever was planned. Moreover such a pogrom would be stupid because the firms and the Reichsbahn would lose valuable workers.

"An hour later I received a summons to appear before the Area Commissioner of Rowno. His deputy, *Stabsleiter* and Cadet Officer (*Ordensjunker*) Beck, subjected me to the same questioning as I had undergone at the SD. My explanation that I had sent the Jews home for urgent delousing appeared plausible to him. He then told me—making me promise to keep it a secret—that a pogrom would in fact take place on the evening of Monday 13 July 1942. After a lengthy negotiation I managed to persuade him to give me permission to take my Jewish workers to Sdolbonov—but only after the pogrom had been carried out. During the night it would be up to me to protect the house in the Ghetto against the entry of the Ukrainian Militia and S.S. As confirmation of the discussion he gave me a document, which stated that the Jewish employees of Messrs. Jung were not affected by the pogrom.

"On the evening of this day I drove to Rowno and posted myself with Fritz Einsporn in front of the house in the Bahnhofstrasse in which the Jewish workers of my firm slept. Shortly after 22:00 the Ghetto was encircled by a large S.S. detachment and about three times as many members of the Ukrainian Militia. Then the electric archlights which had been erected in and around the Ghetto were switched on. S.S. and militia squads of four to six men entered or at least tried to enter the houses. Where the doors and windows were closed and the inhabitants did not open at the knocking, the S.S. men and militia broke the windows, forced the doors with beams and crowbars and entered the houses. The people living there were driven on to the street just as they were, regardless of whether they were dressed or in bed. Since the Jews in most cases refused to leave their houses and resisted, the S.S. and militia applied force. They finally succeeded, with strokes of the whip, kicks, and blows with rifle butts, in clearing the houses. The people were driven out of their houses in such haste that small children in bed had been left behind in several instances. In the street women cried out for their children and children for their parents. That did not prevent the S.S. from driving the people along the road, at running pace, and hitting them, until they reached a waiting freight train. Car after car was filled, and the screaming of women and children, and the cracking of whips and rifle shots resounded unceasingly. Since several families or groups had barricaded themselves in especially strong buildings, and the doors could not be forced with crowbars or beams, these houses were now blown open with hand grenades. Since the Ghetto was near the railroad tracks in Rowno, the younger people tried to get across the tracks and over a small river to get away from the Ghetto area. As this stretch of country was beyond the range of the electric lights, it was illuminated by signal rockets. All through the night these beaten, hounded and wounded people moved along the lighted streets. Women carried their dead children in their arms, children pulled and dragged their dead parents by their arms and legs down the road toward the train. Again and again the cries, 'Open the door!' 'Open the door!' echoed through the Ghetto.

"At about six o'clock in the morning I went away for a moment leaving behind Einsporn and several other German workers who had returned in the meantime. I thought the greatest danger was past and that I could risk it. Shortly after I left, Ukrainian militia men forced their way into 5 Bahnhofstrasse and brought seven Jews out and took them to a collecting point inside the Ghetto. On my return I was able to prevent further Jews from being taken out. I went to the collecting point to save these seven men. I saw dozens of corpses of all ages and both sexes in the streets I had to walk along. The doors of the houses stood open, windows were smashed. Pieces of clothing, shoes, stockings, jackets, caps, hats, coats, etc., were lying in the street. At the corner of a house lay a baby, less than a year old with his skull crushed. Blood and brains were splattered over the house wall and covered the area immediately around the child. The child was dressed only in a little shirt. The commander, S.S. Major Puetz, was walking up and down a row of about eighty to one hundred male Jews who were crouching on the ground. He had a heavy dog whip in his hand. I walked up to him, showed him the written permit of *Stabsleiter* Beck and demanded the seven men whom

I recognized among those who were crouching on the ground. Dr. Puetz was very furious about Beck's concession and nothing could persuade him to release the seven men. He made a motion with his hand encircling the square and said that anyone who was once there would not get away. Although he was very angry with Beck, he ordered me to take the people from 5 Bahnhofstrasse out of Rowno by eight o'clock at the least. When I left Dr. Puetz, I noticed a Ukrainian farm cart with two horses. Dead people with stiff limbs were lying on the cart. Legs and arms projected over the side boards. The cart was making for the freight train. I took the remaining seventy-four Jews who had been locked in the house, to Sdolbonov.

"Several days after the 13 July 1942, the Area Commissioner of Sdolbonov, Georg Marschall, called a meeting of all firm managers, railroad superintendents, and leaders of the Organization Todt and informed them that the firms, etc., should prepare for the 'resettlement' of the Jews which was to take place almost immediately. He referred to the pogrom in Rowno where all the Jews had been liquidated, i.e., had been shot near Kostolpol.

"I make the above statement in Wiesbaden, Germany, on 10 November 1945. I swear by God that this is the absolute truth."

/S/
HERMANN FRIEDRICH GRAEBE

Appendix II

"Der Spiegel and Hermann Graebe—A Correspondence." *Yad Vashem Bulletin,* Volume 19, Jerusalem, October, 1966. (Heshvan 5727)

In the December 29, 1965, issue (53) of the well known German weekly "Der Spiegel," under the main heading "Affairs," and under the subtitle, "A Stormy Life," there appeared a violent attack on the German engineer, Hermann Friedrich Graebe, one of the chief prosecution witnesses in the Nuremberg trials against Nazi criminals. This attack launched by this otherwise liberal-minded and anti-Nazi journal aroused considerable attention and surprise. Graebe's testimony, especially concerning the liquidation of the Rovno and Dubno communities, has become famous the world over. He had been an eyewitness to the atrocities committed inside the ghetto walls and at the death pits outside, and described what he had seen in horrible detail. To a large extent the Nazi criminals he named were convicted on the basis of his testimony which was first published in the proceedings (court records) of the Nuremberg trials and subsequently appeared in various publications. Graebe had made numerous efforts, at the risk of his own life, to save Jews from the clutches of the Nazi assassins, and a number of them survived thanks to his intervention. Some of them are now living in Israel. They were very happy to welcome him in Israel in the summer of 1965, when he came to receive honors from Yad Vashem and to plant a tree in his name in the Avenue of the Righteous in Jerusalem on September 20, 1965, according to the resolution of the Commission for the Righteous.

But in his own country he enjoys little popularity. His people cannot forgive him for his terrible revelations at the Nuremberg trials, and for the fact that a number of criminals received their due punishment on the basis of his testimony. The hostile atmosphere which surrounded him in Germany forced him to emigrate to the United States of America.

The article which appeared in "Der Spiegel" was full of veiled and open accusations, describing Graebe as a person in whom little confidence could be placed and whose words could hardly be relied upon. A photograph of the tree planting ceremony at the Avenue of the Righteous in Jerusalem was reproduced in such a way as to convey the impression that this, too, was an honor attained by unfair means. The reader's obvious conclusion must be that such was the mettle of those on whose evidence the International Court at Nuremberg relied in convicting the "great men" of the Third Reich—people whose own lives were but a lie and a sham.

On October 11, 1965, the editor of "Der Spiegel" had written to Graebe, presenting him a number of questions, some of which were framed in an offensive manner and designed to cast suspicion on him. Graebe had answered all these questions in his letter to "Der Spiegel," dated November 30, 1965. Nevertheless the article which appeared on December 29, 1965, made no mention whatever of Graebe's detailed explanations. Was this omission accidental by chance—or intentional? It is notable that not a single reader's letter referring to this article has been published in the subsequent issues of "Der Spiegel," contrary to its usual custom of printing immediate reaction to practically every article appearing on its pages.

With Mr. Graebe's permission we are printing below the questions addressed to him by "Der Spiegel," together with his replies.

Q1.: First of all, please let us know for what and by whom you are or were recently awarded marks of distinction in Israel, and what is the nature of these awards?

A.: The invitation to visit Israel was sent to me by a group of people—men and women—whom I had saved during the War and who had found shelter with me until the end of the War, as well as by their relatives and families.

These people set up a committee which had a twofold purpose: on the one hand to arrange a meeting between me and those who were saved through my help, and secondly to enable them to take part in the festivities planned in my honor in Israel.

The Remembrance Authority Yad Vashem, which has its seat in Jerusalem, awarded me a Remembrance Medal together with a certificate of merit, and granted me the privilege to plant a tree in my name in the "Avenue of the Righteous."

A further honor was conferred on me by the World Council for the Remembrance of the Deeds of the Righteous which held a festive dinner in Tel Aviv on October 3 this year and presented me with a valuable edition of the Bible.

Since my rescue actions were undertaken during the War, mainly in the territory of Volhynia [Ukraine], former residents of Volhynia now living in Israel, the United States of America, Australia and other countries organized a reception committee for me at Lod Airport. This committee was affiliated to the Association of Emigrants from Volhynia.

These honors were conferred on me for my personal actions for the rescue of Jews in the Ukraine, in Poland, and in Germany during the years 1941–1945, when I managed to save a large number of men, women, and children from certain death.

As a German—and now as before I am proud to have been born and raised as a German in Germany—it was not, to my mind, to the advantage of the German nation to destroy the Jewish population, especially since it was so close to the Germans both in language and in culture.

Q2.: Why did you not come to Nürnberg–Fürth for the Köller trial?

A.: When I was invited to appear as a witness in the Marschall case in 1960, and was ready to appear, I was warned against this readiness on my part by a former lawyer. He was afraid that the Nazis might play the same trick they so successfully applied during the Weimar Republic, of accusing the witnesses of wilful perjury. These tactics were indeed successfully employed in the Marschall trial. This is what prevented me from coming to Nürnberg–Fürth in 1963 and giving evidence there. The same applies to the Marschall affair where the proceedings in the perjury matter have not yet come to an end and I have in addition been threatened with civil action.

The District Court in Nürnberg–Fürth, to dispel my anxiety, offered me "free escort for a period of five days" provided that I make no attempt to escape. The true nature of this "free escort" is self-evident (see also the letter of the District Court of Stade of December 27, 1964 [1963—Ed.], which reached me only on January 14, 1964). Even contrary to the express instructions of my physician, who was afraid that my health would not permit my appearance in that case, I would have been ready to come, and I refer you to the correspondence in this matter:

Letter to the District Court of Stade, dated December 27, 1964 [1963], in re 9-63/1.

Letter of the Landesjustizverwaltungen [District Legal Administration] of Ludwigsburg, dated October 10, 1963. My letter to the Landesjustizverwaltungen of Ludwigsburg, dated September 19, 1963.

Letter of the General Consulate of West Germany in San Francisco, dated April 30, 1963.

My letter to the Attorney General, Nürnberg–Fürth, dated April 30, 1963.

Doctor's certificate of Rubin Gold, M.D., dated April 10, 1963.

Q3.: Are you prepared to come to Germany for the main proceedings due to be held against Georg Marschall and to appear there as a witness?

A.: I am prepared to come to Stade as a witness provided I receive free escort without any conditions, and that I receive due guarantee against my arrest on entering or leaving German territory, i.e., that I should not fall victim to the slander campaign conducted against me, and that the state of my health may permit me to appear as a witness at the murder trial due to be held.

To dispel any doubt I am prepared to submit to the examination of a physician who enjoys the confidence of the General Consulate of West Germany in San Francisco.

Q4.: Why did you several times declare on oath that you were expelled from the Nazi Party in 1932 because of critical remarks against the party, even though it has been proved that you were still a party member in 1935?

A.: I did not "several times declare on oath" that I was expelled from the Party in 1932.

When Marschall's defence counsel, during my examination as a witness at Stade in 1960, asked me whether I was a member of the Party I replied in the affirmative as to my membership as such, and noted that I left in 1932, though in fact I had been a member from 1931 until 1934. The mistake in the dates was apparently due to the fever which had attacked me a few days previously.

I had no reason whatever to give incorrect dates concerning my Party membership. Already at earlier hearings (Spruchkammerverfahren) and before the U.S. authorities, the dates I had mentioned were 1931 to 1934. This was also recorded in the War Crimes Files of the United

States Army, including my personal data. These files were, at my request, forwarded to Germany prior to the 1960 case, and the members of the court in Bremerhaven perused them at the time of the trial.

Dr. F. Schneemann, Marschall's defence counsel, thought he had evidence of my having been a Party member down to 1935. This assumption was based on a letter of the District Administration of the Nazi Party in Solingen to the Supreme Court in Munich, dated March 30, 1935, with reference to me. Obviously I knew nothing of the existence of this correspondence, and the contents of this letter have only now come to my notice. It remains a fact that I was no longer a Party member in 1935. Possibly the Party court made a routine investigation in 1935 of which I, of course, was not informed.

Q5.: Did you ever have a Party membership card? What was your membership number at the Solingen–Gräfrath branch?

A.: I never had a party card and I know nothing of a membership number.

Q6.: Did you in 1933 report Mr. Josef Jansen for stating that the "Heil Hitler" greeting was nonsense? Was Mr. Josef Jansen placed under protective custody following a report of this kind on your part?

A.: Mr. Josef Jansen was the manager of a firm of building contractors. At his suggestion, I entered this firm together with two other gentlemen and became the deputy-manager of the firm. Shortly after having assumed this post I discovered certain abuses of a financial and moral nature.

To the best of my knowledge Mr. Jansen was not taken into protective custody, but together with other employees of the firm was sentenced to imprisonment in regular legal proceedings.

Q7.: Who obtained an "Aryan" passport for Mrs. Bobrow of Zdolbunow—you or Mr. Marschall?

A.: It was I who obtained Aryan papers for Mrs. Bobrow. On the basis of these papers she was registered as an "Aryan" at the municipality of Zdolbunow.

Q8.: How many years had passed since the death of Mrs. Bobrow's husband, who was shot by the S.S. when you appointed her your secretary?

A.: Mrs. Bobrow's first husband was Mr. Warchiwker who was shot in August 1941, in Zdolbunow together with many other Jewish men.

Q9.: Were the Jewish forced laborers employed by you in Zdolbunow beaten? And if so—why did you not try to do anything about it—or did you?

A.: A number of Jews employed by me were beaten. These acts of brutality were usually committed by my former foreman, Max Schmale of Solingen. When I got to hear of his brutality I warned him, and when this did not help I ensured his being enlisted in the Wehrmacht. This was all I could do against Schmale under the Nazis.

Q10.: How did you manage to maintain contact with the Americans in 1944 without getting arrested?

A.: In September 1944, I was working with my (Jewish) team in the Eifel, close to the Western fortifications. This section was conquered by American troops. One of my secretaries who spoke English revealed her identity to the Americans and told them who I was and what I had done for her and her co-religionists. Apparently this was the reason why I was not separated from my men.

Q11.: What is the exact date of your emigration to America and when did you obtain American citizenship? If you emigrated as early as 1947 or 1948 and after a short time became an American citizen, how was this possible for an ex-Party member so soon after the war? Was your emigration and the acquisition of American citizenship made possible by the assistance you rendered to the Allies, and especially the Americans, in supporting the War Crimes Trials at Nürnberg with your evidence on Nazi crimes?

A.: After the War I had no intention and no interest whatever in emigrating. I wanted to take part in the reconstruction of Germany. That was how matters stood in 1946 when I appeared as a witness in Nürnberg. Only afterwards, when I started receiving anonymous threats, apparently from ex-Nazi fanatics, and when my son's life was in danger, I followed the urgent advice of Jewish friends to prepare for emigration to the United States. However, I decided to undertake this step only in 1947, and my application was not approved before 1948 when the Joint Distribution Committee undertook to furnish the necessary guarantee.

I was granted American citizenship at the end of 1954 after I had complied with all the legal provisions and regulations like any other applicant.

Q12.: Did you promise marriage to Mrs. Kosnick?

A.: I did not promise marriage to Mrs. Kosnick. In this connection see her letter sent to me from a mental hospital.

Q13.: Did you through Mrs. Kosnick try to form a "united front" of prosecution witnesses in the anti-Nazi trials in Germany, for instance in the case against Köller?

A.: Although in 1945 I accused Georg Marschall and a number of other people of several crimes before the War Crimes Committee of the United States Army, I did not bring the matter to the attention of the

German authorities. A Jew who came to Zdolbunow during the War put in the charge against Marschall and Schmale after the War, and mentioned my name as a witness.

In the same matter my testimony was also taken in 1957 by the German Consulate General in San Francisco, within the framework of legal aid. When asked about further witnesses I gave such additional names as I was able to recall. At the time I could not remember the name of the Jew who was hanged.

Q14.: Do you maintain contact with hundreds of witnesses who appeared in anti-Nazi trials?

A.: I maintained contact with many witnesses and was also requested by the Attorney General of Nürnberg–Fürth to find additional witnesses. I was thus able to mention a number of witnesses for the purpose of the court. See the attached correspondence.

Q15.: Who was the publisher of "Men In Contemporary Society" and where can the book be obtained?

A.: The book was published by Columbia University. I took no part either in the compilation or publication of this book. I got to know of it only later, just as I was told of a number of other books which mentioned my name.

Q16.: When did you establish your three building companies in the United States? What was the source of the funds for the establishment of these firms?

A.: One year after my immigration I founded an engineering firm. As is well known, no considerable capital is needed to establish a business of this kind. The development and success of these firms were due to much work, technical know-how and self-confidence.

Q17.: How can one explain the many inconsistencies in your evidence concerning the hanging of the Jew Diener, raised against you mainly during your consular examination in 1964? Of course we shall welcome any opinion you may give us exceeding the scope of the questions posed here. Perhaps you might be able to put forward detailed counter-arguments to the investigation proceedings against you on behalf of the Attorney General of Stade.

A.: I am not aware of "many inconsistencies in my evidence concerning the hanging of the Jewish carpenter."

Two proceedings were pending against me, one for wilful perjury and one for perjury by neglect. One of these proceedings has in the meantime been annulled, namely the proceedings instituted at the instigation of Marschall's defence attorney, Dr. Schumann. The second proceedings could not be settled, "unless I was personally examined in Germany by the person in charge of the matter."

My question is, why was it possible to settle one of these proceedings without my presence in Germany, but not the other? All my efforts to stop the proceedings or to have an official charge sheet entered against me have been of no avail. See the correspondence relating to this matter.

In the Marschall murder trial I was one of many witnesses and all their evidence corresponded with mine. All these witnesses testified to the murder of that Jew committed by Marschall in summer, 1942, an event which in 1960 was eighteen years back.

I myself never saw the judgment of the Superior District Court (Oberlandesgericht) of Celle, which reversed the judgment of the District Court of Stade and ordered resumption of proceedings in the Marschall affair. Those, however, who were acquainted with the reasoning of the Court of Celle were surprised at its attitude, seeing fit to accuse me of perjury by neglect in a matter entirely unconnected with the Marschall trial and which had taken place thirty years previously; while on the other hand it accepted the testimony of a man who turned up after Marschall had been tried and sentenced, and who got involved in various contradictions, on the excuse that the events to which he testified lay twenty years back.

May I add here that I was astonished at this entire set of questions, and only the fact that as an old reader of your journal I had found in it a degree of objectivity [that] prevented me from leaving them unanswered.

Apart from that I feel a certain responsibility for preventing the repetition of Nazi customs such as the impartial observer could already notice in the days of the Weimar Republic.

The true legal scandal is not that the "innocent" Georg Marschall is walking about as a sentenced man, awaiting the renewal of legal proceedings, but that a situation of this kind has arisen. Marschall, a former District Governor and the official representative of the Nazis in Zdolbunow, was accused of the murder of the Jew Diener. A large number of witnesses who were living in Zdolbunow at the time and were in contact with Marschall, confirmed this fact in their evidence and he was found guilty and sentenced by lawful trial. Afterwards he was released from prison because his defence counsel discovered in my evidence a mistake in dates which has nothing to do with the murder case, and moreover refers to a period thirty years back.

It stands to reason that certain vested interests, disposing of considerable funds, have enabled Marschall to obtain information about me, although this material is hardly likely to discredit my reliability and casts no light on the Marschall case.

I hope that my description and explanations will help you in your efforts to achieve objective coverage of the news.

/S/

HERMANN GRAEBE

Notes

1. Martin Luther King, Jr., "I've Been to the Mountain Top." 3 April 1968, Memphis, Tennessee. Atlanta: The Martin Luther King, Jr. Center for Social Change, Library Documentation Project.

2. Raul Hilberg, *The Destruction of the European Jews* (New York: New Viewpoints, 1973), p. 192.

3. Rita Thalmann and Emmanuel Feinermann, *Crystal Night, 9–10 November 1938* (New York: Coward, McCann, and Geoghegen, 1974), p. 89.

4. Arthur D. Morse, *While Six Million Died: A Chronicle of American Apathy* (New York: Hart Publishing Company, 1967), p. 51.

5. Robert H. Jackson, *The Nurnberg Case* (New York: Alfred Knopf, 1947), p. 52.

6. Information for this chapter is in part from the forty-two-volume collection *Trial of the Major War Criminals Before the International Military Tribunal: Nuremberg 14 November 1945–1 October 1946* (Nuremberg, Germany: 1947).

7. "Report Nazi Alive in Poland Despite 1959 Death Sentence," *The Northern California Jewish Bulletin* (11 March 1983), p. 17.

8. William L. Shirer, *The Rise and Fall of the Third Reich: A History of Nazi Germany* (New York: Simon and Schuster, 1960), p. 961.

9. Abe Peck, "Elie Wiesel: Still Quarreling with his God," *San Francisco Examiner/Chronicle* (18 March 1979), p. 3.

10. Moshe Bejski, "The Righteous Among the Nations and Their Part in the Rescue of Jews," in *Rescue Attempts During The Holocaust*, Proceedings of the Second Yad Vashem International Historical Conference, April 8–11, 1974 (Jerusalem: "Ahva" Cooperative Press, 1977), p. 627.

11. Perry London, "The Rescuers: Motivational Hypotheses About Christians Who Saved Jews from the Nazis," in *Altruism and Helping Behavior: Social Psychological Studies of Some Antecedents and Consequences*, ed. J. Macaulay and L. Berkowitz (New York: Academic Press, 1970).

12. The background research on this trait is from Dr. Susan Gilmore and Dr. Patrick Fraleigh in their pioneering work with CRICKET International. Further information may be obtained by writing them at 2744 Friendly Street, Eugene, Oregon 97405.

13. The Louis Harris Associates, "Attitudes Toward Racial and Religious Minorities and Toward Women," (New York: National Conference of Christians and Jews, 1979).

14. Henri J.M. Nouwen, *Reaching Out: Three Movements of the Spiritual Life* (New York: Doubleday and Company, 1975), pp. 46–7.

About the Author

Douglas K. Huneke is the pastor of Westminster Presbyterian Church, Tiburon, California. He is a graduate of San Francisco Theological Seminary, San Anselmo, California. He served for eight years as the Presbyterian campus minister at the University of Oregon, Eugene. For five years he was a member of the Honors College faculty at the university. In 1976–1977 he was granted a sabbatical leave to study and to write on the implications of the Holocaust and on the life and writings of Elie Wiesel. He spent a major portion of his leave at the former extermination camps in Poland and East Germany, and studied at the Holocaust memorial and research center, Yad Vashem, in Jerusalem. An unpublished book-length manuscript entitled *Remembering the Victims: A Christian Response to the Holocaust* is a product of the sabbatical. He has written numerous articles on the moral and theological implications of the Holocaust, and on the writings of Elie Wiesel. He is a visiting lecturer and has taught in the Doctor of Ministry program at San Francisco Theological Seminary, and he has been a lecturer for the B'nai B'rith Lecture Bureau.

In 1980, he was awarded a faculty research grant by the Oregon Committee for the Humanities. The grant enabled him to conduct extensive research on the moral and spiritual development of Christians who rescued Jews and other endangered persons during the Nazi era. While conducting research and interviewing in Israel he came across the records of San Franciscan Herman "Fritz" Graebe. The two met, and the process of recording Graebe's story began. To complete the biography, Huneke interviewed Jews rescued by Graebe and reviewed the extensive U.S. Twelfth Army and Nuremberg files on Graebe's activities. The writing and research process have gone on from 1981–1985. In 1981, he was awarded an additional grant from the Memorial Foundation for

Jewish Culture. The grant allowed him to continue gathering the accounts of rescue and to continue interviewing the altruistic persons. Several articles, a privately published manuscript, and a proposed curriculum
have been developed from this study.

Mr. Huneke co-chairs and is a founder of the Marin Interfaith Council. He hosted the interfaith program, "Mosaic," which appears weekly
on the San Francisco Westinghouse network station, KPIX-TV. He holds
several positions within the judicatories of the Presbyterian Church (USA).

In April 1983, Mr. Huneke visited the Soviet Union under a special
program grant sponsored jointly by the Bay Area Council on Soviet
Jewry and the Jewish Community Relations Council of San Francisco.
The purpose of the trip was to make contact with and to assess the
plight of Jewish "refuseniks" and Christian dissidents living in the Soviet
Union.

With his traveling companion to the Soviet Union, Rabbi Sheldon
Lewis of Palo Alto, California, Mr. Huneke received the 1984 Hadassah
Myrtle Wreath Award for "Your devotion on behalf of Soviet Jewry."
The award was presented by the Central Pacific Coast Region of Hadassah.

In 1981, Mr. Huneke was a recipient of The Civil Liberties Awards
presented by the Oregon Chapter of the American Civil Liberties Union.
He is a popular speaker, appearing before civic groups and lecturing in
colleges, universities, and religious institutions in the United States and
Israel.

Printed in the United States
by Baker & Taylor Publisher Services